DATE DUE			

The publishers wish to express
their gratitude to Joan Palevsky
for her most generous contribution
to the publication of this book.

EPIGRAMS OF MARTIAL
ENGLISHED BY
DIVERS HANDS

EPIGRAMS OF MARTIAL ENGLISHED BY DIVERS HANDS

SELECTED AND EDITED
WITH AN INTRODUCTION BY

J. P. SULLIVAN AND PETER WHIGHAM

UNIVERSITY OF CALIFORNIA PRESS

BERKELEY • LOS ANGELES • LONDON

The preparation of this volume was made possible by a grant from the Translations Program of the National Endowment for the Humanities, an independent federal agency.

University of California Press
Berkeley and Los Angeles, California

University of California Press, Ltd.
London, England

© 1987 by The Regents of the University of California

878. 0 / 0 2

M36e

14 5 / 8 9

ort. / 9 8 8

Library of Congress Cataloging-in-Publication Data
Martial.
  Epigrams of Martial Englished by divers hands.
  Bibliography: p.
  Includes index.
    1. Martial—Translations, English. 2. Epigrams,
  Latin—Translations into English. 3. Epigrams,
  English—Translations from Latin. I. Sullivan, J. P.
  (John Patrick). II. Whigham, Peter. III. Title.
  PA6502.S85 1987   878'.0102   86-4301
  ISBN 0-520-04240-9 (alk. paper)
  ISBN 0-520-04241-7 (pbk. : alk. paper)

Printed in the United States of America

1   2   3   4   5   6   7   8   9

J. V. Cunningham: Translations of II.5 and IV.69 from *Collected Poems and Epigrams of J. V. Cunningham*, Swallow Press, 1971. Reprinted by permission of The Ohio University Press, Athens, Ohio.

Dudley Fitts: From his *Sixty Poems of Martial in Translation*: VIII. 69 ("To His Critics") ©1961 by Dudley Fitts; II. 53 ("To Chloe"), VI.57 ("Every Man His Own Absalom"), and XI.85 ("On Zoilus, a Linguist"), ©1967 by Dudley Fitts. Reprinted by permission of Harcourt Brace Jovanovich, Inc.

Brian Hill: Translations reprinted by permission of the author's literary executor, Timothy d'Arch Smith.

Rolfe Humphries: Translations of I.64 and IX.33 from *Selected Epigrams of Martial*, Indiana University Press, 1963. Reprinted by permission of the publisher.

Ralph Marcellino: Translations of I.25 and VII.19 from *Martial: Selected Epigrams*, ©1968 by Macmillan Publishing Company. Reprinted with permission of the publisher.

Philip Murray: Translations of I.103, IV.46, and XII.82 ©1967 by Philip Murray. Reprinted from *Poems after Martial* by permission of Wesleyan University Press.

Peter Porter: From his *After Martial*, Oxford University Press, 1972. Reprinted by permission of the publisher and the author.

J. A. Pott and F. A. Wright: From *Martial, the Twelve Books of Epigrams*, Routledge and Kegan Paul, 1924. Reprinted by permission of the publisher.

Ezra Pound: Translation of V.43 from *Personae*, ©1926 by Ezra Pound. Reprinted by permission of New Directions Publishing Corporation.

Dorothea Wender: From *Roman Poetry: From the Republic to the Silver Age*, ©1980 by Southern Illinois University Press. Reprinted by permission of the publisher and the author.

Omne epigramma sit instar apis; sit aculeus illi;
Sint sua mella; sit et corporis exigui.

The qualities rare in a bee that we meet,
   In an epigram never should fail;
The body should always be little and sweet
   And a sting should be left in its tail.

Lord Chesterfield

Martial, in sooth none should presume to write,
Since time hath brought thy Epigrams to light:
For through our writing, thine so prais'd before
Have this obtained, to be commended more:
   Yet to ourselves although we win no fame,
   We please, which get our master a good name.

Thomas Bastard, Chrestoleros I. 17

And then what proper person can be partial
To all those nauseous epigrams of Martial?

Lord Byron, Don Juan I.43

CONTENTS

PREFACE AND
ACKNOWLEDGMENTS

A work that has been half a decade or more in its gestation is bound to have incurred many debts of various sorts to both friends and strangers. Robert Zachary saw the desirability of a modern Martial that would bring Henry Bohn's classic collection of poetic versions up to date; he started us on the track. H. A. Mason and Peter Jay encouraged us in the undertaking. Then there were those who put us on to obscure sources for versions of Martial, many, though not all, of them now included in this volume: Timothy D'Arch Smith, Roger Lonsdale, Dolores Palomo, and John J. Winkler. Our debt to the contributors who produced new versions of Martial and so patiently awaited their appearance here is more than we can adequately acknowledge.

For their cooperation in some laborious research, one of the editors must also thank the staffs of the Huntington Library in Pasadena; the Bodleian and Cambridge University Libraries; the British Library, which made available the Egerton MS 2982, used by Henry Bohn; and the Interlibrary Loan Service of the University of California, Santa Barbara.

There were others who aided us in practical and scholarly ways too diverse to describe at length: Judy Godfrey, Maeve Binchy, Michiko Yusa, Gordon Snell, Allan Kershaw, and R. C. Colton among them.

The National Endowment for the Humanities provided funds at the inception of the enterprise for the release of time, photocopying, travel, and secretarial aid.

August Frugé devoted many hours to whipping an overlong and overly ambitious text into acceptable shape for the general reader.

No acknowledgments would, however, be complete without a reference to Henry G. Bohn, whose pioneering efforts in bringing together the best poetic versions he could find to supplement the English and Italian prose versions of Martial in the Bohn Classical Library Series (1859) initially inspired this volume. We are grateful to BSB B. G. Teubner Verlagsgesellschaft, publishers of the latest edition of Martial, *M. Valerii Martialis Epigrammaton Libri recognovit W. Heraeus: Editionem correctiorem curavit Iacobus Borovskij* (Leipzig, 1976), for permission to reprint the Latin text for the selection of versions included in this book. The authors of translations previously unpublished or published in journals and private editions have kindly granted permission to print their poems; for the other modern versions, we extend our thanks to those publishers listed on the copyright page.

On the practical side deep gratitude is owed to two people: to Randi Glick, who has been long associated, perhaps to her dismay, with the whole enterprise, and who typed the text from various illegible drafts; and to Margaret Kiers, who compiled the indexes and collated the whole work.

Any errors that remain must rest squarely on our shoulders.

J. P. Sullivan and Peter Whigham
June 1985

INTRODUCTION

MARTIAL'S LIFE AND WORKS

by J. P. Sullivan

The small hill town of Bilbilis Augusta, six kilometers from the modern town of Calatayud, in the part of Hispania Tarraconensis that is now Aragon, was an iron- and gold-mining and manufacturing town whose reputation in the first century A.D. matched that of Toletum, the modern Toledo. It was in this town, or near it, that the poet Marcus Valerius Martialis was born on March 1 in one of the years A.D. 38 to 41. After thirty-four years in Rome he would return to it and die there around 104.

The poet's description of its charms (I.49; IV.55; XII.18), of the hunting, and of the fertile countryside straddling the River Salo (now the Jalón), whose fast-flowing waters meander round the foot of the hills to serve the terraced vineyards and also produce the local steel, may make the reader wonder why he ever left his hometown for the chancy and harassing life of a writer and client in Rome. Fame was the spur, and the metropolis exercised a powerful attraction for Spaniards in the first century of the empire. Seneca, Lucan, and Quintilian, among others, haled from various parts of Spain, and the emperors Trajan (98–117) and Hadrian (117–138) both came from Spanish families. Martial's pride in his national origins, Celtic descent, and Spanish birthplace may be seen in I.49.

The poet's parents, whether or not these were the Fronto and Flaccilla of V.34, were Roman citizens, though natives of Spain, and were prosperous enough to give him a standard Roman education in grammar and rhetoric. Like Ovid, however, Martial did not intend to put his education to professional use when he left

1

for Rome around the age of twenty-five, perhaps in A.D. 64. He doubtless expected, and presumably got, help from the Annaean family, which included the Senecas and Lucan, and through them from other lavish patrons such as the poetically minded Calpurnius Piso. There is some evidence that his Nomentan farm came to him through his Senecan connections. But whatever success he had in those circles of patronage was to be short-lived, since the Pisonian conspiracy of 65 saw the downfall of those great houses and the deaths of Seneca, Lucan, Piso, and numerous others of their acquaintance. How well he lived between then and the accession of Titus in 80 we do not know, except that he seems to have written some poetry for lesser-known patrons, since he mentions in I.113 that his juvenilia are still available for those seriously interested in his work.

He had been somewhat unlucky in his timing. The enormous literary activity that centered round the court of Nero, whose imperial generosity to artists of all kinds, whether poets, musicians, or gladiators, was notorious, might well have found a place for the particular talents of Martial, whose spirit and some of whose themes are reminiscent of Nero's own wide literary circle. Parallels are easily found in his poems to Petronius, the emperor's Arbiter of Elegance, and to the Greek epigrammatists of the Neronian era.

Martial's early associations worked against him in the matter of patronage, and something similar happened to him again after the assassination of Domitian in September 96. Martial's close association with the court of that emperor could not be offset by his rejection of him as a tyrant (Spec. 33; XII.3.11–12) or by his eager compliments to Nerva and Trajan in Books XI and XII (December 96 and early 102) and the revised edition of Book X (mid 98). He reluctantly returned to Bilbilis and spent his last years in an atmosphere of hostility and envy that all his feigned contentment with his situation cannot disguise—compare XII.18 with the prefatory letter to that book. So most of his first and last years in Rome were lean ones. He had a lot of stairs to climb in every sense. Especially in his more prosperous days, surrounded by a comfortable household of slaves, he disliked dancing attendance on his patrons for meager handouts (sportulae) and gifts that always fell below his expectations, even at the height of his fame.

By 85, however, he had managed to reach the honorary rank of military tribune and had thereby become a proud member of the equestrian order, which meant that he had some reasonable financial standing, since a knight's financial worth had to be at least 200,000 sesterces.[1] For his poetic services or merits he was granted the *ius trium liberorum* by Titus around 81 and this was reconfirmed by the latter's successor, Domitian. The evidence drawn from his own work indicates that Martial never married, so the "rights of a parent with three children" became important for the unfettered receipt of legacies from friends. For all this, Martial *felt* poor, even though he resisted the advice of friends to take up a more lucrative and reliable occupation than writing occasional verse in the expectation of subsidies, humiliatingly requested and capriciously bestowed. (This aspect of his writing would have some regrettable consequences for his reputation in later centuries.)

It must be said in Martial's defense that, like Juvenal, he clearly hated the straits imposed by contemporary patronage on indigent poets and other artists. His descriptions of the client's way of life are accurate and heartfelt: trudging across the city to a patron who might not be at home; the grudging invitations to dinner at which different foods and wines were served to those above and those below the salt; the mean and petty rewards for even the most flattering poetic solicitations. These features of Martial's life and the way of living of those like him are poignantly described in his epigrams. The writer's necessary concessions to this milieu, so alien to both our democratic and elitist tastes, would be difficult to swallow or stomach if we were not aware of similar phenomena in English literary history.

Poetry emerges not from a vacuum, however, but from a matrix, and for Roman poets such as Martial and Juvenal, who were not aristocratic dilettantes or retired public figures, patronage was simultaneously an inspiration, a crutch, and a means of livelihood.

---

1. A sesterce at this time would buy two good loaves of bread, so it would have been worth slightly more than the U.S. dollar and slightly less than the English pound in 1985.

In imperial Rome, the rewards for poets, though unreliable and perhaps erratically dispensed, could be much greater than any poet nowadays could hope for. Vergil, according to Suetonius, made ten million sesterces, he and the other famous epic poet Varius Rufus receiving one million from Augustus alone. Horace literally wrote his way out of an inferior post in the Treasury into comparative affluence and a Sabine farm. Even the tight-fisted Vespasian encouraged the arts with a particularly generous grant to the epic writer Saleius Bassus of 500,000 sesterces. Financial rewards from the reigning emperor were not the only compensations for poets; advancement in rank and various other social privileges might be expected as reasonable rewards for service in general and poetic eulogies in particular.

It is easy enough to see how imperial patronage worked: considerable public resources were made available in varying amounts by the imperial throne to suitably talented aspirants to literary fame. But what was the motive? Disinterested encouragement of artists can never be excluded, of course, but the skeptical observer may discern more obvious reasons for this largesse. Most notably, it burnished the imperial image, legitimated a dynasty's claim to supreme power, and affirmed the preeminent suitability of a particular individual to wield power over his putative peers and the Roman world at large. After the first few years of their reigns, most emperors, particularly Nero and Domitian, tended to discount senatorial political attitudes, and looked more and more to control of the army and the praetorian guard and popularity with the people and the middle classes, whose compliance and willingness to serve in official capacities led to their growing power and prominence in the imperial system.

In this "organization of opinion" writers played a large part from the time of Augustus onward. Poetry, particularly of the lighter sort, was hardly a suitable calling, or avocation even, for a senator, as the Younger Pliny's defensive letter on the subject of his own verse writing indicates. Unlike oratory and history, poetry in senatorial eyes was essentially a tool of the regime and the patronage system in general; it was a commodity to be bought and sold, commissioned or rewarded, in accordance with the successful accomplishment of its primary mission, which was, according to Cicero in his speech on behalf of the poet Archias, to extol for contemporaries and posterity the achievements of nations and individuals. It is this accepted purpose that accounts for the praise of Augustus in the *Aeneid*, the fulsome flattery of Nero in Calpurnius Siculus's *Eclogues*, and the gross adulation of Domitian in Martial's *Epigrams* and Statius's *Silvae*. In the case of Domitian, the court poets had to gratify his taste for military glory in Germany and Dacia, praise his attempts to raise the standards of public morality, and accept his pretensions to quasi-divine status in religion and government.

The first book of Martial's epigrams that brought him into the public eye was the so-called *Liber de spectaculis* ("The Book of the Shows"), which was written to celebrate the hundred days of feasts, games, and spectacles put on in A.D. 80 by the open-handed emperor Titus (79–81) at the inauguration of the great Flavian amphitheater we now call the Colosseum. Like the structure itself, Martial's celebratory opus survives in a very truncated form. It consists now of about thirty epigrams in which Martial breathlessly describes the magnificence of the architectural structure, catalogues the huge cosmopolitan crowd that attended the opening ceremonies to honor the emperor, the true father of his country, and ingeniously comments on the various astonishing aspects of the games and the shows themselves. The cruelties of gladiatorial games and wild beast shows are offensive to modern tastes, but we have to understand that to the Romans they provided opportunities for displays of courage, exemplary public punishment of servile criminals, and opportunities for the emperors to display their affection for the people, their generosity, mercy, and commitment to social discipline. Martial's taste for paradox and humorous surprise makes some of the material more palatable. Along with the barbarous spectacle of criminals being executed to add verisimilitude to the plots of stage mimes and farces, less offensive descriptions are featured in the book: the rhinoceros's easy victory over the bull (*Spec.* 9), and the elephant trained to venerate the emperor (*Spec.* 17) by contrast with the deer who does so instinctively (*Spec.* 29).

This book represents only the known beginning of Martial's career, since there were other, less formal modes of publication:

small selections of poems sent to patrons with fulsome dedications, *extempore* compositions at social events, and works presented at the ever-popular public and private recitals. The products of such occasions would be gathered at annual or biennial intervals and issued to the general public, often at some suitable season such as summer or, more often, mid December.

Although numbered XIII and XIV in our texts, Martial's next two publications, which appeared in 84–85, were the *Xenia* and the *Apophoreta*. These contained verse inscriptions for various gifts, such as those that might be sent at the important winter festival of the *Saturnalia* in mid December. These books, about which Martial is suitably modest (XIII.1, 2), are mainly of sociological interest, but gift giving, like testamentary benefactions, was a very important part of the complicated nexus of Roman social relationships. (Both themes occur frequently in satiric contexts in Martial's poetry.) Martial's ingenuity is fully equal to the unpromising material, and the encapsulated judgments on literary classics in presentation copies are particularly striking (XIV.183–196).

Presumably the brilliant wit of Books I and II of the epigrams when they appeared in rapid succession in 85–86 came as no surprise to his general audience. The slimmer volumes, which had been circulated to various patrons and utilized in informal recitations, were now plundered for formal publication by his booksellers. The editions of the first seven books that have come down to us may be in a somewhat different form from their initial publication, since Martial's popularity allowed him the opportunity to revise and reedit his volumes. Despite this, we can have reasonable confidence in the picture Martial wished to present of himself and his genius when they were first published.

The first book sets the pattern for the succeeding eleven volumes, issued at short, irregular intervals over the next two decades of his life. The book contains approximately a hundred epigrams, composed mainly in elegiac couplets, with a scattering of hendecasyllables and an even smaller number of scazons, or limping iambics. The collection is introduced by a significant prose preface addressed to the reader; it is, in effect, a literary manifesto. (Later prose prefaces to Books II, VIII, IX, and XII tend to be ad hominem dedications, and the task of explaining and defending the poet's life and work is accomplished by verses strategically placed throughout the body of his work.)

The main points made in this early statement (see pp. 60–61) provide one key to the understanding of Martial's oeuvre. He has chosen the lowly literary genre of the epigram to display his poetic talents, but in so doing he must follow its conventions of candor and verbal license. In this, he pleads, he is following the established Roman tradition of Catullus and the Augustan or post-Augustan poets Domitius Marsus, Albinovanus Pedo, and Cornelius Lentulus Gaetulicus. Unlike them, he will not indulge in specifically personal attacks, but the sexual frankness he shares with them must be seen in the same light as the ritually sanctified licentiousness of the spring festival of Flora, when actresses appear on the stage naked.

The ramifications and background of this programmatic introduction to Book I, which is amplified by various scattered epigrams throughout his work, need some historical comment. Originally in Greek *epigram* meant any words inscribed on artifacts, votive offerings, graves, monuments, or buildings representing the owner, the maker, the donor, the dedicatee, or simply the message itself. The classical application of the term to sepulchral, commemorative, or dedicatory inscriptions in easily memorable verse prompted the extension of its use in the early Alexandrian period to cover a whole literary genre of brief poems. These productions were reminiscent of, or analogous to, such inscriptions, but they now dealt with almost any subject, sentiment, event, or occasion. There were, of course, models. Short poems of this type—epigrams *avant la lettre*, as it were—by numerous archaic and classical authors were gathered and preserved in later collections.

Such apparently unpretentious poems had been given the general title of *paegnia*, "playthings," as though they were only light and occasional verses by comparison with the elevated genres of epic, lyric, and tragedy. In the Roman tradition of which Martial was part they were defensively termed *lusus* (play), *ioci* (jokes), or even *nugae* (trifles), and epigram never quite lost its apologetic stance, despite its frequent brilliance in the hands of a master and its great popularity.

Important influences on the Hellenistic epigram were the

convivial, hortatory, and erotic themes associated with elegiac
verse in general, and so it was the elegiac couplet that prevailed
over almost all other poetic forms, although meters such as hen-
decasyllables and scazons were popular with Roman epigram-
matists. The elegiac couplet was found preeminently suitable for
a wide range of topics, since its self-contained concision was ar-
tistically adaptable. An epigram would typically consist of one to
five of them, sometimes more, but the unit itself also encouraged
certain characteristics such as wit, terseness, and antithetical
point, enjambment being rare. Indeed it was this quality of the
standard verse for the epigram that led eventually to the use of
the word in English to mean not only an epigraph, sepulchral or
otherwise, but also, after 1583, a short witty poem; and then,
since 1796, any pointed or antithetical sentiment in prose or
verse.

No literary genre in the course of its millennium-long devel-
opment has been put to so many purposes or taken on such pro-
tean shapes. But the mildly pejorative connotation the term still
has, inherited from the sometimes deprecatory use of it by Mar-
tial and his successors, should not hide that fact that we are often
dealing with superb poetry "writ in small."

Real grave inscriptions and dedications had inspired fictitious
examples, but the Alexandrian poets had broken away from any
original limitations the epigram had had in favor of a great variety
of personal, artistic, and general themes, introducing experimen-
tal refinements on their classical precursors and defining by their
example the different types of epigram. Its traditional classifica-
tion by subject is roughly preserved for us in what we now call
the *Greek Anthology*, which was itself amassed from highly pop-
ular earlier anthologies, of which two at least would have been
known to Martial. The main subdivisions of epigram in the *An-
thology*, all of which may be found in Martial, are (1) votive in-
scriptions and dedications (e.g., VI.73); (2) epitaphs or tomb in-
scriptions (e.g., on Erotion, V.34; on Latinus, IX.28); (3) amatory
and pederastic epigrams (e.g., XI.60, 73); (4) "epideictic" epi-
grams, which are clever, rhetorical, or informational poems
on curious facts or incidents, famous personages or places, as
well as "ecphrastic" descriptions of works of art (e.g., XIII.50);

(5) versified reflections and advice on life and morality (e.g., I.15); (6) convivial pieces (e.g., I.71, XI.6); and (7) abusive and satirical epigrams, one of Martial's strengths, exemplified throughout Books I–XII. From the many historical strata of the *Greek Anthology* we can discern fashions and innovations in the development of the genre that provide the background to Martial's achievement.

The most famous Hellenistic writer of epigram was perhaps Callimachus, whose delicate and allusive work was to have a profound effect on Roman literature in general. Already by the time of Ennius (d. 169 B.C.) the elegiac epigram had come to replace earlier Latin meters for Roman funeral inscriptions, and some erotic epigrams were based on Greek models by the early Roman admirers of Alexandrian poetry. These were the immediate predecessors of Catullus (c. 84–c. 54 B.C.), whose genius for short erotic lyric and invective was to make him the main model for Martial. The Catullan circle popularized the epigram. The flexibility and range of the form suited their coterie polemics and the occasions for ad hoc verse presented to them by the social and political scene and their own personal lives.

The most famous example of the genre in Roman hands, and, arguably, one of the finest short poems ever written, is Catullus's poignant expression of his feelings for his mistress Lesbia:

> Odi et amo; quare id faciam fortasse requiris:
> Nescio, sed fieri sentio et excrucior.
>
> *(Carm. 85)*

> I hate and I love. And if you ask me how,
> I do not know: I only feel it, and I'm torn in two.
>
> (trans. Peter Whigham)

Now this elegiac note can be found in Martial,[2] but, as we shall see, the later poet's claim to literary distinction was to be his development of the "pointed" epigram, with its element of surprise or reversal of the reader's expectations.

2. It is interesting that Catullus's poem is glanced at, if not actually parodied, in one of Martial's best-known epigrams:

> Non amo te, Sabidi, nec possum dicere quare:
> Hoc tantum possum dicere, non amo te.
>
> (I.32)

The most important literary phenomenon of the Catullan period had been the anthology, mainly of erotic verses, culled from six centuries of epigram and published as *The Garland of Meleager* sometime around 80 B.C. As a result, Latin epigram, whether erotic or satiric, was firmly established in the Augustan age. Albinovanus Pedo and Domitius Marsus are especially singled out by Martial, but Augustus himself was not above using the form for obscene abuse of his enemies (see XI.20). In fact, satiric epigrams of a highly political nature flourished in the early empire. Often circulated anonymously, they contained attacks on the imperial court and various upper-class Romans besides Augustus made frequent use of them. Of course traditional Greek themes were also borrowed, and the erotic epigram in particular was popular. The Younger Pliny, in his self-conscious defense of the genre (*Epistles* 5.3), gives us a list of more than twenty famous practitioners up to his own day. It includes such names as Cicero, Vergil, and Seneca, as well as most of the first-century rulers, such as Nero and Nerva. The Romans therefore contributed a political dimension to the genre, as well as a certain earthiness and realism.

By the age of Nero, Philippus of Thessalonica could gather his own *Garland* from about fifty poets who had written in Greek since the time of Meleager. The standard divisions are represented: imaginary epigraphs and dedications, epideictic topics and moral exhortations, as well as erotic and satiric epigrams. Apart from the editor himself, its stars are Crinagoras, Philodemus, and the witty Marcus Argentarius, father-in-law of Lucan. One surprising feature of the book is the glimpse afforded, through Crinagoras especially, of aspects of contemporary Roman life. There are even requests for patronage. But perhaps the most important advance in the writing of epigram came slightly later under Nero, when we find in the verses of Lucillius and Nicarchus an upsurge in satiric themes and a noticeable sharpening of the "line of wit," often directed at contemporary literary and dramatic enthusiasms. However obscured by their great successor, all of these writers have left their mark in the scores of allusions, borrowings, and adaptations we can recognize in Martial's fifteen books. And doubtless there are many we cannot trace from Greek epigrammatists now lost.

Why did Martial conceal this obvious debt? Mere snobbish dislike for Greeks in general, a feeling he shared with his friend Juvenal, is only part of the explanation. Rather, Martial wished to set himself firmly in the *Latin* tradition of realistic epigram, which, following Catullus, he describes in various derogatory terms. In this way, by pretending a lack of seriousness, the poet avoids charges of pretentiousness.

The modesty, of course, is feigned. Like Catullus, Martial attacks the conventional long poem as opposed to the carefully crafted miniature, and he goes even further in rejecting mythological tales as subjects for poetry (X.4). Martial claims that his verse reflects Roman life, its values, and the deviation from them, as well as human behavior in general. His epigrams offer a gritty social realism not to be found as a rule in the more artificial and etiolated work of his Greek precursors—*hominem pagina nostra sapit* (X.4.10). One aspect of this realism is of course the blatant sexuality of some of his poems. This was to be justified not only by literary precedent, and by fertility festivals, such as the Floralia, but also by the apotropaic verbal license of the soldiery during a triumph and the acceptable wantonness of the mime (I.4). Martial perhaps believed that his indecent verses similarly provided an acceptable social release of psychological steam.

Unlike Catullus, however, to whose attacks on Julius Caesar, Mamurra, and others Martial presumably alludes, he was in no position to attack notable contemporaries. As Juvenal also knew, the literary and political conditions of the principate were quite different from those of the republic, which had tolerated the satires of Lucilius as well as the lampoons of Catullus.

The defensiveness of his preface to Book I, then, should not hide from the reader Martial's revolutionary poetic ambitions and his high evaluation of his own work. He can admit to faults and unevenness in his prolific output (I.16), but he believes in his own already-established fame, the durability of his work (I.1), and, above all, in the value of his writing (X.4). His carefully muted polemic against mythological epic, in particular that of his hated contemporary rival, Papinius Statius, the author of the *Thebaid* (X.4), subverts the conservative view, as best expressed by Dryden, that "a Heroic poem, truly such, is undoubtedly the greatest work which the son of man is capable to perform." In this opinion

Martial is at one with Catullus and so furthers his own claim to be second only to the republican poet and his successor Domitius Marsus in the more realistic and intrinsically more valuable genre of epigram (VII.99).

Book I, then, provides the paradigm for Martial's later miscellaneous collections, which appeared between 86 (Book II) and early 102 (Book XII). A few new subjects are added to its variety; patrons and addressees change; historical events and personal vicissitudes are recorded; and there are increasing indications of the poet's growing closeness to Domitian and his courtiers. One noticeable change cannot be overlooked: the hasty and unsuccessful attempts after September 96 to ingratiate himself with the new emperors Nerva and Trajan. Perhaps in consequence the proportion of obscene epigrams increases as Martial seemingly despairs of achieving the same rapport with the new regime that he had had with Domitian. A note of bitterness about his fall from grace and his reception by his fellow countrymen may be detected toward the end. Nevertheless the heterogeneity of the first book is reflected in the heterogeneity of its successors, whatever the advances in metrical and linguistic skill or the experiments in versification that may be detected. The critical problem is to find thematic patterns and structures for the whole oeuvre, or any representative selection of it, that will impose some order on a complex mass of material, since only a small proportion of the epigrams may be explained as derivative exercises on subjects already treated by Greek and Roman precursors. Unfortunately most literary evaluations of Martial are content to describe him as a witty observer of Roman society with a taste for the great moral commonplaces and a regrettable penchant for obscenity and adulation, best ignored by his admirers. Adulation was, however, dictated by economic circumstances and the calling he chose, and obscenity, like wit, was for him a traditional, expected, and valid element of the epigrammatist's art. Naturally, neither of these aspects of his writing can be burked in attempting to explain why his critical fortunes have fluctuated so widely through the centuries.

Still, the first task is to find comprehensible patterns and recognizable themes in the striking variety of his poetry. One possibility is to impose on Martial's oeuvre the formal classifications used by the compilers of the *Greek Anthology* and described earlier. Unfortunately such a heuristic classification would tell us nothing except that Martial was adept at all of these eight categories of epigram, and perhaps added a category of his own in the *Xenia* and *Apophoreta*, namely, verse labels for gifts, an extension of the dedicatory subgenre.

Purely formal classifications, then, are of little help, and neither will structural considerations take us much further. We can detect that Martial adopted two complementary principles of organization for his books: variation and juxtaposition, which can be abrupt and startling in their effect. He would compose a cycle of epigrams on the same general topic, but then either divide them and distribute parts of the cycle throughout a whole book or keep some sections together. Obvious examples of cycles are the eight epigrams on the lion and the trained hare (I.6, 14, 22, 44, 48, 51, 60, and 104), where variety is achieved by decisive separation. Another example can be found in the six short poems on Domitian's favorite Earinus (IX.11, 12, 13, 16, 17, and 36), where emphatic juxtaposition is briefly broken by two short unrelated and unexpected epigrams, and an elaborate coda is carefully added later.

Broader principles underlying the structure of the books might be mentioned: compliments to the emperor and his friends and patrons cluster at the beginning of a book; obscene epigrams are generally relegated to the latter third of a volume, sometimes with a warning. There is a tendency to end each collection on a low key, perhaps with an apologetic address to the reader or to the papyrus roll itself; Book VIII, dedicated to Domitian, is the exception to this, as well as being a volume that excludes obscene epigrams entirely.

Such analyses, however, tell us little more than that Martial was neither a careless editor of his own work nor a passionate devotee of almost mathematical balance and arrangement in the manner of the Augustan elegists and Horace. What gives inner shape to Martial's work is his coherent view of Roman life and society and his determination that his chosen literary form best reflect that view.

It must be admitted that his poetic persona and his satirically expressed view of the world of Rome may not be entirely to modern tastes, but at least we will be able to appreciate the consistent philosophical structure that underpins his artistic variety. At the heart of Martial's work is a deep concern for hierarchical order—national, political, social, sexual, and moral. From this springs his concern for private and also public decorum, whether at table or in bed, in manners or in clothing, in relationships between equals, superiors, or inferiors, even in literary composition or in recitations. In this desire for order and decorum, Martial is essentially conservative, resembling such Flavian and post-Flavian writers as Pliny, Tacitus, and Juvenal. Conservatism often goes hand in hand not only with a decided dislike of change, of course, but also with a fear of further change. And this, too, may be found in Martial's poetry beneath the pointed and aggressive wit and the carefully polished eulogy and sentiment. Even his delight in the unexpected often takes the form of pleasure in the discomfiture of the pretentious and greedy.

Once this principle is grasped, the social nature of his poetry becomes apparent. Domitian is a worthy emperor and therefore deserves and earns the loyalty of the people and of the poet, hence Martial's unlimited flattery in such epigrams as VIII.1, IX.3, and so on, and his attack on the rebellious general Antonius Saturninus in IV.11 and XI.84. Domitian's duty is to safeguard the state from external enemies and threats, from Dacians, Sarmatians, and Germans. This successfully achieved, the emperor merits all the pomp of his triumphs, the honorific titles of Germanicus and Dacicus, and all the most lavish secular praises (*rerum salus, terrarum gloria*) that the skilful poet can devise. And since even for an undogmatic Epicurean such as Martial the state religion and the imperial cult were vital conservative elements of social stability, Martial was even ready to call Domitian *dominus et deus* and liken him to various deities of the Roman pantheon, at least until his assassination. On the other hand, by virtue of his supreme position, the emperor also had *his* reciprocal duties, as Seneca had long before pointed out in the *De clementia*, not least that of being the supreme patron of artists, architects, and poets. Martial's pleas, like his thanks, are meant as reminders of this duty. Domitian is later attacked when, in the eyes of the middle class to which Martial precariously belonged, he violates his social contract and becomes a vicious and oppressive ruler.

A little lower in the Roman hierarchy, aristocrats and senators, who are the emperor's clients, are also patrons, who rightly expect from their own clients service, honor, and even flattery. These Martial freely gives, and, equally freely, he reminds them again and again of *their* duty to support their poet-client in the way Maecenas, Seneca, and Calpurnius Piso had supported their literary dependents. Patrons must take pride in being patrons (II.18, 32).

Even further down the scale, freedmen owed their former masters gratitude, loyalty, and service. Their place in the social order was correspondingly and forever fixed. To forget their place, to attempt to usurp their master's position, as it were, and illegally to usurp the privileges of equestrian or senatorial status (II.29) was regarded not only as shameful, but as downright socially disruptive. This largely explains the venomous glee Martial takes in recording the summary ejections of nonequestrians from the reserved equestrian seats at the Circus or theater (e.g., V.8, 14, 25, and 35), and in vilifying anyone, cobbler or merchant, who uses his newfound wealth as an excuse to put on airs and graces. The most frequently pilloried examples of this type are Zoilus (II.16, 42, 58; III.82; V.79; XI.37, 54, 92) and the arrogant shoemaker of Bononia (III.16, 69, 99).

Slaves, lowest of all in the social hierarchy, are expected to know their place, perform their duties conscientiously, and generally behave themselves in accordance with their servile status. Dereliction of duty, insolence, or inefficiency on the part of cooks or barbers should be met with condign punishment (e.g., VIII.23). Conversely, Martial's affections are lavished without reserve on slaves who are young, beautiful, gracious, and present no real threat to the status quo by their impertinence or bad behavior, as witness the moving epitaphs on his young slave secretary Demetrius (I.101), his friend Pudens's slave Encolpus (I.3), and, above all, his dead infant slave Erotion (V.34, 37; X.61). A little sexual blackmail from pretty, spoiled male slaves may be permitted within limits. The important thing is that master and slave should know their social roles. Amorous deviations from them, as in the comedy of Plautus, are a legitimate subject of amusement, since these are the convolutions of lust. Romantic love for an inferior, as seen in the elegists, he regards with contempt (I.62, 68).

There was one particular threat to the long-established hierarchy of Roman social life that aroused both anger and fear in Martial, and later in Juvenal. This was the continuously growing power of the female sex. Between the closing years of the republic and the years when Christianity gained social and then official influence in Roman society, the female sex, in the social strata most visible in our documents and of most concern to Martial, enjoyed a personal, sensual, and economic liberation unparalleled in civilized states before the latter half of the twentieth century in North America, England, and some parts of Europe. This freedom for Roman women sprang predominantly from the instability and casualness of marriage, in particular from the decay of the type of marriage where the legally absolute rights of the father, the paterfamilias, were handed over to the husband. And not the least potent factors in the emancipation of women were the legal developments concerning a wife's dowry. For practical purposes a husband had little more than the right to the income from it so long as the marriage lasted. In the event of divorce or the husband's death, the dowry could be sued for, and so, practically speaking, it belonged in substance to the wife and only in form to the husband. Consequently, women of property had the same sort of power over their husbands that the fear of heavy alimony now inspires in rich Americans. Martial and Juvenal picture wives actually purchasing their husbands' sexual services or marital complaisance. The resulting cynical view that most Romans adopted toward multiple divorces and *mariages de convenance*, whether for political or financial reasons, furnishes another target of Martial's indignant wit. Not unconnected with this is the somewhat strange Roman attitude toward offspring, which was linked with their feelings about abortion, supposititious foundlings, and natural children by female slaves. To the modern reader the frequency, indeed the casualness, of adoption among upperclass Romans must seem surprising. Concern over a cuckoo in the nest, the male-chauvinist desire to be the first and only man in a woman's life, would appear to have been minimal in Roman upper-class males. Indeed the recorded eulogies to a *univira*, a wife who had had but one husband, suggest the rarity of such a marital status in Rome at this period. And a number of Martial's epigrams, for all their epigrammatic hyperbole, make the same point, particularly those that jeer at marriages to rich and ailing widows, or at divorcées who marry so often that their unions seem mere legalized adultery (VI.7). What is also to be divined in Martial, as indeed in Juvenal, is a pervasive fear and resentment of the personal liberty that women now claimed and obtained for themselves in spite of their official legal status vis-à-vis males.

The ready, if not always voluntary, availability of sexual partners in a slave society is difficult to appreciate even in the twentieth century. There are in Martial such revealing epigrams as I.84, directed against a member of the equestrian order who could not be bothered with the problems of a wife, but preferred to produce sons, homebred knights, with the help of female slaves. The point turns more on social snobbery and propriety (he might free these servile sons and adopt them) than on any questioning of Quirinalis's abuse of his power. That Roman women took surreptitious advantage of this servile availability is obvious, not just from the evidence of Martial and Juvenal, but also from the complex and often penal legislation governing the relationships, legal status, and offspring of free women and slave males. A typical, if hyperbolic, epigram to summarize on this point would be VI.39. There Martial claims that Cinna's wife, Marulla, has made Cinna seven times a father—not of free children, for neither friends nor neighbors nor he himself were involved. No, they are all children of slaves, including Cinna's own catamite. And there would be more if two of Cinna's slaves were not eunuchs. Another, more humorous squib (VII.14) concerns a female friend's recent calamity: she has lost her plaything, which was not Lesbia's sparrow or Violentilla's dove, but a twelve-year-old slave whose tool had not reached eighteen inches.

Obviously women were claiming equal rights in their intimate personal lives; among other things, they demanded mutual pleasure from their menfolk as their natural due. The impact of these demands on males in a fundamentally patriarchal society, which may be seen in both our literary and nonliterary evidence, was predictable. Martial's record of the male reaction may be paralleled in the reaction of men to the twentieth-century women's liberation movement. The subsequent jealousy and spying are recorded in several epigrams (e.g., I.73), as are the complaisance and acceptance of this freedom by some husbands (V.61). Martial professes particular disgust for older women who still gratify their sexual urges (III.22), but he also expresses dismay at blatant and excessive sexuality in any female, whatever her age or social status (IV.12).

The strong distaste Martial expresses for oral sex, particularly the pleasuring of females, is part of this hostile attitude. Such practices are to be expected only in societies where women are accustomed to demand and receive extensive foreplay, orgasm, and all the sexual satisfactions arrogated in other ancient societies by the male. For the male to indulge in cunnilingus, then, was to reverse the male and female roles, and it therefore incurs Martial's wittiest contempt.

Martial's fear and dislike of emancipated women and his general cynicism about contemporary female chastity were attitudes he shared with most of his audience. Epigrams I.62, IV.71, and IV.81 are variations on Ovid's theme that the only chaste woman is one who has never been asked (casta est quam nemo rogavit). Caelia's xenophiliac promiscuity (VII.30) is another aspect of the theme. The obverse of the coin is Martial's professed admiration for Lucan's faithful widow, Polla Argentaria, and other models of wifely and matronly decorum who knew their place. Such women were safe and no threat to socially insecure males like Martial. Besides making hostile allusions to female adultery (II.39, 56), he attacks fellation by females (I.94, II.50, III.87, IV.84, VI.69) and directs particularly biting barbs at aged widows hoping to remarry (III.93) and aging Lady Chatterleys who buy sexual pleasure by purchasing handsome young slaves (II.34). (We note that there is no criticism of grizzled centurions or aging poets, such as Martial himself, who have, or hope for, similar pretty slave boys [II.48, 49; III.65; IV.7, 42; V.46, 48; VI.34; VII.29].) Martial also severely criticizes the nonservile lovers of such aging women (e.g., III.76; IV.5.6, 28; V.45), although it must be remembered that what a Roman male and what a modern man would characterize as "an old woman" differs considerably, since the median age of mortality for Roman matrons was only thirty-four years.

We may detect then in Martial a strong fear of women other than prostitutes and respectable wives, and his most telling epigram on this topic, whether it is most revealing about himself or his audience, is surely VIII.12, which concludes with the ringing chauvinist sentiment:

> Inferior matrona suo sit, Prisce, marito:
> Non aliter fiunt femina virque pares.
>
> (3–4)

In Robert Fletcher's version:

> Let matrons to their spouse inferior be,
> Else man and wife have no equality.

By the lights of his age, Martial was fairly conventional in his sexual values as regards the opposite sex, although his frank, and sometimes crude, language had to be defended on grounds of literary tradition and the demands of the genre.

The same may be said of his frequent use of homosexual topics. There was clearly a standard assumption in this classical period of Rome that men were promiscuously heterosexual *and* homosexual, and the easy sexual access to charming slaves of both sexes, again plain in Martial, would partially explain this automatic assumption, which can be paralleled in Catullus, Horace, Vergil, Tibullus, Ovid, Petronius, and Juvenal.

On the other hand, Martial displays strong animosity toward lesbians, toward what he calls *tribades*, just as he is equally against the idea that anal sodomy with a female (this in an epigram to his fictitious wife!) could be a substitute for active pederasty. This, too, would be an unnatural role reversal. In one of his more vicious and artificial epigrams he characterizes lesbianism as a monstrous and enigmatic form of female adultery (I.90).

If we juxtapose this attitude with his approving attitude toward pederasty (I.92), the keeping of boy slaves as catamites, his own request to a patron for a young Alexis such as Vergil had enjoyed, and his sad epitaphs for some of those pretty favorites, then his double standard is plain. It is typical of Roman patriarchal society and is consonant with other literary evidence from the first and second centuries A.D.

His objection to female perversion, including exhibitionism, is unqualified, but Martial is not tolerant of all forms of male homosexuality either. The association of philosophy and homosexuality, a traditional charge since the days of Socrates, is the butt of several of Martial's epigrams (and Juvenal's second satire), although it was the hypocrisy involved rather than the homosexuality itself that Martial, and presumably his readers, disliked. Again, while a number of epigrams provide evidence that there was no personal or social disapproval of active pederastic behavior, generally with handsome young slaves, the behavior that *was* regarded as unseemly and disreputable was passive homosexuality, whether anal or oral, in a mature citizen. Oral sex was associated with a pale complexion, as was the writing of poetry, so the perverted Oppianus had to write verses to cover up his profligate disposition. The social disapproval of passive male homosexuality (VII.7) is again evident from both our Greek and Latin sources.

These dominating themes, along with literary polemic and the venting of personal spleen against plagiarists and detractors, explain the thrust of Martial's satiric epigrams, but every satirist has to convey, implicitly or explicitly, his own positive values or at least the values that would awaken sympathetic echoes in the minds of his audience.

In what we may call his "protreptic" epigrams we find expressed in memorable form a typically Roman epicureanism, very similar to that of Horace and his Greek precursors: *carpe diem*, enjoy the present and be content with a modest, if gentlemanly, sufficiency. It is best summed up in his most admired (and most translated) poem, X.47.

There are no hopes of heaven or fears of hell, no deep religious feelings, merely an acceptance of the traditional Roman religion as reformed by imperial exigencies. Of sympathies toward foreign or mystery cults, such as those of the Magna Mater or Cybele, or Judaism, there is no trace, except as material for sardonic humor. There is, then, nothing to compensate for Martial's pagan sense of the fragility of human existence. Such a note later found more reverberations in the England of the Reformation than in Catholic Spain. And his gnomic brevity in variations on the theme were to be repeated in epigraphs, prefaces, and sundials: *pereunt et imputantur; vivere bis vita est posse priore frui; non est vivere, sed valere vita; cineri gloria sera venit;* and many others. This was the elegiac note on life's transiency that attracted so many of the Tudor poets, accustomed as they were to the life at court being often "nasty, brutish, and short."

MARTIAL'S INFLUENCE ON ENGLISH POETRY
by J. P. Sullivan

Martial not only survived the advent of Christianity and the drastic and arbitrary destruction of Greek and Roman authors by the Middle Ages but came to enjoy, as a rediscovered classic in the Tudor period, almost the popularity of Ovid and Seneca, despite his unevenness in comparison with those more elevated authors, an unevenness he frankly admitted (I.16). Martial's contemporary and patron, the Younger Pliny, on hearing the sad news of his death in Spain in A.D. 104, professed admiration for his combination of sincerity, acuity, and wit, but he doubted whether Martial's works would long survive, even though he had written them as though they would (*Ep.* 3.21.1). How wrong Pliny's judgment was!

Indeed, Martial seems from the beginning to have been extremely popular. Despite the mock-modest pose about the literary value of his "trifles" and his elaborate *apologia* for its occasional obscenity, Martial describes the epigram, as Juvenal describes satire, as a true and educational commentary on life and morality. There is in epigram more social realism and criticism than is to be found in mythological epics such as Statius's *Thebaid* or in abstruse works such as the *Aetia* of Callimachus (IV.49, X.4). Martial can therefore boast of his status as an accepted contemporary classic in Rome and the provinces (V.13, 16; VI.60), and that status and his influence did not cease with his death. The satires of his friend and near contemporary Juvenal relied heavily on Martial's wit and observation. Indeed, as one critic has said, an understanding of Juvenal is impossible without a profound knowledge of Martial. This, of course, was the way Roman authors worked, and sixteenth- and seventeenth-century poets in England were to do the same. Inserted into a new production, allusions, indeed outright thefts, were flattering compliments to the classical status or superior art of the original poet. As T. S. Eliot says, "Bad poets plagiarize; good poets steal." Martial had done the same with his Greek and Latin predecessors.

Juvenal was clearly most impressed by the unexpected and witty concluding twist to Martial's epigrams, what was later to be called "point," and a majority of Martial's imitators established this as the paradigm of verse epigram. Many of Martial's own poems are not of this type at all, but all were characterized by him as "epigrams," even when fifty lines long, so that the practice of Ben Jonson and his contemporaries in Elizabethan times conforms to Martial's broader (rather than the modern) definition: for example, Jonson has as a coda to his *Epigrams* a poem two hundred lines long. Clearly an epigram was any short (or not so short) poem its author decided to call an epigram. The usage narrowed later to mean specifically the short witty poems that comprise a large part, but not the whole, of the *Greek Anthology* and Martial. From the success of this tradition finally evolved the secondary meaning of *epigram*, signifying any pointed or pithy saying at all, whether in speech, prose, or verse.

Martial's popularity in the ancient world and even in late antiquity is, however, beyond dispute. Our text comes down to us in three separate families of manuscripts, one descending from a copy emended in A.D. 401 by a lawyer, Torquatus Gennadius; all furnish confirmation that a number of different copies were available in very early times to the curious. It is significant that the anthologies expurgate some of the sexual words used in the epigrams, and Martial was to be exposed to similar bowdlerization later. Nevertheless, already in the second century L. Aelius Caesar, Hadrian's adopted son, had called him his Vergil, and this imperial cachet and numerous references and quotations, as well as patent forgeries, bear witness to his popularity. Though excoriated by Christian writers such as Marius Mercator for his obscenity, toward the end of antiquity he was still cited by grammarians such as Servius and Priscian and by the encyclopaedist Isidorus, bishop of Seville (602–636); he was plagiarized and imitated by such pagan and Christian poets as Ausonius (d. c. 395), Prudentius (c. 348–405), Sidonius Apollinaris (c. 430–480), Venantius Fortunatus (c. 540–600) and the Vandal encomiast Luxorius (c. 450). His literary presence was felt in the Carolingian revival of learning in the late eighth century, and in the twelfth and thirteenth centuries he provided quotations and even vicious turns of phrase for such learned wits as John of Salisbury, Walter Map, Peter of Blois, Godfrey of Winchester (whose work was often confused with that of Martial himself), Giraldus Cambrensis, and Vincent de Beauvais. But as with other authors, it was the Renaissance, when the search for lost classics was pursued in earnest, that restored him to his former glory. Appropriately, the author of the *Decameron*, Giovanni Boccaccio, may be given some of the credit for rediscovering Martial at the monastery of Monte Cassino about 1361, and so bringing him back into circulation, this time among the most distinguished Italian humanists, such as Coluccio Salutati, Niccolò Niccoli, Poggio Bracciolini, and Lorenzo Valla.

With the advent of printing, about 1450, Martial was among the first Latin classics off the press: the *editio princeps* was printed perhaps in Rome about 1471, followed by editions in Ferrara and Venice. Editions began appearing in France (1502, Lyons), where in later centuries Martial would have such enormous literary impact, his *sal Romanus* being an appropriate condiment for *l'esprit français*. England waited until 1615 for its first native edition, from the schoolmaster Thomas Farnaby. But continental editions had long been available to his admirers.

Besides the complete editions of Martial in Italy, France, and Holland, there also appeared various anthologies and supposed editions which eliminated material that might offend the prudish or corrupt the young. The most popular was the condensed collection of the Jesuit André Frusius, which was put to press by his confrere Edmond Auger in 1558 in Rome and steadily reprinted until 1702. Another Jesuit, Matthaeus Rader, produced another bowdlerized and frequently reprinted edition in 1599, to the indignation of John Donne, who wrote:

> Why this man gelded *Martiall* I muse
> Except himselfe alone his tricks would use,
> As *Katherine*, for the Courts sake, put downe Stewes.

The Delphin edition was produced in 1680 by Vincent Colleson, who, to Byron's amusement, printed all the obscene epigrams conveniently at the end of the volume. Naturally the parts of Martial's poetry that prompted such expurgation were to present even greater difficulties to translators and critics, particularly in the nineteenth and early twentieth centuries.

Now why did a fairly voluminous, frequently tedious, sometimes obscure poet such as Martial, part of whose literary persona was that of a flatterer, pederast, and place seeker, whose language, though cosmopolitan and innovative, smacked often of the gutter, whose attitudes to the opposite sex were, to say the least, denigrating—why did such a writer exercise such an influence on post-Renaissance literature in Europe, particularly on English poetry in the sixteenth and seventeenth centuries? For Martial attracted not only translators, although there were enough of these, but also imitators and emulators, courtiers and clergymen. Robert Herrick, a man of the cloth, aspired to become the English Martial and almost succeeded. John Heywood, Sir John Davies, and the neo-Latin epigrammatist John Owen were all hailed as the English Martial, and the title was obviously much coveted.

The unabashed flattery of emperors and other patrons to which Martial's economic circumstances and social views impelled him was not a feature of Martial's work that perturbed either sixteenth- or seventeenth-century poets and critics. They, too, knew the mechanics and requirements of power and patronage.

A more positive consideration for Martial's popularity may be advanced. The sixteenth century was the great age of the amateur poet. It was a perfect time for the short poem, specifically the epigram as now popularly conceived, to come into its own. And a long list could be compiled of writers whose chosen genre was the short, ingenious, witty poem, whether dedicatory or derisory, sentimental or sententious, amorous or invidious, directed at the living or the dead, the real or the fictitious. Among the more distinguished practitioners were Sir John Davies; Sir John Denham; John Donne; Sir John Harrington; John Heywood; Henry Howard, earl of Surrey; Mathew Prior; John Wilmot, earl of Rochester; and Sir Henry Wotton. For one who took to the writing of short poems or epigrams, Martial was clearly the ancient epigrammatist par excellence: the treasures of the Palatine Anthology, like lace, were accessible to few. So Martial became to epigram what Ovid was to love poetry, Horace to lyric, and Vergil to epic. Sir John Harrington (1560–1612), who based at least eighty of his four hundred and thirty epigrams on Martial's work, expressed the sentiment of most of his fellow practitioners of polite poetry when he said:

> It is certain, that of all poems, the Epigram is the pleasantest, and of all that writes epigrams, Martial is counted the wittiest.

At this time there was a close connection between poetry and translation, which was to be drawn even tighter by free adaptation and, later, by the poetic mode of imitation. As Ezra Pound puts it in his "Notes on Elizabethan Classicists": "A great age of literature is also a great age of translations; or follows it." For Ben Jonson "creative translation" was as demanding a task for a poet or "maker" as the production of supposedly original lyrics, which are, in any case, partially dependent on earlier models and verse forms.

Contemporary attitudes toward translation and its relationship to original poetry, then, had much to do with Martial's unexpected popularity. It was very tempting to steal from Martial, or adapt him, or "make him new," in Pound's phrase, by introducing fresh instances and contemporary material. If one of Martial's strengths is the witty, and yet almost Dickensian, depiction of Roman life, there is also a universality in Martial's depiction of the society around him that made his portraits and vignettes excellent models, *mutatis mutandis*, for his Elizabethan and Jacobean imitators. These found little trouble in adapting the detailed satiric portraits and sketches of patrons and clients, dandies, upstarts, fortune hunters, connoisseurs, dinner cadgers, lawyers, schoolmasters, doctors, debtors, bores, poisoners, nymphomaniacs, hypocritical intellectuals, and the like to depict the analogous types of their own eras; the street-walking Convent Garden Abbesses, the credulous cullies and gulls, and the fat fussocks had their precursors in Flavian Rome. A few changes of description and names were all that was needed. Similarly, for the Roman poet's sexually perverse or homosexual motifs the Elizabethans substituted the dreaded imagery of the pox, that ever-present fear, as D. H. Lawrence remarks, in the literature of the Elizabethan and Jacobean eras.

The multifariousness of Martial's talent made different aspects of his work attractive in turn to his admirers in these centuries, although many of the English epigrammatists toned down Martial's obscenity even in plain heterosexual matters and there were very few who translated, except in the most delicate ways, Martial's satiric allusions to pederasty, lesbianism, or oral sex. The Reverend Thomas Bastard even boasted:

> I have taught Epigrams to speak chastlie . . .
> Barring them of their olde libertie . . .
>
>   (*Epist. dedic.*)

But beyond this Martial's careful modulations on the age-old themes of life and death, happiness and the joys of the countryside offered useful, compact models for these writers. The sadness Martial could express in some of his epitaphs is duplicated in Sir Henry Wotton's famous epigram *Upon the Death of Sir Albert Morton's Wife*, which is a masterpiece of compression and pathos in Martial's style:

> He first deceased; she for a little tried
> To live without him, liked it not, and died.

Martial's impact on the literary consciousness of Elizabethan England was of the utmost significance for the *progress* of English poetry, not just its matter. Early Elizabethan writing, simple and direct though its thinking was, tended to be stylistically expansive and diffuse. The classical Latin formalism of Martial was to refine and chasten this tendency and also gratify and further stimulate the taste for quick and amusing turns of thought, one of the main attractions of the epigram. The exemplification by John Donne of "metaphysical wit" represents the triumph of epigram over allegory, and in the work of Sir John Harrington and Ben Jonson, Martial's influence is even plainer, more extensive, and more critically absorbed. Harrington brought the development of the epigram as we know it in English literature to its highest point so far. Ben Jonson had a high regard for his own ventures into this area: "the ripest of my studies" he termed his *Epigrammes*. Jonson's aim was to be a radical and serious innovator in the now-established tradition of English epigram, or rather, since epigram was well on its way to developing its satiric connotations, the short poem. He therefore took even greater liberties than Martial in the length of his poems. On the other hand, he restored to his work the eulogistic epigrams that Martial had gladly written for his potential patrons, and took up freely the thematic cycles of epigrams that had been a feature of some of Martial's books.

This restoration of eulogy as an appropriate subject for epigram does not, however, hide the fact that a slight preponderance (60 to 65 percent) of the poems are bitingly or comically satiric. These satiric epigrams are directed, like Martial's, against social rather than political targets, against those addicted to avarice, gluttony, and lechery. This last deadly sin prompted some quite offensive epigrams in Jonson, and they had a somewhat disproportionate effect on the work of his friend the Reverend Robert Herrick, whose volume of epigrams, *Hesperides* (1648), contains even more direct translations of Martial and the *Greek Anthology* and more offensive poems (150 out of 1,100), anticipating in this at least the predilections of modern translators of Martial. Martial thus gave flattery, obscenity, satire, compliment, and social and literary comment a convenient and compact classical base, and the English poets of the period were able to pick and choose among these possibilities almost as they wished. And with the

Restoration, license, rather than liberty, became the order of the
day. The satiric epigram was freed from any fetters it had felt in
Tudor times. The earl of Rochester could produce this epigram
on his king, which is surely in the spirit of Martial but goes far
beyond the freedom of the Flavian poet and his Elizabethan imi-
tators:

> Here lies our Sov'ran Lord the King,
>   Whose word no Man relies on,
> Who never said a Foolish Thing
>   Nor ever did a Wise one.

The satiric possibilities Martial offered his English succes-
sors, his adaptability to climes and times, suggest one key to his
success, but Martial's unexpected influence flowed also from an-
other quality, less political, less social, but more verbal and for-
mal; a quality that was, if intermittent, certainly pervasive in his
better books. There is no word to describe it other than "wit."
Latin brevity may aid it; linguistic ambiguity, even puns nourish
it; but the quality of mind that it represents is unmistakable. And
this quality above all attracted the practitioners of English poetry
in their struggle toward the apparent formal perfection presented
them, for good or ill, by the poetry of Greece and Rome. Metri-
cally and linguistically, Martial gave some verse practitioners an
achievable goal: perfect formal control, with that sting in the tail,
the punchline. The poet who looked to Martial could decide more
easily when he had achieved his poetic purpose most economi-
cally. It is scarcely an exaggeration to claim that the lineal de-
scendants of Martial's biting elegiac distichs are the couplets of
John Dryden and Alexander Pope, the greatest satirists and among
the best coiners of poetic epigram in the language. The sure En-
glishing of satiric wit would have scarcely been possible without
the earlier work of Martial's devoted admirers.

In the post-Augustan period of English literature Martial
could rely on the same attractions he held for the audiences who
appreciated the wit and poetic skills of Dryden and Pope. Adap-
tations, imitations, and translations of Martial remained popular,
and many may be found in *The Rambler* and *The Gentleman's
Magazine*. But with the advent of the romantic movement in

England a century later, Martial's social and political values, not
to mention his sexual attitudes, became disreputable. The poetic
revolution preferred odes to couplets, and Shelley found more
inspiration in Greek tragedy than in the less elevated genres of
satire and epigram, just as Wordsworth turned more to the beau-
ties of nature than to the imperfections of urban man. Even By-
ron, somewhat ironically, referred to "all those nauseous epi-
grams of Martial."

Worse was to follow in the Victorian age. Its verdict on the
epigrammatist is summarized in Macaulay's damning judgment
in one of his letters:

> I have now gone through the first seven books of Martial, and have
> learned about 360 of the best lines. His merit seems to me to lie, not
> in wit, but in the rapid succession of vivid images. I wish he were
> less nauseous. He is as great a beast as Aristophanes. He is certainly
> a very clever, pleasant writer. Sometimes he runs Catullus himself
> hard. But, besides his indecency, his servility and his mendicancy
> disgust me. In his position,—for he was a Roman knight,—some-
> thing more like self-respect would have been becoming. I make large
> allowance for the difference of manners; but it can never have been
> comme il faut in any age or nation for a man of note,—an accom-
> plished man,—a man living with the great,—to be constantly asking
> for money, clothes, and dainties, and to pursue with volleys of abuse
> those who would give him nothing.

This was the sort of critical evaluation that was to hold sway
in scholarly histories of Latin literature almost up to the present.
Nevertheless Martial still had his admirers even in the nine-
teenth century. The blameless Henry Bohn took especial pains in
presenting him to the British public in his Classical Library
(1859), ferreting out verse translations from old editions and man-
uscripts to accompany the standard prose versions. Naturally he
left the most indecent poems in "the decent obscurity of a
learned language," providing there only the Latin text, a boon to
prurient schoolboys, and sometimes an Italian translation by
Giuspanio Graglia. Some "Other Victorians," most prominently
George Augustus Sala, hurried to supply poetic renderings of
these (with imaginative annotations) in the Index Expurgatorius
to Martial a year or two later. Somewhat later still, Robert Louis

Stevenson, a number of whose versions are well worth reprinting in this volume, also defied the prevailing disapproval by translating a generous selection of Martial's more acceptable epigrams among his own poetry.

In the modernist reaction to nineteenth-century and post-romantic notions of poetry, Martial was to some degree rehabilitated along with Catullus and Propertius by Ezra Pound, who detected in his shorter poems manifestations of Imagism and the appropriate application of language to material without unnecessary verbiage or rhetorical clutter. Although Pound translated only one, rather insignificant, humorous epigram, reprinted in this volume, the Roman poet's influence may be seen clearly in the pointed satiric sketches he published in *Personae*. This critical cachet was reaffirmed by T. S. Eliot.

Of course not all of Martial could be assimilated by twentieth-century poets, but what could be accepted in the new atmosphere of candid realism and social consciousness was the satirical obscenity that had so offended Victorian sensibilities. Martial's verses in search of patronage and reward, congenial enough in the seventeenth and eighteenth centuries, had no attractions and provided no models in the different economic circumstances of the modern age. Consequently the selections translated by Peter Porter, James Michie, Tony Harrison, Dudley Fitts, and others represented in this book show a perhaps disproportionate emphasis on the grotesque, the sexual, and the disreputable aspects of Martial's genius. (After all, the avowedly sexual or frankly obscene epigrams of Martial constitute scarcely a tenth of his oeuvre.) But then it was impossible for Martial to reach the twentieth century whole, and the modern reader perhaps can appreciate him best in an anthology such as this, compiled by modern editors from the versions of mainly modern translators. The Appendix in some small fashion tries to provide an insight into his somewhat different appeal to earlier tastes.

ON TRANSLATING MARTIAL

by Peter Whigham

PRINCIPLES

There is a story of an American lady who called on Victor
Hugo to ask him to autograph a volume of his works. The great
man was all but deaf, and they had to communicate through an
interpreter. "Just tell him," the lady said, "I can't wait to get back
to the States to read some of his books." Whereupon the inter-
preter bellowed in the bard's ear: "Cher Maitre, Madame m'a dit
que vous êtes l'aigle de la belle France, mère des armes et des
arts."

Did the interpreter fail in his task? Was the translation ade-
quate? He did not translate what the lady actually said. But then,
given the circumstances, that was hardly possible. He translated,
it may be supposed, what she would have wished to have said,
even, one may aver, what she should have said. The moral is clear:
circumstance is the great dictator. Under certain circumstances
there are certain things one just doesn't say, and contrariwise,
other things that insist on being said and on no account may be
left unsaid. From this point of view, Richmond Lattimore's aim
of translating each word, exactly as in the original, appears im-
practical to the point of irrelevance. Robert Lowell, in the intro-
duction to his *Imitations*, is nearer the mark. He says he has tried
to write as though the original author were alive and writing in
English. Of course, were Martial alive and writing in English—or
any other language—it is supremely doubtful that he would de-
vote his anecdotal skill to jokes about infibulation (which served
in place of chastity belts for male slaves). However, there are var-
ious devices by which such difficulties can be overcome, notably
"transposition." Lowell, no doubt consciously, was paraphrasing
Dryden, who said almost exactly the same thing, the difference
being that for Lowell it meant allowing himself to be possessed
by his originals, turning himself into them, a mediumistic pro-
cess, which, insofar as it is possible, leaves the poor originals very
much astray in the modern world. For Dryden it was just the
other way around: *he* sought to possess *them*, turning them into

himself. The distinction is radical and one I shall elaborate on in a minute. The point here is not to compare Dryden with Lowell, but both with Lattimore.

It is not simply a matter of transposition, conjuring Latin names and customs into their modern equivalents, a technique Peter Porter has used with some success in his translations of Martial. Martial has suffered more than most from this sort of treatment. It is a method that has its uses, particularly, and paradoxically, when equivalents are lacking. It also has its dangers. Litters, for the most part, are best permitted to remain such and need not be referred to as taxicabs; taverns are not cocktail bars; nor are slave girls waitresses, or even parlor maids. When transposition is used merely to make the reader feel more at home in the remote, strange world of antiquity, the result is too often a factitious cozying-up to what becomes even more remote and strange for not being perceived as such. On the other hand, when equivalents are made not to cosset the lazy or fearful reader but to reveal moral similarities between the past and present, the method is justified. Locally, it should be applied with caution; on a wide scale, in Johnson's use of Juvenal, or Pound's of Propertius, it becomes "imitation" or "homage," an explicit interlocking of past and present by means of which the classic can realize its function of invoking the present.

If, then, it is not a question of transposition, what is it? We must turn to Borges's fable of Pierre Ménard, which puts the matter clearly. Were, by some bizarre force of circumstance, a work from the past to be produced again today, exactly, word for word, as in its original composition, it would not be the same work. For Cervantes to conceive Don Quixote in sixteenth-century Spain was one thing; for you or me—or him—to produce Don Quixote today would be something quite other. What we translate is not some original, pristine work, slumbering out there in the past, waiting for the miracle translator with his magic xerox machine to whisk it into the present. The opposite is true. We know the poem only in the present, as it has come to us, with the patina of time adhering to it, not to be stripped away. We can no longer know Sappho's "*Phainetai moi*" as it was before Catullus translated it, nor can we know Catullus's own kissing poems as they were before passing through Ben Jonson's hands. And we should not wish to. To do so would be to fall for the notion that the past is somehow *there*, separate from us. This is a misconception that has been widespread since the invention of historical perspective at the beginning of the nineteenth century. The past is not there at all—at least, not in any static sense. It does not exist except in our knowing it. Far from being static, it shifts precisely as the present shifts. Hence the need for our continual reassessment of it as self-validation. Which is precisely what translation is: a validation of today in relation to yesterday.

From this it follows that there are no definitive translations. Each age is under the necessity of making its own. The watershed here is what I have just referred to as "the invention of historical perspective." Before that, as far back as one cares to go, the past was felt to have close kinship with the present, to be, indeed, alive in it. This is evident in the common approach to translation of all ages before the nineteenth century. And this unselfconscious sense of possessing the past prompted the translator to treat his original as part of his own world. Catullus, in the poem from Sappho, inserts an entire line—*ille si fas est superare divos*—that has no source in the Greek. The liberty has nothing to do with transposition, or veneer of detail, but is the result of a perceived affinity. It is what Sappho would have said had she been a Roman, for Romans were always more cautious in such matters as comparing themselves to the gods than were the Greeks. Chaucer dressed his Trojan and Greek heroes up as Red Cross knights, pricking beneath the battlements of Troy, not because he thought that by doing so he would make them more acceptable to his mediaeval readers. He did so because that was how he perceived them—as part of his world. The baroque interludes of Gavin Douglas, bishop of Dunkeld, sandwiched between the books of his *Aeneid*, do not come amiss, since Vergil's characters have become renaissance figures and their exploits are such as to be found in a book of wonders of the period. Much the same may be said of Chapman. His tortured syntax, lingering over the minutest details in the Homeric picture, may retard the forward movement of the narrative, but we are made to feel that Homer's vigor has found fresh roots, native Elizabethan ones, and with this

the pedantry falls away. And so with Pope. The Homeric hexa-
meter, moving through the mazes of the Popean paragraph, to-
gether with Homer's clear outline in description and event, ani-
mate, in the foreign context of a Newtonian universe, what is
arguably the finest poem of the century. The influence in such
works—in all translations of any consequence—is two-way. The
translator interprets his Homer or his Vergil in the light of where
they have arrived at that time. And the original makes, in the
mouth of the translator, new work in the new language, which
would not otherwise have been possible. So the translator—and
it has been said that all art is in some sense translation—me-
diates between past and present, preventing the present from
going dead by constant refocussing on and readjusting to the past.

The whole subject of poet/translator as mediator between
past and present is first laid out by Homer himself in the episode
at the court of King Alcinous. Homer/Demodocos sings of the
past happenings at Troy. The stranger, revealing himself as Odys-
seus, takes up the tale. What for others was closed history is still
for Odysseus in process of enactment, so much so that he weeps
as the tale unfolds. For them, the wanderer, whom they have
known only as a figure of the present, suddenly becomes a figure
of history. He steps backward into the past as the past steps for-
ward into their midst. This attitude, first to be discerned in
Homer, in abeyance through the nineteenth century, has been
given rebirth in our time by Pound, not simply in his translations,
but in his entire oeuvre, and particularly his *Cantos*—the whole
concept of them. It is an attitude that dispenses with the distinc-
tion between "original" and "translated" work, and that would
in fact hold that the most original work is as often as not trans-
lated.

If, with the coming of the romantics and historical perspec-
tive, the sense of nonlinear development, of still on various levels
possessing the same world as one's originals—originals, at least,
of the classical world—was lost, was anything gained? The an-
swer would be: adherence to the letter, though whether this can
be considered as anything other than an archeological gain is
questionable. The idea that there is a past that we can come to
know in its own terms by strenuous acts of historical imagination

led in literary matters to a scrupulous regard for texts and, in poetic translation, for preserving the strict prose meaning of one's originals. Not surprisingly a conflict was discovered between the claims of the translator's living language, his spirit of composition, and those of literalness. As a result, translatorese was born. At its best, it aimed at a so-called timeless style, vaguely modeled on the King James version of the Bible and known as "Wardour Street," from the district in London where theatrical costumes are sold. At its worst, it was merely unreadable. Soon the idea took root that poetic translation was impossible. The chasm that had been philosophically created between past and present made such an idea inevitable. But it was unfortunate, for it removed translation, in the minds of most readers, and many poets, from the center of literary activity, a position it had always held from Chaucer through Shakespeare to Johnson. "Nothing changes," said Oscar Wilde to the shocked delight of his audience, "but fashion and adjectives." To an Elizabethan or Restoration audience, who might have been amused by the excess of the remark, but no more, translation was a natural way of "breaking bread with the past" (in W. H. Auden's phrase), and so finding one's bearings in the present. By Wilde's time it had become a specialized activity, even a slightly shady one (*traditore/traduttore*) and unworthy of the serious attention given to original work.

This changed attitude to translation was particularly unfortunate as far as Martial was concerned. The Victorian ideal of literalness spawned difficulties. The sense of day-by-day moral experience shared with the ancients had considerably diminished, if not evaporated, but it is just such a spectacle of the world's passing show that Martial's work presents. The *De spectaculis* of Titus's amphitheater spills over in the subsequent twelve books into the streets of Rome. The shifting images of sand, chariots, animals, and gladiators give place to the scarcely less stimulating kaleidoscope of metropolitan life, public and private, social, literary, and domestic, conducted with tooth and talon. It is all this, reported directly as he saw it, that Martial gives us. For the Victorians, this was natural material for the historical novel, a new form that, with the new historical consciousness, they developed so avidly. It was too strong a dose for poetry.

The obscene poems were not the real problem, for they amount to a very small proportion of the total work; nor are they in any way essential to it, as the obscene poems of Catullus are to his work. They are, as is well known, excessively coarse. Even the Elizabethan and Restoration translators found it necessary to soften them. The Victorians found them impossible. But this was not the point. Martial's world was dead and gone, fit study for archeologists. Had he written about *himself* like Catullus, they would have said, we could have found something to respond to, human nature being ever fresh and engaging. We could perhaps—as with Catullus—have forgiven the obscenities, even if we could not have translated them. The response to this is to point to Jonson's "Penshurst" or Herrick's *Hesperides*, the latter modeled expressly on Martial. Herrick, as a whole poet, was largely destroyed by the Victorian anthologists, who could handle him only sentimentally. It is interesting to observe that neither Jonson nor Herrick, the two poets who have adapted Martial most fruitfully, finds an echo in the nineteenth century. The only poet of the age through whom Martial speaks in those abrasive tones, but with a formality like a piece of well-oiled machinery, is Walter Savage Landor. But then, despite his dates (1775–1864), Landor remained all his life an eighteenth-century man. The editors of his collected works distinguish between "Poems" and "Epigrams," as used to be the fashion. Needless to say (*pace* Ben Jonson on *his* epigrams) much of the best poetry is to be found under the head of "Epigrams":

> Thy skin is like an unwashed carrot's.
> Thy tongue is blacker than a parrot's.
> Thy teeth are crooked, but belong
> Inherently to such a tongue.

Martial is there.

If the Victorians lacked sympathy for Martial's subject matter, they lacked sympathy in equal degree for the form in which that subject matter is presented. Epigrams were not, by definition, poetry. In an essay on his friend Pound, T. S. Eliot notes Martial's influence, specifically in the epigrams in *Lustra*, and declares his taste to be "possibly too romantic" to appreciate them fully. He went on to assert that an appreciation of Pope as poetry was, at the time he was writing, a test of the ability to judge poetry. That was in 1928. Today, the Augustans are once again a touchstone of the permanent. Byron's *Don Juan* is no longer a mildly scandalous romp, but the greatest comic poetic masterpiece we have. The classicism T. E. Hulme, Pound, and the men of 1914 proclaimed may not have been in them. To many of us now they probably appear irremediable romantics. But whether it is that we have moved nearly a century from the romantic Victorians, or whether it is the example of at least the desire of the founding fathers of modernism, we no longer, in Eliot's phrase, compare all poetry to the "Ode to a Nightingale" before passing judgment on it. Pound as usual bears much of the responsibility.

> When I consider the curious habits of dogs
> I am compelled to conclude
> That man is the superior animal.
> When I consider the curious habits of man
> I confess, my friend, I am puzzled.

Martial is there.

If we are not exactly preromantics, much that enabled poets as diverse as Jonson, Herrick, and Landor to find bearings for their own day in Martial's works has been restored to us. The physical mundanities of daily life are back, center stage. If a "Penshurst" is beyond us, something at heart similar, such as quite eluded the Victorians, is not impossible to imagine. In fact Auden in much of his work has shown the way here, admirably transposing many of Jonson's ethical and even aesthetic loci. Wit, liberated from the Victorian whimsy to which it was shackled, is again a weapon. Common sense and shared experience are no longer attitudes reserved for prose. Most important of all, the whole spectacle of life is again poetry's sphere. Appearances are less than reality, surfaces superficial, only to people with superficial minds, as Jonson and Herrick understood well. The witches of exclusion, taste, and gentility have beaten a retreat. What is there to be reported may be reported. With such a catalogue of Martialesque virtues not foreign to reader or writer for the first time in two hundred years, the occasion ripens for a new English edition of Martial.

The admirable Dr. Bohn did his best in the mid nineteenth century, but the age was against him. Though his book has been, and still is, of considerable value, it is our intent to replace it. To trace the effect that the translated poet has on his translators, and vice versa, was beyond Bohn. Our book, we hope, will illustrate this.

There is a final point. Martial is technically adept, but formally he is neither very varied nor inventive. In substance he is both these things. It seems to us that to portray Martial, formally, in the rather unvaried manner in which he has traditionally been rendered in any given age is to do him a disservice. His varied substance can, and should, be presented by means of a wide variety of formal approaches. As one draws on all those who have Englished Martial, from Wyatt on, a whole range of possible ways of assimilating him begins to emerge. And after the recent era of experimentation, we are in a good position to add to these, whether by pastiche, "work in the manner of," variations on old themes, or striking out on our own in fresh experiment—whatever may seem best to define substance. Clarity of definition, a sharp eye and sharper tongue, the poetry of the intensive use of language, rather than of association, the modulations of syntax in familiar rhythms, these are the hallmarks of the style the translator, free as seldom before in selection of technique, has as his "prime material." If what we have made of Martial over the centuries and what he has made of us are illustrated here, the new versions—approximately half the whole—also show what he is continuing to do. Unforeseen poetic opportunities offer themselves as one submits to his schooling. The old Spaniard's voice still sounds, even in our foreign accents, teaching us new ways to use our own tongue.

TECHNIQUES

It will be noted that few translators of Martial over the centuries have tried to adapt his varied meters in their English renderings. The commonest meters we encounter in the Roman poet's work are the scazon, or limping iambic line, the elegiac distich, consisting of an hexameter followed by a pentameter, and the Phalaecian hendecasyllable. The English poets, as we might expect, have relied on various forms of iambic verse: initially, the rhymed couplet that we associate with Dryden and Pope; then, later, the looser iambic line, with or without various patterns of rhyming. Here and there an English translator, particularly when given the greater freedom of imitation, has experimented with quatrains in different rhyme schemes, but these are the exception rather than the rule. The line of wit, so to speak, seemed the ideal medium for Martial, at least until the twentieth century, when careful use of rhythm and irregular line length allowed greater suppleness and often accuracy. But a disquisition on either Latin or English verse forms would be too lengthy to indulge in here.

What can be said of the technique of verse translation is that if the translator has failed to write a poem, he has done nothing. But if that is all he has done, he has not done enough. A poem that is a translation is required to be continually illuminating of its original. Although it is true that the poetry of the original remains inviolate in the original language, locked up in the Latin or Greek, it is also true that the act of Englishing in itself represents a form of violation, leaving the original both more and less than it was before. And as for the language of translation, that too undergoes a similar violation in the attempt to accommodate the original's foreignness. The assertion that it is the translator's duty first and foremost to write a poem needs to be accompanied by a reminder that every poem (that *is* a poem) is a new poem. Every poem is an experiment. An urgent original, one that, in Osip Mandelstam's phrase, *disturbs meanings*, must not be turned into something the opposite of urgent, something faded, that does not press to be uttered. Which is what most often happens. Poems that once were disturbers of meanings are turned into faded imitations of themselves, where all meanings lie deathly quiet. Any technique that prevents the Englishing of a poem in this way is fit for use. Any that distracts from the translator's prime duty is to be eschewed. With that caveat in mind, here is a small litany of *Do's and Don'ts*.

1. *Don't confound your fidelities.* The translator's fidelity is bound to one thing and one thing only—the poetry. Of the three elements in any poem—sound, sense, and image—none takes precedence; the important thing is the relation between them,

which is the poem. As Pound observed, images often carry over quite well; sound almost never. As for sense, there are the dictionary meanings of words, which is their prosaic sense, and the sense they acquire through their relations with the other two elements, sound and image, which is their poetic sense. It cannot be too strongly stated that the prose content of a poem is not coterminous with the poetry. If it were, one would be able to paraphrase any poem and lose next to nothing; while translating poetry would differ little, except in effort, from reading it. But this, as is generally agreed, is not the case.

2. *Don't insert images not in the original.* Possible exceptions may be made in the case of latent images—allusions you perceive as such.

3. *Don't tamper with the order in which the images occur.* The dynamic architecture of the image, as one emerges from another, is the heart of the poem.

4. *Don't count the number of syllables in a line, but the time it takes to say them.* Specifically, a line of Latin or Greek will almost invariably contain more syllables, though fewer words, than the same line in English. This has led translators in search of metrical equivalence to pad. Time, not number, is the key.

5. *Don't put your foot in your mouth just because your model has put his in his.* Pound comments on this somewhere. You are not required to ape bêtises, but to recreate beauty.

6. *Don't obfuscate for the sake of so-called "scholarly accuracy."* Your business is to keep your man in the marketplace, not preserve him for professorial entombment.

7. As corollary to 6 above, *be ready with insertions that will save footnotes.*

8. *Don't feel that because you have started translating in metaphrase you cannot therefore switch to paraphrase, or even imitation.* Pound frequently did so, earning much opprobrium from scholars of his day. But they are dead, and he lives.

9. *Don't be seduced by the "music" of a poem into trying to make a carbon copy of that music.* It is what the music signifies that is important. I use the inclusive word "music" to denote

the mélange of time, pitch, and beat all speech presents. The
translator must decide which of these elements do what, their
relative functions, and then what he can do about it, making En-
glish, not Latin or Greek, music.

10. *Hew as closely as possible to the way end-stopped and
carry-over lines, lines with heavy internal caesurae, and lines
with no caesurae at all, balance and interlock.* Remember that
there are as many varieties of carry-over lines as there are gram-
matical connections between lines. Such arrangements form the
basic units of articulation and should not be allowed to disappear,
even in a radical reordering of syntax.

11. *Don't seek to convey the accuracy of a strict form by
vague adumbrations thereof.* Cumulatively, the aesthetic effects
of unerringly hitting the nail on the head in line after line of hex-
ameters, or in line after line half doing so, lead in opposite direc-
tions.

12. *When working with closed forms, you may wish to ren-
der form by form—a sonnet by a sonnet.* Where this is possible I
believe it to be desirable, even though a sonnet today may be a
different animal from what it was in Dante's, or even Ronsard's,
day. Campion's "Observations in The Art of English Poesy"
should be studied in this connection, particularly as regards
Sapphics.

13. *You may wish to find an analogue for the form,* a form in
the English tradition that will provide something of the same ef-
fect, or will "place" the original in some way. We do not have
elegiacs or alexandrines in English: the heroic couplet has tradi-
tionally been held fit for both.

14. Should the original be hopelessly foreign, as in Chinese
poetry or an ode by Pindar, *you may want to abandon all notion
of closed form in favor of vers libre,* hoping there to contrive
some echo, but always remembering Eliot's warning: "no vers is
libre." Almost certainly the most difficult of forms.

15. There is a fourth approach, too seldom used: *Analyze the
form in question.* Does a sonnet have to have a set number of
syllables? Does it have to rhyme in a certain way? Or rhyme at
all? And so on. Strip the form of its encrustations. Reduce it to its

essence and translate that. No longer will the sonnet seem a different animal from what it was in Dante's day. It will have been made new.

16. *Develop a talent for mimicry.* It is one of the most valuable tools in the translator's kit. Not in the language of the original, but in that of the translation. The whole range of expressiveness from all ages, in all styles, must be the translator's to call on. How else to lay a hand on the required analogue or be able to place the foreign poem in a different tradition? Pound's *Odes* are the great example.

17. *Treat proper names with great deference.* "Each man is a poet when he names his cat" (Auden). Poems are proper names for states of mind. Inside the poem, each proper name (I exclude the addressees), as it falls, sets off vibrations—ripples such as the pebble you throw in the pond makes. Poets delight in proper names. You know you are very close to the poet when you are translating one of these lists strewn across the page like colored pebbles. Catullus's *Carmen* XI is an example, as is poem after poem of Martial's. They represent par excellence, and in purest form, the mantic power of language. "No ideas but in things," as William Carlos Williams says. Every child is aware that names carry with them power over the objects they denote. Treat proper names with great deference. Whenever possible rhyme on them.

18. Finally, the translator must bear in mind that the syntax of one language consorts ill with that of another. And it is in syntax that the roots of the untranslatable rhythms of language lie. Polysyllabic lines disguise this fact, introducing the tonic element, but in monosyllabic lines the dominant influence of syntax is plain—pitch and quantity being, as it were, in attendance. In a sense, the syntax, the ordering of the thought, *is* the rhythm—that irreducible quiddity that sets one language apart from another. It was not for nothing that Swinburne, the master of us all in meter, resorted so extensively to monosyllabic structures.

If translation all too often seems, from beginning to end, nothing more than an interminable succession of choices between an infinite variety of evils, it—the act of possession it represents—is also the only way to experience from the inside what is not our own. The translator is no "mere translator," nor are the poems "mere translations." We know that we shall wake, with the work done, to find that the one we have loved and lived with and learned to treat as ourselves has remained intractably inviolate after all. But while we are at work we shall, like any other artist, have beaten back temporality. The result will not be complete. No book is perfect. But, as Martial puts it, choose what there is for you to read, and leave the rest on one side.

PRINCIPLES OF SELECTION AND EDITING
by J. P. Sullivan and Peter Whigham

A complete, unexpurgated translation in verse of the whole of Martial's epigrams, with the very best represented in several versions, is a desirable enterprise, despite the poet's own warning, *sunt mala plura*. But if the Latin text is also to be provided, the enterprise becomes, for obvious practical reasons, unfeasible. We offer instead a generous selection, fairly representative but largely critical, of the fifteen hundred and more epigrams that make up the extant corpus.

Individual epigrams are available in English translations from the middle of the sixteenth century to the present day, some by distinguished poets, some by talented dilettantes. Most of these writers produced just one or two; others translated whole blocks of the epigrams. And it would be easy enough to represent each century by its proportionate number of good or adequate versions. But that method of selection would have distorted the critical presentation of Martial for reasons we shall see presently. The final decision was to offer the reader a predominantly modern selection, using available, solicited, or editorial versions.

What was to be regarded as "modern"? It was tempting to settle on whatever "sounds" modern. But English poetic diction, for twentieth-century ears at least, is not so easily classified: an Elizabethan version of a very short epigram might well sound more modern than a twentieth-century archaizing translation. The resolution of the dilemma, simultaneously ruthless and compromising, was to constitute the body of the book from twentieth-century versions, along with some nineteenth-century translations, whether these last were modern in tone, like those of Byron, Leigh Hunt, and Stevenson, or somewhat old-fashioned, like the contributions to the *Index Expurgatorius.*

The Appendix provides a selection of versions from earlier centuries. Here we have tried to represent both the dedicated translators of Martial, such as Robert Fletcher and William Hay and even the ill-starred James Elphinston, and also the minor and major poets—Sir Charles Sedley and Pope, for example, who produced only a few casual, even anonymous, translations.

Many thousand of versions in older manuscripts and printed translations of Martial, dating between 1540 and 1985, had to be read to produce this selection. The collections in the British, Bodleian, and Huntington Libraries should be singled out for special praise, and *The Gentleman's Magazine* and *The Rambler* contained some excellent efforts over the many years of their existence. The solid, at times exciting, volumes of Hay, Fletcher, Bohn, Thomas May, Henry Killigrew, J. A. Pott and F. A. Wright, A. L. Francis and H. F. Tatum, and later James Michie were always at hand to help in time of need when the editors could not fill certain gaps themselves or the indefatigable Anon. did not come to the rescue. But generally various modern translators submitted or were encouraged to submit for our consideration renderings both published and unpublished. For every Latin poem Martial wrote we had, we may say confidently, several English versions or imitations to examine. And it was not always easy to choose from this *embarras de richesses,* even in an attempt to represent, briefly or at length, every side of Martial's multifaceted talents. Obviously we could have supplied several renderings of the more famous, pathetic, or amusing pieces.

We had to jettison much from several categories: the trivial poems that revolve around plays on Greek and Latin words; the nervous jibes at the hairless and the toothless; brief eulogies of exemplary figures in Roman history; exaggerated compliments to

the emperor Domitian and other patrons; the often extempora-
neous compositions to celebrate objets d'art; epigrams based on
purely temporary and local considerations of little interest except
to the scholar, and so on. This left us free to add our own empha-
sis in providing versions of the substantial poems that illumi-
nated Martial's life and times, his art and wit, and his philosophy
and prejudices, not least those involving sex. The supposedly ob-
scene epigrams of Martial pushed him almost entirely outside
the pale of Victorian reading and critical scholarship, even though
these represent but a fraction of his total output. Yet, unlike the
flattery of the emperor and rich, important friends, readily under-
standable and congenial enough to ages with similar social and
economic structures, this side of Martial does interest the mod-
ern audience because of the increasing sexual frankness of our
own literature and a greater curiosity about subjects formerly
kept from historical and critical inspection. *Quot saecula, tot
Martiales!*

We have therefore only minimally represented the *Liber de
spectaculis* and we had to discard many excellent versions of his
"trifles" (*apinates*) from the *Xenia* and *Apophoreta* (Books XIII
and XIV). Enough, however, of the literary and historically impor-
tant distichs are given to provide a representative sample, along
with a few illustrating Roman diet and the sometimes bizarre
gifts the Romans gave one another on special occasions.

In compiling the Appendix we have tried to represent as best
we could, given the limitations of space, the many talents, fa-
mous and obscure, who took up the challenge of Martial in the
sixteenth, seventeenth, and eighteenth centuries. The Index of
Translators will show how varied these were.

Following the excellent principle of F. W. Bateson, increas-
ingly adopted by editors of sixteenth-, seventeenth-, and eigh-
teenth-century texts, we have modernized the spelling, capitali-
zation, and punctuation of the older versions in the Appendix, so
that, as far as possible, nothing extraneous or adventitious would
hinder the interaction between the reader and the poem. An ob-
vious exception had to be made for metrical purposes with the
more archaic translations: so in these, *loved*, for example, is to

be pronounced as a dissyllable (*lov-ed*) in contradistinction to the monosyllable *lov'd*. We have also restored those words translators in earlier centuries saw fit to conceal by asterisks or dashes.

We have made no attempt to draw attention to the mistakes or freedoms that may be detected in the versions. Sometimes young boys are metamorphosed into young girls, and many of the versions were written in the heyday of imitation, when it was almost de rigueur to use fresh names and modern instances. (This is a practice that shows some signs of reviving among twentieth-century interpreters of Martial.) Such creative translations we regarded as appropriate to the many-sided genius of Martial, who himself adapted to Roman contexts Greek epigrams he borrowed from the various collections circulating in his day. Despite his carping at fellow poets who appropriated his work as their own, Martial, like his admirer Ben Jonson, knew when to appropriate the inspiration of others.

The notes added are few; they serve only to gloss rare or archaic English words or throw light on some out-of-the-way facet of Roman life. It would have been intolerably cumbersome to explain all the mythological allusions to gods, heroes, and places, and the information is easily supplied from any classical dictionary or handbook.

Except in the case of the *Xenia* and *Apophoreta*, where the titles were deliberately put there by Martial to serve as lemmata or subject headings, we have not prefaced the translations with the titles often given them by our English authors. The older translators used them as a convenient way of omitting from the body of the epigram the sometimes awkward names of Martial's addressees or victims; that want may be supplied from the Latin texts. Modern titles, on the other hand, have tended to be simply for convenience of reference or ingenious, sometimes whimsical, summaries of the subject matter.

Naturally the final arbiter in all these matters has been our own literary tastes. Many will find their favorite poems or areas of our poet meagerly represented, but, to borrow a phrase from Martial: *aliter non fit liber.*

EPIGRAMS OF MARTIAL
ENGLISHED BY
DIVERS HANDS

LIBER DE SPECTACULIS

(A.D. 80)

SPEC. I

Barbara pyramidum sileat miracula Memphis,
    Assyrius iactet nec Babylona labor;
Nec Triviae templo molles laudentur Iones,
    Dissimulet Delon cornibus ara frequens;
Aere nec vacuo pendentia Mausolea
    Laudibus inmodicis Cares in astra ferant.
Omnis Caesareo cedit labor amphitheatro,
    Unum pro cunctis fama loquetur opus.

Memphis, forbear anent your *Pyramids*
nor *Syria* boast your highrise skyline;
Lax *Ionians,* vaunt not *Dian's* shrine,
and may her trophies *Phoebus' Delos* hide;
Pendant in space the *Mausoleum* hangs—
let modest *Carians* play down the fact:
O'er mankind's monuments tow'rs *Caesar's Ring.**
the fame of each proclaimed in that of one.

Peter Whigham

* That is, the Amphitheatrum Flavium; being near the Colossus Neronis, it became known in the Middle Ages as the Colosseum. Begun by Vespasian and finished by Titus and Domitian, it was dedicated by Titus in June A.D. 80, so prompting this first short book of Martial's epigrams. The Pyramids, the Temple of Diana of the Ephesians, and the Mausoleum were three of the seven ancient wonders of the world.

SPEC. 7

Qualiter in Scythica religatus rupe Prometheus
  Adsiduam nimio pectore pavit avem,
Nuda Caledonio sic viscera praebuit urso
  Non falsa pendens in cruce Laureolus.
Vivebant laceri membris stillantibus artus
  Inque omni nusquam corpore corpus erat.
Denique supplicium ⟨dignum tulit: ille parentis⟩
  Vel domini iugulum foderat ense nocens,
Templa vel arcano demens spoliaverat auro,
  Subdiderat saevas vel tibi, Roma, faces.
Vicerat antiquae sceleratus crimina famae,
  In quo, quae fuerat fabula, poena fuit.

Just as Prometheus, bound tight on a Russian crag
   Fed with his ever healing and regrowing heart
   The bird that never tires of eating
               So,
                  cast as
   Laureolus, the bandit-king, nailed to a cross—no stage
   prop this—
A man offered his exposed guts to a Highland bear.
   His shredded limbs clung onto life though
Their constituent parts gushed with blood;
   No trace of body—but the body lived.
Finally he got the punishment he deserved . . .*
   Maybe he'd slit his master's throat,
   Maybe he'd robbed a temple's treasury of gold,
   Maybe he'd tried to burn our city, Rome.
That criminal had surpassed all ancient folklore's crimes.
   Through him what had been merely myth
      Became real punishment.

Frederick Ahl

---

* Part of the line is lost from the manuscripts.

SPEC. 18

Lambere securi dextram consueta magistri
   Tigris, ab Hyrcano gloria rara iugo,
Saeva ferum rabido laceravit dente leonem:
   Res nova, non ullis cognita temporibus.
Ausa est tale nihil, silvis dum vixit in altis:
   Postquam inter nos est, plus feritatis habet.

SPEC. 22/23

Sollicitant pavidi dum rhinocerota magistri
   Seque diu magnae colligit ira ferae,
Desperabantur promissi proelia Martis;
   Sed tandem rediit cognitus ante furor.
Namque gravem cornu gemino sic extulit ursum,
   Iactat ut inpositas taurus in astra pilas:
Norica tam certo venabula derigit ictu
   Fortis adhuc teneri dextera Carpophori.
Ille tulit geminos facili cervice iuvencos,
   Illi cessit atrox bubalus atque vison:
Hunc leo cum fugeret, praeceps in tela cucurrit.
   I nunc et lentas corripe, turba, moras.

Tonguing its trusting keeper's hand,
The vaunted *Caspian* Tigress sprang
Mangling with bleak tooth a lion.

Occurrence strange in Time unknown,
Foreign to forest fastnesses.

Come live with us and learn our ways . . .

Peter Whigham

Cautiously the keeper poked the rhino;
    long it took to rouse the giant beast,
And the crowd's hope of Mars, his fray, faded,
    till the old rage—all knew—returned:
The double horn tosses an outsize bear,
    as bulls toss bladders to the stars—
Thrust as sure as young Carpophorus makes,
    his stout fist driving the Noric shaft.
Flexible neck sporting a brace of bullocks . . .
    fierce bison, buffalo, turning tail . . .
The fleeing lion impaled on ready spears . . .
    Chide, crowd, the drawn-out prologue, still?

Peter Whigham

SPEC. 29

Concita veloces fugeret cum damma Molossos
  Et varia lentas necteret arte moras,
Caesaris ante pedes supplex similisque roganti
  Constitit, et praedam non tetigere canes.
. . . .
  Haec intellecto principe dona tulit.
Numen habet Caesar, sacra est haec, sacra potestas,
  Credite: mentiri non didicere ferae.

SPEC. 33

Flavia gens, quantum tibi tertius abstulit heres!
  Paene fuit tanti, non habuisse duos.

When a doe was started by the hounds
and ran from them using all her instinctive skill
to throw them off the scent, at last she stopped
in front of the emperor's throne, and stood still there,
like one asking pardon. The hounds
held back from attacking her.
And surely such immunity was the gift of Caesar,
of his awesome presence; for his power is sacred
and makes its subjects sacrosanct:
Animals cannot lie.

Palmer Bovie

How damned was the Flavian line by that third heir!
Was it worth the benefits of the earlier pair? *

J. P. Sullivan

* This attack on Domitian, contrasting his reign with the more benevolent
reigns of Vespasian and Titus, indicates that the epigram was an addition (written
after A.D. 96) to the main body of the *Liber de spectaculis*. The work as we have it
was, in any case, probably a mere distillation of a greater number of epigrams
written by Martial on the opening of the Flavian amphitheater.

BOOK I

(A.D. 85–86)

I. PREFACE

Spero me secutum in libellis meis tale temperamentum, ut de illis queri non possit quisquis de se bene senserit, cum salva infimarum quoque personarum reverentia ludant; quae adeo antiquis auctoribus defuit, ut nominibus non tantum veris abusi sint, sed et magnis. Mihi fama vilius constet et probetur in me novissimum ingenium. Absit a iocorum nostrorum simplicitate malignus interpres nec epigrammata mea scribat: inprobe facit qui in alieno libro ingeniosus est. Lascivam verborum veritatem, id est epigrammaton linguam, excusarem, si meum esset exemplum: sic scribit Catullus, sic Marsus, sic Pedo, sic Gaetulicus, sic quicumque perlegitur. Si quis tamen tam ambitiose tristis est, ut apud illum in nulla pagina latine loqui fas sit, potest epistula vel potius titulo contentus esse. Epigrammata illis scribuntur, qui solent spectare Florales. Non intret Cato theatrum meum, aut si intraverit, spectet. Videor mihi meo iure facturus, si epistulam versibus clusero:

Nosses iocosae dulce cum sacrum Florae

Festosque lusus et licentiam volgi,

Cur in theatrum, Cato severe, venisti?

An ideo tantum veneras, ut exires?

I hope that, in my slim volumes, I have adopted such an attitude that no-one who is comfortable with himself can take exception to them, since their humour goes along with a respect for even people of very humble station. This respect was so lacking in the ancient authors that they abused not only real, but even prominent people. I would prefer that my reputation would cost me less and that cleverness should be the last thing to gain me the reader's approval. I do not want any malicious interpreters of the frankness of my humorous verses: they should not write my epigrams for me. I would apologize for their lewd language, the language of epigram after all, if I had been the first to employ it. But this is the way Catullus wrote, and Marsus, and Pedo, and Gaetulicus,* indeed anyone who holds the reader's attention to the end. If anyone, however, is so extraordinarily moral that for him plain Latin is not allowable in any of these pages, he will have to make do with this letter or, even better, the book title. Epigrams are written for those who attend the Festival of Flora.† I urge Cato not to come into my show, or if he does come in, let him watch it. I feel that I will be within my rights if I close my epistle with some verses:

This day is Flora's sweet fiesta well you know,

When the crowd cuts loose and bawdy jokes can flow.

Cato you prude, did you come to watch girls strip

Or to stalk straight out, curling your lip?

J. P. Sullivan

* Catullus (84–54 B.C.) and the three Augustan poets, Domitius Marsus, Albinovanus Pedo, and Cornelius Lentulus Gaetulicus, all wrote short erotic poems. Martial does not deign to mention his Greek models.

† The licentious spring festival of the Floralia, at which prostitutes performed on stage, took place on April 28.

I.1

Hic est quem legis ille, quem requiris,
Toto notus in orbe Martialis
Argutis epigrammaton libellis:
Cui, lector studiose, quod dedisti
Viventi decus atque sentienti,
Rari post cineres habent poetae.

I.2

Qui tecum cupis esse meos ubicumque libellos
Et comites longae quaeris habere viae,
Hos eme, quos artat brevibus membrana tabellis:
Scrinia da magnis, me manus una capit.
Ne tamen ignores ubi sim venalis, et erres
Urbe vagus tota, me duce certus eris:
Libertum docti Lucensis quaere Secundum
Limina post Pacis Palladiumque forum.

He unto whom thou art so partial,
O reader, is the well-known Martial,
The epigrammatist: while living,
Give him the fame thou wouldst be giving
So shall he hear, and feel, and know it:
Post-obits rarely reach a poet.

George Gordon, Lord Byron

You'ld have my poems ever beside you,
    friends when the journey drags?
Invest, then, in these handy paperbacks,
    save hardbacks for your shelves.
And take directions where I'm sold, rather
    than citywide comb Rome.
Lucensis, the learned freedman, stocks them
    —back of *Pax* & *Pallas.*

Peter Whigham

1.3

Argiletanas mavis habitare tabernas,
    Cum tibi, parve liber, scrinia nostra vacent.
Nescis, heu, nescis dominae fastidia Romae:
    Crede mihi, nimium Martia turba sapit.
Maiores nusquam rhonchi: iuvenesque senesque
    Et pueri nasum rhinocerotis habent.
Audieris cum grande sophos, dum basia iactas,
    Ibis ab excusso missus in astra sago.
Sed tu ne totiens domini patiare lituras
    Neve notet lusus tristis harundo tuos,
Aetherias, lascive, cupis volitare per auras:
    I, fuge; sed poteras tutior esse domi.

1.4

Contigeris nostros, Caesar, si forte libellos,
    Terrarum dominum pone supercilium.
Consuevere iocos vestri quoque ferre triumphi,
    Materiam dictis nec pudet esse ducem.
Qua Thymelen spectas derisoremque Latinum,
    Illa fronte precor carmina nostra legas.
Innocuos censura potest permittere lusus:
    Lasciva est nobis pagina, vita proba.

So, they've summed you up, my little book.
You're now "a milestone in ironic outlook."
This the price of your publicity:
MARTIAL VIEWS LIFE VERY SAUCILY.
Whatever they say is a load of balls
Certain to send you to second-hand stalls,
Unaware, little book, of the comforts of home
Your "low key wit" now belongs to Rome.
What today's "an incandescent event"
Soon winds up "a minor supplement."
To set you off on the proper foot
Some shit's written "Magic, a classic to boot."

                                        W. S. Milne

Caesar, if my small book should reach your hands,
    Relax the frown that dominates all lands.
Jokes are the custom at your triumphs too—
    The general's not ashamed the jokes are blue.
As you watch mimes or dancers on the stage—
    With that expression look upon my page.
These games are harmless, censor: let them pass.
    My poems play around; but not my life.

                                        Alistair Elliot

1.16

Sunt bona, sunt quaedam mediocria, sunt mala plura
Quae legis hic: aliter non fit, Avite, liber.

1.18

Quid te, Tucca, iuvat vetulo miscere Falerno
    In Vaticanis condita musta cadis?
Quid tantum fecere boni tibi pessima vina?
    Aut quid fecerunt optima vina mali?
De nobis facile est, scelus est iugulare Falernum
    Et dare Campano toxica saeva mero.
Convivae meruere tui fortasse perire:
    Amphora non meruit tam pretiosa mori.

Good work you'll find, some poor, and much that's worse;
It takes all sorts to make a book of verse.

J. A. Pott

What ails you, Tucca, that you mix
In with your old and fine
Falernian, those musty dregs
Of awful Vatican wine?
Did the priceless wine mistreat you once?
What harm did it ever do
To merit this? Or the other stuff,
Does it have some hold on you?
Forget your Roman guests; it is
A heinous crime to throttle
A Falernian, or give strong poison
To a Campanian—bottle.
No doubt your drinking-friends deserved
To die in deadly pain:
That precious amphora should not
Have been so foully slain.

Dorothea Wender

I.23

Invitas nullum nisi cum quo, Cotta, lavaris
Et dant convivam balnea sola tibi.
Mirabar, quare numquam me, Cotta, vocasses:
Iam scio, me nudum displicuisse tibi.

I.24

Aspicis incomptis illum, Deciane, capillis,
Cuius et ipse times triste supercilium,
Qui loquitur Curios adsertoresque Camillos?
Nolito fronti credere: nupsit heri.

Cotta will not choose dinner-guests, till viewed
Down at the Public Baths, completely nude;
So, since I'm never bidden to a meal,
My private parts must lack some sex-appeal.

Anthony Reid

You see that fellow with his roundhead crop,
    His godly talk and manner dignified?
Do not be duped. Why, only yesterday
    He acted as a "bride."

Brian Hill

1.25

Ede tuos tandem populo, Faustine, libellos
   Et cultum docto pectore profer opus,
Quod nec Cecropiae damnent Pandionis arces
   Nec sileant nostri praetereantque senes.
Ante fores stantem dubitas admittere Famam
   Teque piget curae praemia ferre tuae?
Post te victurae per te quoque vivere chartae
   Incipiant: cineri gloria sera venit.

1.30

Chirurgus fuerat, nunc est vispillo Diaulus.
   Coepit quo poterat clinicus esse modo.

Faustinus, why not publish them,
   Those masterpieces of a mind
Which Athens cannot but commend,
   To which Rome cannot but be kind.

Why do you hesitate to open
   Wide the gates Fame stands before
And take the prize she long has offered,
   Long has held for you in store?

Let works that will survive you after
   You have trod the path all dread
Live now while you still are living.
   Fame comes too late to the dead.

                     Ralph Marcellino

Once a surgeon, Dr. Baker
Then became an undertaker,
Not so much his trade reversing
Since for him it's just re-hearsing.

                     T. W. Melluish

I.33

Amissum non flet cum sola est Gellia patrem,
    Si quis adest, iussae prosiliunt lacrimae.
Non luget quisquis laudari, Gellia, quaerit,
    Ille dolet vere, qui sine teste dolet.

I.35

Versus scribere me parum severos
Nec quos praelegat in schola magister,
Corneli, quereris: sed hi libelli,
Tamquam coniugibus suis mariti,
Non possunt sine mentula placere.
Quid si me iubeas talassionem
Verbis dicere non talassionis?
Quis Floralia vestit et stolatum
Permittit meretricibus pudorem?
Lex haec carminibus data est iocosis,
Ne possint, nisi pruriant, iuvare.
Quare deposita severitate
Parcas lusibus et iocis rogamus,
Nec castrare velis meos libellos.
Gallo turpius est nihil Priapo.

Alone, Gellia never weeps over her father's death;
if someone's there, her tears burst forth at will.
Mourning that looks for praise, Gellia, is not grief:
true sorrow grieves unseen.

Jim Powell

Cornelius sighs . . . the lines I write
Are such no dominie would recite:
They are not "prim" . . . but epigrams,
As men for wives, no pleasure can
Procure without what makes a man.
You'ld have me write a Hymen hymn
Nor use the words for hymning him?
We clothe ourselves at Flora's feast,
In chaste stole let whores go dressed?
One rule for witty songs like these:
They may not, without prurience, please.
Then stifle primness, I must ask;
Take not my toys & jests to task.
Nor bowdlerise my pretty verses—
Than Priapic Gallus naught there's worse is.

Peter Whigham

1.37

Ventris onus misero, nec te pudet, excipis auro,
    Basse, bibis vitro: carius ergo cacas.

1.38

Quem recitas meus est, o Fidentine, libellus:
    Sed male cum recitas, incipit esse tuus.

You've a golden pot for your arse
But you drink your wine from glass—
You value your stink
Far more than your drink.

Olive Pitt-Kethley

That verse is mine, you know, which you're
    Reciting. But you quote it
So execrably, that I believe
    I'll let you say *you* wrote it.

Dorothea Wender

1.49

Vir Celtiberis non tacende gentibus
   Nostraeque laus Hispaniae,
Videbis altam, Liciniane, Bilbilin,
   Equis et armis nobilem,
Senemque Caium nivibus, et fractis sacrum
   Vadaveronem montibus,
Et delicati dulce Boterdi nemus,
   Pomona quod felix amat.
Tepidi natabis lene Congedi vadum
   Mollesque Nympharum lacus,
Quibus remissum corpus adstringes brevi
   Salone, qui ferrum gelat.
Praestabit illic ipsa figendas prope
   Voberca prandenti feras.
Aestus serenos aureo franges Tago
   Obscurus umbris arborum;
Avidam rigens Derceita placabit sitim
   Et Nutha, quae vincit nives.
At cum December canus et bruma impotens
   Aquilone rauco mugiet,
Aprica repetes Tarraconis litora
   Tuamque Laletaniam.
Ibi inligatas mollibus dammas plagis
   Mactabis et vernas apros

Whom Spain cannot refrain from praising,
   sprig of Celtiberia,
Licinianus!—set soon to see tall
   Bilbilis, famed mounts, famed armour,
Famed for its snow-caps, Caius, and
   its cleft slopes, Vadavero,
Sweet Boterdus, its ringing copses
   by ripe Pomona bless'd.
I' the genial Congedus you'll bathe
   & the silk lake, haunt of nymphs;
Your limbs relaxed, a dip in iron-
   chastening Salo follows.
Vobesca's nearby woods shall yield
   the wild beast speared for lunch.
From glitt'ring sun, in golden Tagus
   by boughs o'erhung you'll cool;
Dercenna's, Nutha's snow-cold fresh-
   ets shall assuage your thirst.
December frosts & savage winter,
   north blasts harshly sounding—
Taragon, Laletania'll find
   you sunning on their beaches.
There with flexible net you'll trap
   the doe, the home-grown pig,

Leporemque forti callidum rumpes equo,
   Cervos relinques vilico.
Vicina in ipsum silva descendet focum
   Infante cinctum sordido.
Vocabitur venator et veniet tibi
   Conviva clamatus prope.
Lunata nusquam pellis et nusquam toga
   Olidaeque vestes murice;
Procul horridus Liburnus et querulus cliens,
   Imperia viduarum procul;
Non rumpet altum pallidus somnum reus,
   Sed mane totum dormies.
Mereatur alius grande et insanum sophos:
   Miserere tu felicium
Veroque fruere non superbus gaudio,
   Dum Sura laudatur tuus.
Non inpudenter vita quod relicum est petit,
   Cum fama quod satis est habet.

On a stout mount outrun the wily
    hare, —stags left for the serfs.
The close wood shall come to your fire
    circled by raggedy kids.
You call in the huntsman, and he
    comes on cue as your guest.
Absent the senatorial slipper,
    toga & purple hem,
Court's courier (brusque), quarrelsome
    client, imperious widow.
Sleep unbroken by defendants,
    you shall lie in of mornings.
Not yours th' idle, hoarse "Huzzahs"—
    bear with the fortunate,
Modestly true gladness garn'ring
    while Sura laurels gains.
Nor crass is it Life drain the dregs,
    when fame has its reward.

              Peter Whigham

1.55

Vota tui breviter si vis cognoscere Marci,
   Clarum militiae, Fronto, togaeque decus,
Hoc petit, esse sui nec magni ruris arator,
   Sordidaque in parvis otia rebus amat.
Quisquam picta colit Spartani frigora saxi
   Et matutinum portat ineptus Have,
Cui licet exuviis nemoris rurisque beato
   Ante focum plenas explicuisse plagas
Et piscem tremula salientem ducere saeta
   Flavaque de rubro promere mella cado?
Pinguis inaequales onerat cui vilica mensas
   Et sua non emptus praeparat ova cinis?
Non amet hanc vitam quisquis me non amat, opto,
   Vivat et urbanis albus in officiis.

1.57

Qualem, Flacce, velim quaeris nolimve puellam?
   Nolo nimis facilem difficilemque nimis.
Illud quod medium est atque inter utrumque probamus:
   Nec volo quod cruciat, nec volo quod satiat.

Who shines in battlefield & forum, Fronto
   needs briefly know what Marcus needs.
This: to farm his own (not swollen) acres,
   to live at ease on lowly means.
Who tills chill halls of colored Spartan marble,
   yields the naive client's first kiss,
When, blessed with spoils of wood & chase, that man
   can crammed nets empty by the fire,
From quivering line unhook the twitching fish,
   from red jars draw golden honey,
Whose plump housekeeper piles the rough board and
   on homeburnt charcoal fries his eggs?
This life is not for you? You're not for me:
   tend, pray, your pallid chores of town.

Peter Whigham

My taste in women, Flaccus? Give me one
Neither too slow nor yet too quick to bed.
For me, the middle sort: I've not the will
To be Love's Martyr—nor his glutton either.

Peter Whigham

1.58

Milia pro puero centum me mango poposcit:
   Risi ego, sed Phoebus protinus illa dedit.
Hoc dolet et queritur de me mea mentula secum
   Laudaturque meam Phoebus in invidiam.
Sed sestertiolum donavit mentula Phoebo
   Bis decies: hoc da tu mihi, pluris emam.

1.61

Verona docti syllabas amat vatis,
   Marone felix Mantua est,
Censetur Aponi Livio suo tellus
   Stellaque nec Flacco minus,
Apollodoro plaudit imbrifer Nilus,
   Nasone Paeligni sonant,
Duosque Senecas unicumque Lucanum
   Facunda loquitur Corduba,
Gaudent iocosae Canio suo Gades,
   Emerita Deciano meo:
Te, Liciniane, gloriabitur nostra
   Nec me tacebit Bilbilis.

They asked a hundred thousand for the lad;
   I laughed; but Phoebus paid the price and bought him.
Whereat my penis grumbled, limp and sad,
   Comparing me to Phoebus. But I taught him:
"His cock has golden coins to stoke his fire;
Give me as much and, trust me, I'll bid higher."

                                    Brian Hill

Verona loves each vatic syllable.
   Mantua in Maro counts her blessings.
Aponan soil from Livy wins its measure,
   from Flaccus, Stella too, no less.
Apollodoran plaudits swell the Nile.
   Paelignians think naught but Naso.
Lettered Cordobans of both Senecas,
   & the one & only Lucan.
Mirthful Gades—happy in her Canius;
   Emerita, in Decianus mine.
Of you, Licinianus, shall Bilbilis
   boast—nor pass me by in silence.

                                    Peter Whigham

1.62

Casta nec antiquis cedens Laevina Sabinis
  Et quamvis tetrico tristior ipsa viro
Dum modo Lucrino, modo se permittit Averno,
  Et dum Baianis saepe fovetur aquis,
Incidit in flammas: iuvenemque secuta relicto
  Coniuge Penelope venit, abit Helene.

1.63

Ut recitem tibi nostra rogas epigrammata. Nolo.
  Non audire, Celer, sed recitare cupis.

1.64

Bella es, novimus, et puella, verum est,
Et dives, quis enim potest negare?
Sed cum te nimium, Fabulla, laudas,
Nec dives neque bella nec puella es.

Laevina, more than Sabine maid,
Renowned as pure and chaste,
(Her husband was both stern and staid—
Yet she was more straight-laced,)

Went bathing in the Lucrine Lake,
And then in dark Avernus,
And, seeking still her heat to slake,
Fell straight into a furnace,

Broke vows, to youthful love a prey,
In cooling Baiae burned—
Penelope she went away,
A Helen she returned.

                    Olive Pitt-Kethley

Read you my epigrams? No, I decline!
You want me to read yours, not hear mine.

                    Hubert Dynes Ellis

You're beautiful, oh yes, and young, and rich;
But since you tell us so, you're just a bitch.

                    Rolfe Humphries

1.67

"Liber homo es nimium," dicis mihi, Ceryle, semper.
  In te qui dicit, Ceryle, liber homo est?

1.70

Vade salutatum pro me, liber: ire iuberis
  Ad Proculi nitidos, officiose, lares.
Quaeris iter, dicam. Vicinum Castora canae
  Transibis Vestae virgineamque domum;
Inde sacro veneranda petes Palatia clivo,
  Plurima qua summi fulget imago ducis.
Nec te detineat miri radiata colossi
  Quae Rhodium moles vincere gaudet opus.
Flecte vias hac qua madidi sunt tecta Lyaei
  Et Cybeles picto stat Corybante tholus.
Protinus a laeva clari tibi fronte Penates
  Atriaque excelsae sunt adeunda domus.
Hanc pete: ne metuas fastus limenque superbum:
  Nulla magis toto ianua poste patet,
Nec propior quam Phoebus amet doctaeque sorores.
  Si dicet "Quare non tamen ipse venit?",
Sic licet excuses "Quia qualiacumque leguntur
  Ista, salutator scribere non potuit."

You often say my work is coarse. It's true;
But then it must be so—it deals with you.

J. A. Pott

Go, book! To Proculus, greetings: hence to his
    smart townhouse. The way? I'll tell you.
Past Castor's, venerable Vesta's, fanes
    (the Vesta's residence nearby),
Head for sacred Palatine, up the hill
    where the statues of the *duce* gleam.
Skirt the aureoled bulk of the Colossus
    basking in bettering Rhodes' work.
By bibulous Bacchus' dome, Cybele's
    Corybantic cupola, turn,
Where, hard on the left, a fine fronted hearth
    with tall entrance hall awaits you.
Approach those proud portals with no shyness—
    no door so readily swings wide,
And none's more loved of Phoebus and the Nine.
    Should one note: "He comes not here himself . . .",
Excuse me thus: "Even this poem you read,
    had not been written had he called."

Peter Whigham

1.77

Pulchre valet Charinus, et tamen pallet.
Parce bibit Charinus, et tamen pallet.
Bene concoquit Charinus, et tamen pallet.
Sole utitur Charinus, et tamen pallet.
Tingit cutem Charinus, et tamen pallet.
Cunnum Charinus lingit, et tamen pallet.

1.83

Os et labra tibi lingit, Manneia, catellus:
Non miror, merdas si libet esse cani.

Charinus bloomingly thrives
 and yet he's pale,
Charinus sparingly drinks
 and yet he's pale,
Charinus' digestion's sound
 and ditto he's ditto.

Charinus employs the sun
 and yet he's pale,
Charinus paints his face
 and ditto he's ditto,
Charinus bibs vagina
 and ditto ditto ditto.

W. G. Shepherd

Your little dog licks you from head to foot. ✶
Am I surprised, Manneia?
                              Not a bit.
I'm not surprised that dogs like shit.

Richard O'Connell

1.93

Fabricio iunctus fido requiescit Aquinus,
   Qui prior Elysias gaudet adisse domos.
Ara duplex primi testatur munera pili:
   Plus tamen est, titulo quod breviore legis:
Iunctus uterque sacro laudatae foedere vitae,
   Famaque quod raro novit, amicus erat.

1.96

Si non molestum est teque non piget, scazon,
Nostro rogamus pauca verba Materno
Dicas in aurem sic ut audiat solus.
Amator ille tristium lacernarum
Et baeticatus atque leucophaeatus,
Qui coccinatos non putat viros esse
Amethystinasque mulierum vocat vestes,
Nativa laudet, habeat et licet semper
Fuscos colores, galbinos habet mores.
Rogabit, unde suspicer virum mollem.
Una lavamur: aspicit nihil sursum.
Sed spectat oculis devorantibus draucos
Nec otiosis mentulas videt labris.
Quaeris quis hic sit? Excidit mihi nomen.

Now by Fabricius let Aquinus rest,
   Glad to be first to reach Elysium's shore;
Twin altar-tombs the comrades' rank attest—
   Both chief centurions; yet there is more
Engraved upon the stone: *These men professed*
   A sacred bond of honour to the ends
Of their two lives; and (rare to fame) were friends.

                                        Brian Hill

My hobbling metre, if it's not a task
Too onerous for you, not too much to ask,
Go and drop a few words in Maternus' ear
Just loud enough for him alone to hear.
He favours drab, dark cloaks, he has a passion
For wearing Baetic wool and grey; the fashion
For scarlet he calls "degenerate," "un-Roman,"
And, as for mauve, that's "only fit for women."
He's all for "Nature"; yet, though no one's duller
In dress, his morals sport a different colour.
He may demand the grounds of my suspicion.
We bathe together, and his line of vision
Keeps below waist-level, he devours
Ocularly the boys under the showers,
And his lips twitch at the sight of a luscious member.
Did you ask his name? How odd, I can't remember!

                                        James Michie

1.102

Qui pinxit Venerem tuam, Lycori,
Blanditus, puto, pictor est Minervae.

1.103

"Si dederint superi decies mihi milia centum?"
    Dicebas nondum, Scaevola, iustus eques,
"Qualiter o vivam, quam large quamque beate!"
    Riserunt faciles et tribuere dei.
Sordidior multo post hoc toga, paenula peior,
    Calceus est sarta terque quaterque cute:
Deque decem plures semper servantur olivae,
    Explicat et cenas unica mensa duas,
Et Veientani bibitur faex crassa rubelli,
    Asse cicer tepidum constat et asse Venus.
In ius, o fallax atque infitiator, eamus:
    Aut vive aut decies, Scaevola, redde deis.

Whoever painted your Venus, Lycoris, had no desire to serve
  her.
I think he only wanted to curry favour with Minerva.

John Adlard

"Ye gods," you cried, "If I had the money,
How lavishly I should live."
The gods, who enjoy being funny,
Granted your wish. You're rich.
Yet your clothes are coarse; your manners, worse.
Your shoes are patched; your socks don't match;
You need a comb, you constantly scratch;
You live in rooms abandoned by rats.
A stingy dinner for six serves eleven;
Out of ten large olives, you hoard seven.
That tepid brine you call pea soup
Costs as little as your penny love-whoops.
You drink nothing but the worst red wine,
Neatest when returned to the jar as urine.
As a wealthy man you're a foolish fraud,
The butt of bored and playful gods.
If you're only going to live like a beggar,
Give me the money. I'll show them better.

Philip Murray

1.105

In Nomentanis, Ovidi, quod nascitur arvis,
    Accepit quotiens tempora longa, merum
Exuit annosa mores nomenque senecta:
    Et quidquid voluit, testa vocatur anus.

1.106

Interponis aquam subinde, Rufe,
Et si cogeris a sodale, raram
Diluti bibis unciam Falerni.
Numquid pollicita est tibi beatam
Noctem Naevia sobriasque mavis
Certae nequitias fututionis?
Suspiras, retices, gemis: negavit.
Crebros ergo licet bibas trientes
Et durum iugules mero dolorem.
Quid parcis tibi, Rufe? dormiendum est.

With years, upon my *Nomentan* estate
The yield that in the cellar's laid unmixed,
Aging in bottle, transubstantiates
And tastes as per the labelling affixed.

Peter Whigham

You drink when you are asked, my friend,
   And water well your wine,
Falernian well diluted
   You sip from time to time.

'Tis *Naevia* has promised you
   The freedom of her bed,
Which better t' enjoy you've vowed
   To keep a sober head.

And now the lady's stood you up
   You've sighs and moans and weeping,
So stifle sorrow in the cup,
   Naught there's a-bed but sleeping.

Peter Whigham

1.108

Est tibi—sitque precor multos crescatque per annos—
  Pulchra quidem, verum transtiberina domus:
At mea Vipsanas spectant cenacula laurus,
  Factus in hac ego sum iam regione senex.
Migrandum est, ut mane domi te, Galle, salutem:
  Est tanti, vel si longius illa foret.
Sed tibi non multum est, unum si praesto togatum:
  Multum est hunc unum si mihi, Galle, nego.
Ipse salutabo decuma te saepius hora:
  Mane tibi pro me dicet havere liber.

1.110

Scribere me quereris, Velox, epigrammata longa.
  Ipse nihil scribis: tu breviora facis.

Gallus, your house will stand, I pray,
And grow in splendour every day.
For me, one little thing it lacks—
Trans-Tiber's wrong side of the tracks.
Here, from my garret I can show
Where the Vipsanian laurels grow.
Here I've grown old—I've not the power
To call at such an early hour;
Not that I'd be averse to take
A longer journey for your sake,
That you another guest may see—
Not much to you, but much to me!
Expect me when your dinner's spread;
Earlier, I'll send my book instead.

Olive Pitt-Kethley

My epigrams are wordy, you've complained;
But you write nothing. Yours are more restrained.

Richard O'Connell

I.114

Hos tibi vicinos, Faustine, Telesphorus hortos
  Faenius et breve rus udaque prata tenet.
Condidit hic natae cineres nomenque sacravit
  Quod legis Antullae, dignior ipse legi.
Ad Stygias aequum fuerat pater isset ut umbras:
  Quod quia non licuit, vivat, ut ossa colat.

I.116

Hoc nemus aeterno cinerum sacravit honori
  Faenius et culti iugera pulchra soli.
Hoc tegitur cito rapta suis Antulla sepulchro,
  Hoc erit Antullae mixtus uterque parens.
Si cupit hunc aliquis, moneo, ne speret agellum:
  Perpetuo dominis serviet iste suis.

Telesphorus Faenius owns these gardens near you,
    Faustinus: the short field, the water-meadows.
He buried here his daughter's bones, and hallowed
    The name you read—Antulla—his own more fitting.
The father should have joined the Stygian shadows:
    Not granted; he must live, to tend her ashes.

                                  Alistair Elliot

This grove, these pretty acres of tilled land,
    Faenius gave the dead, perpetual honour.
Here the tomb guards Antulla, snatched too soon;
    Here shall be mixed the ashes of her parents.
Who wants this field? I warn him not to hope:
    These are the masters it will serve forever.

                                  Alistair Elliot

1.117

Occurris quotiens, Luperce, nobis,
"Vis mittam puerum" subinde dicis,
"Cui tradas epigrammaton libellum,
Lectum quem tibi protinus remittam?"
Non est quod puerum, Luperce, vexes.
Longum est, si velit ad Pirum venire,
Et scalis habito tribus, sed altis.
Quod quaeris propius petas licebit.
Argi nempe soles subire letum:
Contra Caesaris est forum taberna
Scriptis postibus hinc et inde totis,
Omnis ut cito perlegas poetas.
Illinc me pete. Nec roges Atrectum
—Hoc nomen dominus gerit tabernae—:
De primo dabit alterove nido
Rasum pumice purpuraque cultum
Denaris tibi quinque Martialem.
"Tanti non est" ais? Sapis, Luperce.

Lupercus, when we meet you say,
"I'll send my lad round if I may,
Your book of epigrams to borrow,
To read, and give you back tomorrow."
Lupercus, please don't tire him out,
The way is long and round about,
To reach the Pear Tree takes some time,
And then there are three flights to climb,
And, what is more, those stairs are high.
So I suggest you look more nigh.
At Argiletum first you stop;
Near Caesar's Forum there's a shop
Doors covered with a Poets' List—
Look for me there. I can't be missed.
No need to ask Atrectus which
Shelf I am on—first, second niche?
Ah! there's your Martial—lovely job
Smooth, purple-trimmed and—just five bob!
"Oh, it's not worth it," you will cry.
You are a knowing man, say I.

Olive Pitt-Kethley

BOOK II

(A.D. 85–86)

II.1

Ter centena quidem poteras epigrammata ferre,
  Sed quis te ferret perlegeretque, liber?
At nunc succincti quae sint bona disce libelli.
  Hoc primum est, brevior quod mihi charta perit;
Deinde, quod haec una peraget librarius hora,
  Nec tantum nugis serviet ille meis;
Tertia res haec est, quod si cui forte legeris,
  Sic licet usque malus, non odiosus eris.
Te conviva leget mixto quincunce, sed ante
  Incipiat positus quam tepuisse calix.
Esse tibi tanta cautus brevitate videris?
  Ei mihi, quam multis sic quoque longus eris!

II.3

Sexte, nihil debes, nil debes, Sexte, fatemur.
  Debet enim, si quis solvere, Sexte, potest.

Three hundred epigrams you might have borne,
But who, my book, would then have borne with you?
I keep books short, I make no readers yawn,
Save paper and the busy copyist too.
He'll run you off within an hour maybe,
I'd say you could be read, too, in no more,
And—last good reason for your brevity—
If bad, a shorter book's a shorter bore.
A guest, five measures at his elbow, will
Skim through before his final cup has cooled.
You're reassured? Oh no, for many still
Will find you much too long, so don't be fooled.

Olive Pitt-Kethley

Sextus, you keep on saying
You're not in debt. I know.
Without the means of paying
One can't be said to owe.

James Michie

II.5

Ne valeam, si non totis, Deciane, diebus
  Et tecum totis noctibus esse velim.
Sed duo sunt quae nos disiungunt milia passum:
  Quattuor haec fiunt, cum rediturus eam.
Saepe domi non es, cum sis quoque, saepe negaris:
  Vel tantum causis vel tibi saepe vacas.
Te tamen ut videam, duo milia non piget ire:
  Ut te non videam, quattuor ire piget.

II.6

I nunc, edere me iube libellos.
Lectis vix tibi paginis duabus
Spectas eschatocollion, Severe,
Et longas trahis oscitationes.
Haec sunt, quae relegente me solebas
Rapta exscribere, sed Vitellianis,
Haec sunt, singula quae sinu ferebas
Per convivia cuncta, per theatra,
Haec sunt aut meliora si qua nescis.
Quid prodest mihi tam macer libellus,
Nullo crassior ut sit umbilico,
Si totus tibi triduo legatur?
Numquam deliciae supiniores.
Lassus tam cito deficis viator,
Et cum currere debeas Bovillas,
Interiungere quaeris ad Camenas?
I nunc, edere me iube libellos.

Believe me, sir, I'd like to spend whole days,
    Yes, and whole evenings in your company,
But the two miles between your house and mine
    Are four miles when I go there and come back.
You're seldom home, and when you are deny it,
    Engrossed with business or with yourself.
Now, I don't mind the two mile trip to see you;
    What I do mind is going four to not to.

                                    J. V. Cunningham

You bid me publish pamphlets now, go on!
    You've hardly read the first two pages when
You, Severus, turn to the colophon
    Yawning. These verses, which, read out again
By me, you used to snatch and copy out
    Upon Vitellian tablets. These, of old,
You took to dos and theatres round about,
    Tucked away singly in your toga's fold—
These ones, or better ones as yet untold.
    If you must take three days to read it through,
What good's a book, thin as a rod, to me?
    Never was dilettante slacker. You
Give up so soon, a tired traveller. You'd be
    For changing at Camenae if you'd gone
To Bovillae upon some business, too.
    You bid me publish pamphlets now, go on!

                                    Fiona Pitt-Kethley

II.11

Quod fronte Selium nubila vides, Rufe,
Quod ambulator porticum terit seram,
Lugubre quiddam quod tacet piger voltus,
Quod paene terram nasus indecens tangit,
Quod dextra pectus pulsat et comam vellit:
Non ille amici fata luget aut fratris,
Uterque natus vivit et precor vivat,
Salva est et uxor sarcinaeque servique,
Nihil colonus vilicusque decoxit.
Maeroris igitur causa quae? Domi cenat.

II.29

Rufe, vides illum subsellia prima terentem,
    Cuius et hinc lucet sardonychata manus
Quaeque Tyron totiens epotavere lacernae
    Et toga non tactas vincere iussa nives,
Cuius olet toto pinguis coma Marcellano
    Et splendent volso bracchia trita pilo,
Non hesterna sedet lunata lingula planta,
    Coccina non laesum pingit aluta pedem,
Et numerosa linunt stellantem splenia frontem.
    Ignoras quid sit? splenia tolle, leges.

Observing Selius pacing to and fro
And up and down Europa's portico
Late in the day, brow clouded, listless air
Hinting at secret sorrows, grotesque nose
Grazing the ground, hand clutching at his hair
Or pummelling his breast, one might suppose
He'd lost a friend or a brother. But the fact
Is that his sons are flourishing—long life
To both of them!—his property's intact,
His slaves are in good health, likewise his wife,
His tenants pay, his bailiff doesn't cheat.
What's wrong, then? No one's asked him out to eat.

James Michie

Rufus, look at those front seats! Do you see
That man whose purple cloak hangs past the knee;
Whose jewels dazzle, even to our row;
Whose well-scrubbed toga humbles purest snow;
Whose hair's so oiled it permeates the air
In the theater; whose limbs have been plucked bare;
Whose laces bind red leather shoes; whose ankles
Show crescents; and whose starry face must rankle
The firmament? What meaning? Peel the stars,
And read the text, Rufus: an ex-slave's scars.

R. L. Barth

II.32

Lis mihi cum Balbo est, tu Balbum offendere non vis,
    Pontice: cum Licino est, hic quoque magnus homo est.
Vexat saepe meum Patrobas confinis agellum,
    Contra libertum Caesaris ire times.
Abnegat et retinet nostrum Laronia servum,
    Respondes "Orba est, dives, anus, vidua."
Non bene, crede mihi, servo servitur amico:
    Sit liber, dominus qui volet esse meus.

II.33

Cur non basio te, Philaeni? calva es.
Cur non basio te, Philaeni? rufa es.
Cur non basio te, Philaeni? lusca es.
Haec qui basiat, o Philaeni, fellat.

I'm taking Balbus to court, and hoped that you . . .
    "Balbus is someone I'd rather not offend."
Ponticus, I need aid with Licinus too . . .
    "He's a great man as well," explains my friend.
Patrobas next door trespasses on my field . . .
    "He's Caesar's freedman. 'Fraid we'll have to yield."
Laronia borrowed my slave—which she denies
And keeps him . . .
                    "Piquant. Rich, old, no dependents?
Someone should marry her before she dies . . ."
Really, a patron who must dance attendance
On other patrons is no friend for me.
The friend who wants my service must be free.

Alistair Elliot

Why no kiss, Phyllis? Your bald head.
Why no kiss, Phyllis? Your skin's red.
Why no kiss, Phyllis? Your one eye.
Kissing you, Phyllis, I'd suck. That's why.

J. P. Sullivan

II.36

Flectere te nolim, sed nec turbare capillos;
  Splendida sit nolo, sordida nolo cutis;
Nec tibi mitrarum nec sit tibi barba reorum:
  Nolo virum nimium, Pannyche, nolo parum.
Nunc sunt crura pilis et sunt tibi pectora saetis
  Horrida, sed mens est, Pannyche, volsa tibi.

II.38

Quid mihi reddat ager quaeris, Line, Nomentanus?
  Hoc mihi reddit ager: te, Line, non video.

Not Afro—not crewcut
and no way out new cut
but something betwixt and between.

Please don't look too hippy
or boondocks Mississippi
and try if you can to keep clean.

Shave so close but no closer,
no *eau-de-mimosa*,
be macho, not mucho, enough.

I'm a little bit wary
of hirsute and hairy
and your sort of chestrug's so rough—

but one place they don't sprout
as all growth's been plucked out
is, Mr. REDNECK, your mind!

                                        Tony Harrison

You wonder if my farm pays me its share?
It pays me this: I do not see you there.

                                        Raymond Oliver

II.42

Zoile, quid solium subluto podice perdis?
  Spurcius ut fiat, Zoile, merge caput.

II.48

Coponem laniumque balneumque,
Tonsorem tabulamque calculosque
Et paucos, sed ut eligam, libellos:
Unum non nimium rudem sodalem
Et grandem puerum diuque levem
Et caram puero meo puellam:
Haec praesta mihi, Rufe, vel Butuntis,
Et thermas tibi habe Neronianas.

II.49

Uxorem nolo Telesinam ducere: "quare?"
  Moecha est. "Sed pueris dat Telesina." Volo.

Zoilus, if you want to pollute the public
    bathing place,
Don't stick in your ass first; stick in
    your face.

    Richard O'Connell

A pub, a meatshop, and a sauna,
A little barber round the corner,
A playing-board (with all the men),
Books (a small helping—I'll say when),
And one not-too-unlettered friend,
And a tall boy who can unbend
And isn't bristly, and a dear
Young girl to satisfy my dear:
Promise me these—Bututni's home,
And you can keep the baths of Rome.

    Alistair Elliot

"I won't marry Betty: she's too fond of men."
"Well, boys find her charming." I'll marry her then.

    F. A. Wright

II.51

Unus saepe tibi tota denarius arca
  Cum sit et hic culo tritior, Hylle, tuo,
Non tamen hunc pistor, non auferet hunc tibi copo.
  Sed si quis nimio pene superbus erit.
Infelix venter spectat convivia culi
  Et semper miser hic esurit, ille vorat.

II.54

Quid de te, Line, suspicetur uxor
Et qua parte velit pudiciorem,
Certis indiciis satis probavit,
Custodem tibi quae dedit spadonem.
Nil nasutius hac maligniusque.

II.55

Vis te, Sexte, coli: volebam amare.
Parendum est tibi: quod iubes, coleris:
Sed si te colo, Sexte, non amabo.

You've got just one coin alone in your box,
As smooth as your asshole, worn down by cocks.
This won't go on bread and it won't go on booze,
But a well-hung young stud will soon pry it loose;
So your poor empty stomach will look on in vain,
As your asshole is feasted again and again.

                                        J. P. Sullivan

Your wife her husband knows, Linus,
And what in you she'ld have more chaste.
Your tastes (it's plain) are plain to her:
She's bought a spaded valet for you!
What shrewder, what more bitter pill?

                                        Peter Whigham

You ask for deference when I offer love;
So be it; you shall have my bended knee.
But, Sextus, by great Jupiter above,
Getting respect, you'll get no love from me.

                                        Brian Hill

II.59

Mica* vocor: quid sim cernis, cenatio parva:
    Ex me Caesareum prospicis ecce tholum.
Frange toros, pete vina, rosas cape, tinguere nardo:
    Ipse iubet mortis te meminisse deus.

II.62

Quod pectus, quod crura tibi, quod bracchia vellis,
    Quod cincta est brevibus mentula tonsa pilis:
Hoc praestas, Labiene, tuae—quis nescit?—amicae.
    Cui praestas, culum quod, Labiene, pilas?

II.67

Occurris quocumque loco mihi, Postume, clamas
    Protinus et prima est haec tua vox "Quid agis?"
Hoc, si me decies una conveneris hora,
    Dicis: habes puto tu, Postume, nil quod agas.

---

* In Roman as in modern society names were sometimes given to houses and
rooms. *Mica*, a grain, e.g., of salt, may have been the *mica aurea* or Golden Grain
room we hear of in later sources. The room overlooked either the Templum gentis
Flaviae or the Mausoleum of Augustus.

Look round: You see a little supper room;
But from my window, lo! great Caesar's tomb!
And the great dead themselves, with jovial breath,
Bid you be merry and remember death.

Robert Louis Stevenson

If your arms, legs and chest are all shaved bare,
And your smooth tool has close-cropped pubic hair,
Is it, Labienus, for your female chum?
That's fine! For whom, though, do you shave your bum?

Anthony Reid

Whenever, Postumus, you meet me
You rush forward and loudly greet me
With "How do you do?" Even if we meet
Ten times in an hour you still repeat
"How do you do?" How does one do
As little with one's time as you?

James Michie

II.68

Quod te nomine iam tuo saluto,
Quem regem et dominum prius vocabam,
Ne me dixeris esse contumacem:
Totis pillea sarcinis redemi.
Reges et dominos habere debet,
Qui se non habet atque concupiscit
Quod reges dominique concupiscunt.
Servom si potes, Ole, non habere,
Et regem potes, Ole, non habere.

II.82

Abscisa servom quid figis, Pontice, lingua?
    nescis tu populum, quod tacet ille, loqui?

II.83

Foedasti miserum, marite, moechum,
Et se, qui fuerant prius, requirunt
Trunci naribus auribusque voltus.
Credis te satis esse vindicatum?
Erras: iste potest et irrumare.

Call me not rebel, though in what I sing
If I no longer hail thee Lord and King,
I have redeemed myself with all I had,
And now possess my fortunes poor but glad.
With all I had I have redeemed myself,
And escaped at once from slavery and pelf.
The unruly wishes must a ruler take,
Our high desires do our low fortunes make:
Those only who desire palatial things
Do bear the fetters and the frowns of Kings;
Set free thy slave; thou settest free thyself.

> Robert Louis Stevenson

Why cut his tongue out, Ponticus,
And nail your slave upon the cross?
Aren't you aware that people shout
The very things he can't let out?

> A. G. Carrington

You took a dire revenge, one hears,
On him who stole your wife,
By cutting off his nose and ears—
It's marred his social life.
Still there's one thing you didn't get
And that could cause you trouble yet.

> Olive Pitt-Kethley

II.89

Quod nimio gaudes noctem producere vino,
   Ignosco: vitium, Gaure, Catonis habes.
Carmina quod scribis Musis et Apolline nullo,
   Laudari debes: hoc Ciceronis habes:
Quod vomis, Antoni: quod luxuriaris, Apici.
   Quod fellas, vitium dic mihi cuius habes?

Gaurus, you have a fault for which
   I freely pardon you:
You love to drink too much, too late;
   That vice was Cato's too.
I'll even praise your scribbling
   Verses, instead of prose,
With NO help from the Muses, for
   That fault was Cicero's.
You vomit: so did Antony,
   You squander: records *may* show
Apicius as your model—now,
   Who led you to fellatio?

Dorothea Wender

II.90

Quintiliane, vagae moderator summe iuventae,
   Gloria Romanae, Quintiliane, togae,
Vivere quod propero pauper nec inutilis annis,
   Da veniam: properat vivere nemo satis.
Differat hoc, patrios optat qui vincere census
   Atriaque inmodicis artat imaginibus.
Me focus et nigros non indignantia fumos
   Tecta iuvant et fons vivus et herba rudis.
Sit mihi verna satur, sit non doctissima coniunx,
   Sit nox cum somno, sit sine lite dies.

O chief director of the growing race,
Of Rome the glory and of Rome the grace,
Me, O Quintilian,* may you not forgive
Though, far from labour, I make haste to live?
Some burn to gather wealth, lay hands on rule,
Or with white statues fill the atrium full.
The talking hearth, the rafters swart with smoke,
Live fountains and rough grass, my love invokes:
A sturdy slave: a not too learned wife:
Nights filled with slumber, and a quiet life.

Robert Louis Stevenson

*Marcus Fabius Quintilianus (born ca. A.D. 30–35), like Martial a Spaniard, was the first famous teacher of rhetoric to receive an imperial salary.

BOOK III

(A.D. 87–88)

III.5

Vis commendari sine me cursurus in urbem,
    Parve liber, multis, an satis unus erit?
Unus erit, mihi crede, satis, cui non eris hospes,
    Iulius, assiduum nomen in ore meo.
Protinus hunc primae quaeres in limine Tectae:
    Quos tenuit Daphnis, nunc tenet ille lares.
Est illi coniunx, quae te manibusque sinuque
    Excipiet, tu vel pulverulentus eas.
Hos tu seu pariter sive hanc illumve priorem
    Videris, hoc dices "Marcus havere iubet,"
Et satis est: alios commendet epistula: peccat
    Qui commendandum se putat esse suis.

III.7

Centum miselli iam valete quadrantes,
Anteambulonis congiarium lassi,
Quos dividebat balneator elixus.
Quid cogitatis, o fames amicorum?
Regis superbi sportulae recesserunt.
"Nihil stropharum est: iam salarium dandum est."

Since, little book, you're bent on leaving home
Without me, do you want, when you reach Rome,
Lots of introductions, or will one suffice?
One will be quite enough, take my advice—
And I don't mean some stranger, but the same
Julius whom you've often heard me name.
Go to the Arcade entrance—right beside it
You'll find his house (Daphnis last occupied it).
He has a wife, who even if you land
Dust-spattered at the door will offer hand
And heart in hospitable welcome. Whether
You see her first, or him, or both together,
All you need say is, "Marcus Valerius sends
His love." A formal letter recommends
Strangers to strangers; there's no need with friends.

James Michie

Domitian's banned our money dole. Adieu
The worn-out client's pitiful revenue
For being obsequious, which some half-drowned
Superintendent of the bath dealt round.
We've seen the last of "princely" dividends.
What do you think of the news, my starving friends?
"Let's face the facts," they say, "we're on our uppers:
We want a fixed wage, not uncertain suppers."

James Michie

III.8

"Thaida Quintus amat." Quam Thaida? "Thaida luscam."
Unum oculum Thais non habet, ille duos.

III.9

Versiculos in me narratur scribere Cinna.
Non scribit, cuius carmina nemo legit.

III.11

Si tua nec Thais nec lusca est, Quinte, puella,
    Cur in te factum distichon esse putas?
Sed similest aliquid? pro Laide Thaida dixi?
    Dic mihi, quid simile est Thais et Hermione?
Tu tamen es Quintus: mutemus nomen amantis:
    Si non vult Quintus, Thaida Sextus amet.

His one-eyed Thais sets his love aglow;
She's half-blind—he's entirely so!

J. A. Pott

Cinna attacks me, calls me dirt?
Let him. Who isn't read, can't hurt.

Richard O'Connell

I was silly enough to use your name
    in a recent epigram, Quintus,
and I spoke of your Thais (perhaps as
    a change from Lais)—after all,
I could have chosen Hermione or any
    other name. To make amends,
I've revised the epigram: Book 3, No. 8:
    "Sextus loves Hermione." "Which Hermione?"
"Hermione, the one-eyed." "Hermione lacks
    one eye, but Sextus both!" Now the names
are changed, you won't see any similarities.
    Didn't a satirist say that satire
is a sort of glass, wherein beholders do
    generally discover everybody's face
but their own? Names are another matter!

Peter Porter

III.12

Unguentum, fateor, bonum dedisti
Convivis here, sed nihil scidisti.
Res salsa est bene olere et esurire.
Qui non cenat et unguitur, Fabulle,
Hic vere mihi mortuus videtur.

III.17

Circumlata diu mensis scribilita secundis
    Urebat nimio saeva calore manus;
Sed magis ardebat Sabidi gula: protinus ergo
    Sufflavit buccis terque quaterque suis.
Illa quidem tepuit digitosque admittere visa est,
    Sed nemo potuit tangere: merda fuit.

III.26

Praedia solus habes et solus, Candide, nummos,
    Aurea solus habes, murrina solus habes,
Massica solus habes et Opimi Caecuba solus,
    Et cor solus habes, solus et ingenium.
Omnia solus habes—hoc me puta velle negare!—
    Uxorem sed habes, Candide, cum populo.

Last night, at your house, you drowned us all in a
Beautiful perfume, but gave us no dinner.
To be scented so well but not eat at all—
Was it a feast or our funeral?

John Adlard

The tart passed round for sweet's so hot
no-one touches it. No-one but NOT
Sabidius whose greed burns more.

He blows on it 1-2-3-4.
It's cool. Still no-one touches it.
Sabidius's breath turns all to shit.

Tony Harrison

Candidus, all this land is yours alone,
Wealth, golden plate, and murrine cups you own;
For you alone the noble Massic wine,
And Caecuban, Opimian vintage fine.
Yours, yours alone, all talent and all powers,
You have a wife too, who is yours—and ours!

Olive Pitt-Kethley

III.32

Non possum vetulam. Quereris, Matrinia? possum
  Et vetulam, sed tu mortua, non vetula es.
Possum Hecubam, possum Niobam, Matrinia, sed si
  Nondum erit illa canis, nondum erit illa lapis.

III.35

Artis Phidiacae toreuma clarum
Pisces aspicis: adde aquam, natabunt.

III.37

Irasci tantum felices nostis amici.
Non belle facitis, sed iuvat hoc: facite.

Screw old women? Sure I do! But YOU,
Matrinia, you're more a corpse than crone
and necrophilia I'm not into.

Hecuba, Niobe, both of them I'd screw
till one became a bitch, the other stone.

Tony Harrison

Instant Fish
  by Phidias!
Add water
  and they swim.

Peter Porter

The rich feign wrath—a profitable plan;
'Tis cheaper far to hate than help a man.

J. A. Pott

III.43

Mentiris iuvenem tinctis, Laetine, capillis,
    Tam subito corvus, qui modo cycnus eras.
Non omnes fallis; scit te Proserpina canum:
    Personam capiti detrahet illa tuo.

III.45

Fugerit an Phoebus mensas cenamque Thyestae
    Ignoro: fugimus nos, Ligurine, tuam.
Illa quidem lauta est dapibusque instructa superbis,
    Sed nihil omnino te recitante placet.
Nolo mihi ponas rhombos mullumve bilibrem,
    Nec volo boletos, ostrea nolo: tace.

You were a swan, you're now a crow.
Laetinus, why deceive us so,
With borrowed plumage trying?
The Queen of Shades will surely know
When she strips off your mask below—
In Death there's no more dyeing.

Olive Pitt-Kethley

Whether Phoebus fled from Thyestes' table and meat,
I do not know. We fly, Ligurinus, from yours.
It is grand, of course, and set with splendid feasts—
but nothing at all is pleasant while you recite.

I don't want you to serve me with turbot, a two-
pound mullet, I don't want mushrooms,
I do not want oysters—
BE QUIET!

W. G. Shepherd

III.47

Capena grandi porta qua pluit gutta
Phrygiumque Matris Almo qua lavat ferrum,
Horatiorum qua viret sacer campus
Et qua pusilli fervet Herculis fanum,
Faustine, plena Bassus ibat in raeda,
Omnis beati copias trahens ruris.
Illic videres frutice nobili caules
Et utrumque porrum sessilesque lactucas
Pigroque ventri non inutiles betas,
Illic coronam pinguibus gravem turdis
Leporemque laesum Gallici canis dente
Nondumque victa lacteum faba porcum.
Nec feriatus ibat ante carrucam,
Sed tuta faeno cursor ova portabat.
Urbem petebat Bassus? immo rus ibat.

Where Aqua Marcia drips a great
Bead-curtain down the Capua gate,
And Almo washes once a year
Mother Cybele's gelding-gear,
Where the Horatian brothers lie
And save their honoured greenery,
And where the heated pilgrims press
To worship Hercules the Less,
There in his coach, cram-full of all
The country treasures it can haul,
Bassus was riding. Cabbages,
With noble heads as fine as his,
Bounced on the left-hand door and hit
Soft lettuces (the kind that sit)
About his ears, and leeks (both types),
And beets (so good for blocked-up pipes),
While on the right there hung a frame
Heavy with plumply-feathered game,
A hare that got its mortal wound
Being mouthed by someone's Gallic hound,
And a wee sucking-pig too young
To turn a horse-bean into dung.
Even the footman walked before
The cart, with eggs packed safe in straw.
Was Bassus heading into Rome?
No, leaving for his country home!

                              Alistair Elliot

III.51

Cum faciem laudo, cum miror crura manusque,
    Dicere, Galla, soles "Nuda placebo magis,"
Et semper vitas communia balnea nobis.
    Numquid, Galla, times, ne tibi non placeam?

III.52

Empta domus fuerat tibi, Tongiliane, ducentis:
    Abstulit hanc nimium casus in urbe frequens.
Conlatum est deciens. Rogo, non potes ipse videri
    Incendisse tuam, Tongiliane, domum?

III.53

Et voltu poteram tuo carere
Et collo manibusque cruribusque
Et mammis natibusque clunibusque,
Et, ne singula persequi laborem,
Tota te poteram, Chloe, carere.

I praise your body's beauty. "Quite enough,"
Galla, you say, "it's better in the buff."
Let's go a-bathing then, but you decline.
Galla, are you afraid you won't like mine?

Mollie Barger

For twenty grand you bought yourself a home,
Destroyed by fire, a frequent chance in Rome.
A hundred grand your friends made up in purse:
To think of arson's by no means perverse.

Roy F. Butler

Take oh take that face away,
    That neck away, those arms away,
Hips and bottom, legs and breast—
    Dear, must I catalogue the rest?
Take, Chloe, take yourself away.

Dudley Fitts

III.55

Quod quacumque venis, Cosmum* migrare putamus
   Et fluere excusso cinnama fusa vitro,
Nolo peregrinis placeas tibi, Gellia, nugis.
   Scis, puto, posse meum sic bene olere canem.

III.65

Quod spirat tenera malum mordente puella,
   Quod de Corycio quae venit aura croco;
Vinea quod primis floret cum cana racemis,
   Gramina quod redolent, quae modo carpsit ovis;
Quod myrtus, quod messor Arabs, quod sucina trita,
   Pallidus Eoo ture quod ignis olet;
Glaeba quod aestivo leviter cum spargitur imbre,
   Quod madidas nardo passa corona comas:
Hoc tua, saeve puer Diadumene, basia fragrant.
   Quid si tota dares illa sine invidia?

---

*Cosmus was the most famous *parfumier* and purveyor of skin lotions in
first century Rome. The name may have been used by more than one establish-
ment.

Wherever you come, we think Olfactor
Is transmutating and cinnamon
Flowing, diffusing from shaken glass . . .

I do not wish you to pique yourself,
Gellia, on foreign rubbish. You know,
I think my dog can smell sweet thus.

W. G. Shepherd

They smell of Corycian saffron, of a
   girl's tooth biting a fresh apple,
Of first bunches of white grapes & sheep-cropped
   grass & myrtle leaves & chafed amber.
They're in the herb harvest. They're in the flame
   Golden with myrrh. Earth smells of them
In summer after rain, and jewelry
   reeking of expensive heads.
Your kisses, my cold jewel, smell thus. How would
   they smell if love had warmed their giving?

Peter Whigham

III.68

Huc est usque tibi scriptus, matrona, libellus.
    Cui sint scripta, rogas, interiora? mihi.
Gymnasium, thermae, stadium est hac parte: recede.
    Exuimur: nudos parce videre viros.
Hinc iam deposito post vina rosasque pudore,
    Quid dicat, nescit saucia Terpsichore:
Schemate nec dubio, sed aperte nominat illam,
    Quam recipit sexto mense superba Venus,
Custodem medio statuit quam vilicus horto,
    Opposita spectat quam proba virgo manu.
Si bene te novi, longum iam lassa libellum
    Ponebas, totum nunc studiosa leges.

Madam: my little book, so far,
  In its entirety
Up to this point, has been for you;
  From now on, it's for me.
The gym, the locker-room, the baths
  Are next; you'd better skip
This part and go away, my dear,
  The men are going to strip.
Terpsichore is staggering
  From all the wine and roses,
She lays aside her shame and starts
  Assuming naughty poses,
In no ambiguous terms she names
  Quite openly, that Thing
Which haughty Venus welcomes
  In the rituals, in spring,
That Thing which stands in gardens
  Scaring thieves with its great size,
Which virgins peek at modestly
  With almost-covered eyes.
I know you, Madam: you were tired
  And just about to quit
My lengthy little book: *now* you'll
  Devour all of it!

  Dorothea Wender

III.70

Moechus es Aufidiae, qui vir, Scaevine, fuisti;
  Rivalis fuerat qui tuus, ille vir est.
Cur aliena placet tibi, quae tua non placet, uxor?
  Numquid securus non potes arrigere?

III.71

Mentula cum doleat puero, tibi, Naevole, culus,
  Non sum divinus, sed scio quid facias.

III.72

Vis futui, nec vis mecum, Saufeia, lavari.
  Nescio quod magnum suspicor esse nefas.
Aut tibi pannosae dependent pectore mammae,
  Aut sulcos uteri prodere nuda times,
Aut infinito lacerum patet inguen hiatu,
  Aut aliquid cunni prominet ore tui.
Sed nihil est horum, credo, pulcherrima nuda es.
  Si verum est, vitium peius habes: fatua es.

You're fucking Aufidia, your ex
who's married to the guy who gave *you* grounds.
Adultery's the one way you get sex.
You only get a hard-on out of bounds.

Tony Harrison

Your lad is sore in front
    And you itch at the rear;
I'm no clairvoyant, but
    I see things crystal-clear!

Brian Hill

You want a fuck, Saufeia
But not the hot-tub larks.
Something is very queer.
Is it sagging boobs?
Or is it just stretch marks?
A gaping gash from overuse?
A clitoris that's hanging loose?
None of these. Stripped, you'd turn on guests
And you'd look real cool.
You have a worse fault, though—
You are just a fool.

J. P. Sullivan

III.73

Dormis cum pueris mutuniatis,
Et non stat tibi, Galle, quod stat illis.
Quid vis me, rogo, Phoebe, suspicari?
Mollem credere te virum volebam,
Sed rumor negat esse te cinaedum.

III.87

Narrat te, Chione, rumor numquam esse fututam
    Atque nihil cunno purius esse tuo.
Tecta tamen non hac, qua debes, parte lavaris:
    Si pudor est, transfer subligar in faciem.

III.88

Sunt gemini fratres, diversa sed inguina lingunt.
    Dicite, dissimiles sunt magis, an similes?

To sleep with well-hung lads' your stunt,
  And whilst you're flabby, they're erect.
  You want to know what I suspect?
That you love boys—but back to front.

Anthony Reid

Rumor has it your twat is pure
  As snow, and you've never screwed;
But nonetheless when you take a bath
  You won't go in the nude.
You're acting very foolish
  If you really fear disgrace,
If you're so modest, take your pants
  And cover up that face!

Dorothea Wender

Say, when twin brothers diverse groins would kiss,
Do they more twinlike grow, or less, in this?

Peter Whigham

III.94

Esse negas coctum leporem poscisque flagella.
  Mavis, Rufe, cocum scindere, quam leporem.

III.96

Lingis, non futuis meam puellam
Et garris quasi moechus et fututor.
Si te prendero, Gargili, tacebis.

III.98

Sit culus tibi quam macer, requiris?
Pedicare potes, Sabelle, culo.

The whip! for Rufus finds the hare too rare to eat,
will sooner cut his cook than carve his meat.

W. G. Shepherd

You lick, you don't fuck my baby doll's puss,
Yet you talk like a macho, a goat.
Let me just catch you, Gargilius,
You'll gargle—Deep Throat!

J. P. Sullivan

You know how thin your ass-hole's gone?
You could stuff it, Sabellus, up another one.

J. P. Sullivan

BOOK IV

(A.D. 89 DECEMBER)

IV.7

Cur, here quod dederas, hodie, puer Hylle, negasti,
    Durus tam subito, qui modo mitis eras?
Sed iam causaris barbamque annosque pilosque.
    O nox quam longa es, quae facis una senem.
Quid nos derides? here qui puer, Hylle, fuisti,
    Dic nobis, hodie qua ratione vir es?

IV.8

Prima salutantes atque altera conterit hora,
    Exercet raucos tertia causidicos,
In quintam varios extendit Roma labores,
    Sexta quies lassis, septima finis erit,
Sufficit in nonam nitidis octava palaestris,
    Imperat extructos frangere nona toros:
Hora libellorum decuma est, Eupheme, meorum,
    Temperat ambrosias cum tua cura dapes
Et bonus aetherio laxatur nectare Caesar
    Ingentique tenet pocula parca manu.
Tunc admitte iocos: gressu timet ire licenti
    Ad matutinum nostra Thalia Iovem.

Why, Hyllus, do you deny to me today
What you so freely gave just yesterday?
Last night you were a soft and yielding youth;
Today you greet me with a sullen mouth.
You've grown a bristly beard and manly hairs?
What lingering night could last so many years?
You're joking, Hyllus! Tell me how you can
Turn yesterday's boy today into a man.

Mollie Barger

The first, second hours grind down petitioners politely,
    The third sets on barking advocates,
On through the fifth, Rome extends like a handshake her
    labors,
    The sixth, rest to the weary; the seventh, the end.
The eighth to the ninth suffices for oil-gleaming wrestling,
    The ninth crushes the couches heaped high;
The tenth is the hour, Euphemus, for my little volumes,
    While care metes out the ambrosial feast,
And good Caesar, softened with heavenly nectar,
    swallows the sparing cup in mighty grip.
Then let my jokes in. A morning Jove
    stays Thalia at the threshold, a-tremble.

Helen Deutsch

IV.12

Nulli, Thai, negas, sed si te non pudet istud,
Hoc saltem pudeat, Thai, negare nihil.

IV.13

Claudia, Rufe, meo nubit Peregrina Pudenti:
Macte esto taedis, o Hymenaee, tuis.
Tam bene rara suo miscentur cinnama nardo,
Massica Theseis tam bene vina favis;
Nec melius teneris iunguntur vitibus ulmi,
Nec plus lotos aquas, litora myrtus amat.
Candida perpetuo reside, Concordia, lecto,
Tamque pari semper sit Venus aequa iugo:
Diligat illa senem quondam, sed et ipsa marito
Tum quoque, cum fuerit, non videatur anus.

To everyone, Thais, you say Yes—
Where's the blame?
But never a No to *anything*—
Have you no shame?

J. P. Sullivan

Now Claudia to my Pudens comes as bride:
   blessings on their Hymen torches!
Cinnamon blends well with cinnamon oil,
   Massic with Attic honey blends.
Vine is not more closely twined to elm; no
   myrtle more loves coast; lotus, pool.
May constant Harmony attend their bed,
   likewise Venus their like pledge.
Let her still love him old, and him not see
   her old age come, though old she be.

Peter Whigham

IV.18

Qua vicina pluit Vipsanis porta columnis
    Et madet adsiduo lubricus imbre lapis,
In iugulum pueri, qui roscida tecta subibat,
    Decidit hiberno praegravis unda gelu:
Cumque peregisset miseri crudelia fata,
    Tabuit in calido volnere mucro tener.
Quid non saeva sibi voluit Fortuna licere?
    Aut ubi non mors est, si iugulatis aquae?

Near the Vipsanian columns where the aqueduct
    drips down the side of its dark arch,
the stone is a green and pulsing velvet
    and the air is powdered with sweat
from the invisible faucet: there winter
    shaped a dagger of ice, waited till
a boy looked up at the quondam stalactites,
    threw it like a gimlet through his throat
and as in a murder in a paperback the clever
    weapon melted away in its own hole. Where
have blood and water flowed before from one wound?
    The story is trivial and the instance holy—
what portion of power has violent fortune
    ever surrendered, what degraded circumstance
will she refuse? Death is everywhere
    if water, the life-giving element,
will descend to cutting throats.

Peter Porter

IV.22

Primos passa toros et adhuc placanda marito
   Merserat in nitidos se Cleopatra lacus,
Dum fugit amplexus. Sed prodidit unda latentem;
   Lucebat, totis cum tegeretur aquis:
Condita sic puro numerantur lilia vitro,
   Sic prohibet tenuis gemma latere rosas.
Insilui mersusque vadis luctantia carpsi
   Basia: perspicuae plus vetuistis aquae.

After her wedding-night, the nymph,
   avoiding what she seeks (her husband's touch),
Runs to the bright concealments
   of her pool. But water (like glass) betrays
The hidden woman. Cleopatra
   glitters through her cloak of water. So
Ornamental flowers in glass
   or crystal, shroud themselves in the same cheat-
ing clearness. I joined her there. I
   tore up water-kisses. Transparent
Crystal robbed us of the rest.

Peter Whigham

IV.30

Baiano procul a lacu, monemus,
Piscator, fuge, ne nocens recedas.
Sacris piscibus hae natantur undae,
Qui norunt dominum manumque lambunt
Illam, qua nihil est in orbe maius.
Quid, quod nomen habent et ad magistri
Vocem quisque sui venit citatus?
Hoc quondam Libys impius profundo,
Dum praedam calamo tremente ducit,
Raptis luminibus repente caecus
Captum non potuit videre piscem,
Et nunc sacrilegos perosus hamos
Baianos sedet ad lacus rogator.
At tu, dum potes, innocens recede
Iactis simplicibus cibis in undas,
Et pisces venerare delicatos.

IV.32

Et latet et lucet Phaethontide condita gutta,
    Ut videatur apis nectare clusa suo.
Dignum tantorum pretium tulit illa laborum:
    Credibile est ipsam sic voluisse mori.

Fisher, I warn, from Baiae's lake fly far,
Lest you with guilt depart. These waters swim
With sacred fish who know their lord and are
Obedient to his call. They come to him
And suck that hand, than which there can be none
More great on earth. Each fish is named and they
Swim to their master's voice. Here, some time gone,
An impious Libyan pulling in his prey
From depths, his line quivering, was robbed of sight
And couldn't see the fish, deprived of light,
Loathing his sacrilegious hooks, he sits
And begs by Baiae's lake. At any rate,
Go while you can, still guiltless. Throw plain bits
Of food. The dainty fishes, venerate.

Olive Pitt-Kethley

Encased & shining in a bead of amber
The bee looks trapped in its own nectar:
A fit close to sweet toils, it lies
Coffined in honey—as any bee would wish.

Peter Whigham

IV.38

Galla, nega: satiatur amor, nisi gaudia torquent:
Sed noli nimium, Galla, negare diu.

IV.43

Non dixi, Coracine, te cinaedum:
Non sum tam temerarius nec audax
Nec mendacia qui loquar libenter.
Si dixi, Coracine, te cinaedum,
Iratam mihi Pontiae lagonam,
Iratum calicem mihi Metili:
Iuro per Syrios tibi tumores,
Iuro per Berecyntios furores.
Quid dixi tamen? Hoc leve et pusillum,
Quod notum est, quod et ipse non negabis,
Dixi te, Coracine, cunnilingum.

Galla, say No, for Love will cloy
Without some torment mixed with joy.
But, Galla, do not get me wrong—
Please don't say No to me too long.

Mollie Barger

Coracinus,
I never said you were nasty
to women,
I never said you bad-mouthed
the fair sex
or carried on unnaturally
with females.

All I said was
now and then
you like to get
a few licks in.

Donald Goertz

IV.44

Hic est pampineis viridis modo Vesbius umbris,
   Presserat hic madidos nobilis uva lacus:
Haec iuga, quam Nysae colles, plus Bacchus amavit,
   Hoc nuper Satyri monte dedere choros.
Haec Veneris sedes, Lacedaemone gratior illi,
   Hic locus Herculeo numine clarus erat.
Cuncta iacent flammis et tristi mersa favilla:
   Nec superi vellent hoc licuisse sibi.

This is Vesuvius, yesterday green with shady vines.
Here notable grapes weighed down the wine-steeped vats.
These the heights that Bacchus loved more than Nysa's
   hills.
On this mountain the Satyrs began their dances lately.
This was Venus' seat, more pleasing to her than Sparta.
This place was made renowned by Hercules' godhead.
All lies sunk in flames and bleak ash. Even the high gods
Could wish that this had not been allowed to them.

                                        W. G. Shepherd

IV.46

Saturnalia divitem Sabellum
Fecerunt: merito tumet Sabellus,
Nec quemquam putat esse praedicatque
Inter causidicos beatiorem.
Hos fastus animosque dat Sabello
Farris semodius fabaeque fresae,
Et turis piperisque tres selibrae,
Et Lucanica ventre cum Falisco,
Et nigri Syra defruti lagona,
Et ficus Libyca gelata testa
Cum bulbis cocleisque caseoque.
Piceno quoque venit a cliente
Parcae cistula non capax olivae,
Et crasso figuli polita caelo
Septenaria synthesis Sagunti,
Hispanae luteum rotae toreuma,
Et lato variata mappa clavo.
Saturnalia fructuosiora
Annis non habuit decem Sabellus.

Sabellus is rich;
What holiday gifts!
He's bragging up and down
There's no luckier lawyer in town.
And the cause of all this windy pride
Is a half-peck of crushed beans,
Three half-pounds of frankincense and pepper,
A flagon of black must and a string of sausages,
One jar of fig jelly, some snails and a cheese;
Not to mention a small box of large olives,
A set of seven clay cups from Spain, *embossed,*
And a handkerchief with broad vulgar stripes,
The kind bald Senators blow their distinguished noses in.
Lucky, lucky him!

> Philip Murray

IV.49

Nescit, crede mihi, quid sint epigrammata, Flacce,
　　Qui tantum lusus ista iocosque vocat.
Ille magis ludit, qui scribit prandia saevi
　　Tereos, aut cenam, crude Thyesta, tuam,
Aut puero liquidas aptantem Daedalon alas,
　　Pascantem Siculas aut Polyphemon ovis.
A nostris procul est omnis vesica libellis,
　　Musa nec insano syrmate nostra tumet.
"Illa tamen laudant omnes, mirantur, adorant."
　　Confiteor: laudant illa, sed ista legunt.

IV.54

O cui Tarpeias licuit contingere quercus
　　Et meritas prima cingere fronde comas,
Si sapis, utaris totis, Colline, diebus
　　Extremumque tibi semper adesse putes.
Lanificas nulli tres exorare puellas
　　Contigit: observant quem statuere diem.
Divitior Crispo, Thrasea constantior ipso
　　Lautior et nitido sis Meliore licet:
Nil adicit penso Lachesis fusosque sororum
　　Explicat et semper de tribus una negat.

Who deem epigrams mere trifles,
  Flaccus, know not epigram.
He trifles who describes the meal
  wild *Tereus,* rude *Thyestes* ate,
The *Cretan Glider* moulting wax,
  the one-eyed shepherd herding sheep.
Foreign to my verse the tragic sock,
  its turgid, ranting rhetoric.
"Men praise—esteem—revere these works."
  True: them they praise . . . while reading me.

Peter Whigham

Collinus, crowned with oak-leaves fair
With well-earned garlands in your hair,
Live all your days, if you are wise,
As if no morrow's sun would rise.
No man can move the Fates, my friend;
Strictly to business they attend.
Join Melior's grace with Crispus' store,
In spirit Thrasea's self outsoar,
One sister still unrolls your thread,
Another slits and you are dead.

A. L. Francis and H. F. Tatum

IV.55

Luci, gloria temporum tuorum,
Qui Caium veterem Tagumque nostrum
Arpis cedere non sinis disertis:
Argivas generatus inter urbes
Thebas carmine cantet aut Mycenas,
Aut claram Rhodon aut libidinosae
Ledaeas Lacedaemonos palaestras:
Nos Celtis genitos et ex Hiberis
Nostrae nomina duriora terrae
Grato non pudeat referre versu:
Saevo Bilbilin optimam metallo,
Quae vincit Chalybasque Noricosque,
Et ferro Plateam suo sonantem,
Quam fluctu tenui sed inquieto
Armorum Salo temperator ambit,
Tutelamque chorosque Rixamarum,
Et convivia festa Carduarum,
Et textis Peterin rosis rubentem,
Atque antiqua patrum theatra Rigas,
Et certos iaculo levi Silaos,
Turgontique lacus Perusiaeque,
Et parvae vada pura Tvetonissae,
Et sanctum Buradonis ilicetum,
Per quod vel piger ambulat viator,
Et quae fortibus excolit iuvencis
Curvae Manlius arva Vativescae.
Haec tam rustica, delicate lector,
Rides nomina? rideas licebit,
Haec tam rustica malo, quam Butuntos.

Lucius Licinianus, friend,
Adornment of our days! securing
for *Gaius, Tagus,* poetic
Palms that *Arpi* would pre-empt,
Let *Greeks* of *Thebes, Mycenae,* sing—
The wrestling pitches of permissive
Spartans—Rhodes, the world's *Colossus* . . .
Let's not, as *Celtiberians,* laggard
Be in filial verse proclaiming
Our own more homely names, to wit:
Bilbilis, its fell mines outstripping
What *Norici,* what *Chalybes* boast . . .
Plataea, where smithies ring and steel
Is tempered in *Salo's* waters,
Scant but swift, washing *Plataea's* walls . . .
Ramaxae's Ghost, its choruses . . .
At *Carduae,* the festal gath'rings . . .
Peteris, pink with woven roses . . .
Regae's ancestral arena . . .
The *Silai,* deadly with light lance . . .
The *Perusian, Turgontan* Lakes . . .
Small *Tuetonissa's* limpid shoals . . .
Buradon's holy oaks where e'en
The flagging traveller cares to wander . . .
The field on *Vativesca's* slopes
Manlius with stout bullocks furrowed . . .
Names outlandish? Names to smile at,
Sophisticate? Smile on! They're mine—
Mine more than *Roman* names can be.

Peter Whigham

IV.56

Munera quod senibus viduisque ingentia mittis,
　　Vis te munificum, Gargiliane, vocem?
Sordidius nihil est, nihil est te spurcius uno,
　　Qui potes insidias dona vocare tuas:
Sic avidis fallax indulget piscibus hamus,
　　Callida sic stultas decipit esca feras.
Quid sit largiri, quid sit donare, docebo,
　　Si nescis: dona, Gargiliane, mihi.

You want me to call you *generous*
   Because you shower gold
On widows, and send costly gifts
   To none but the very old?
There's nothing quite so nasty
   Or so sordidly unpleasant
As what you do and what you say
   When you call a snare a "present."
The treacherous hook is "generous"
   To the greedy fishes, too;
Trappers lay bait for stupid beasts—
   They're generous just like you.
You want to learn the meaning of
   True generosity?
I'll teach you about pure largesse:
   Just send your gifts to me!

               Dorothea Wender

IV.64

Iuli iugera pauca Martialis
Hortis Hesperidum beatiora
Longo Ianiculi iugo recumbunt:
Lati collibus eminent recessus,
Et planus modico tumore vertex
Caelo perfruitur sereniore
Et curvas nebula tegente valles
Solus luce nitet peculiari;
Puris leniter admoventur astris
Celsae culmina delicata villae.
Hinc septem dominos videre montis
Et totam licet aestimare Romam,
Albanos quoque Tusculosque colles
Et quodcumque iacet sub urbe frigus,
Fidenas veteres brevesque Rubras,
Et quod virgineo cruore gaudet
Annae pomiferum nemus Perennae.
Illinc Flaminiae Salariaeque
Gestator patet essedo tacente,
Ne blando rota sit molesta somno,
Quem nec rumpere nauticum celeuma
Nec clamor valet helciariorum,

The modest poles of J. Martial,
Than Gardens of the West *more blest,*
Line Janiculum's *lengthy beam.*

Remote heights command the foothills,
And the top, rolling & smooth lies
Open to serener heavens . . .
Mist covering the curved valleys,
It shines in radiance alone, while
Delicate roofs of the tall house
Soar, tapering, to th' unveiled stars.

From here the *Seven Peerless Hills,*
Here all of *Rome* herself—appraise,
The *Tusculan,* th' *Alban Hills,*
Cooling Parks fringing the City,
Old *Fidena,* little *Rubra,*
Orchards of the nymph, *Perenna*
(Pleasaunces for lustful ladies).

There *Flaminia,* there *Salernia,*
Soundlessly coach-travellers passing—
Wheels not touching softest slumbers
Boatmen's, bargees' sing-songs touch not,

Cum sit tam prope Mulvius sacrumque
Lapsae per Tiberim volent carinae.
Hoc rus, seu potius domus vocanda est,
Commendat dominus: tuam putabis,
Tam non invida tamque liberalis,
Tam comi patet hospitalitate:
Credas Alcinoi pios Penates
Aut facti modo divitis Molorchi.
Vos nunc omnia parva qui putatis,
Centeno gelidum ligone Tibur
Vel Praeneste domate pendulamque
Uni dedite Setiam colono,
Dum me iudice praeferantur istis
Iuli iugera pauca Martialis.

Though nearby hangs the *Mulvian Bridge,*
With river craft that skim down *Tiber.*

This country lodge—more truly "seat,"—
Its Master yields: you'll feel it's yours,
So lacking meanness, filled with cheer,
The genial welcome spread for you.
You'll dream *Alcinous'* hearth, or be
(Like *Hercules*) *Molorchus'* guest.

If nowadays, such seem small fry,
Exploit *Tivoli* with gangs
Of mattocks! Try cool *Praeneste!*
Rent hillside *Setia* out to farm!
M. V. shall still more blessed judge
The modest poles of *J. Martial.*

Peter Whigham

IV.66

Egisti vitam semper, Line, municipalem,
    Qua nihil omnino vilius esse potest.
Idibus et raris togula est excussa Kalendis
    Duxit et aestates synthesis una decem.
Saltus aprum, campus leporem tibi misit inemptum,
    Silva gravis turdos exagitata dedit.
Captus flumineo venit de gurgite piscis,
    Vina ruber fudit non peregrina cadus.
Nec tener Argolica missus de gente minister,
    Sed stetit inculti rustica turba foci.
Vilica vel duri conpressa est nupta coloni,
    Incaluit quotiens saucia vena mero.
Nec nocuit tectis ignis nec Sirius agris,
    Nec mersa est pelago nec fuit ulla ratis.
Subposita est blando numquam tibi tessera talo,
    Alea sed parcae sola fuere nuces.
Dic ubi sit decies, mater quod avara reliquit.
    Nusquam est: fecisti rem, Line, difficilem.

IV.69

Tu Setina quidem semper vel Massica ponis,
    Papyle, sed rumor tam bona vina negat:
Diceris hac factus caelebs quater esse lagona.
    Nec puto nec credo, Papyle, nec sitio.

Life in the provinces is simple, cheap,
And, Linus, that's the sort of style you keep;
You, once or twice a month, shake out its fold,
And dine out in a toga ten years old.
You've woods with boars, and hares to hand—unbought—
And plump field-fares just asking to be caught,
Fish in your rivers; foreign wines you bar,
And drink rough wine poured from an earthen jar.
You never choose your slaves from dear Greek boys,
But keep a crowd of country hobbledehoys.
If, after too much wine, your passions swell,
Housekeeper, farmers' wives, will do quite well.
You've never had a fire, had fields turn brown
In summer drought, nor had your ship go down
—But then you've never had one—nor lost much,
Playing with knucklebones for nuts and such.
Your greedy mother's million—really gone!
What on earth, Linus, have you spent it on?

Olive Pitt-Kethley

You serve the best wine always, my dear sir,
     And yet they say your wines are not so good.
They say you are four times a widower.
     They say . . . A drink? I don't believe I would.

J. V. Cunningham

IV.70

Nihil Ammiano praeter aridam restem
Moriens reliquit ultimis pater ceris.
Fieri putaret posse quis, Marulline,
Ut Ammianus mortuum patrem nollet?

IV.71

Quaero diu totam, Safroni Rufe, per urbem,
    Si qua puella neget: nulla puella negat.
Tamquam fas non sit, tamquam sit turpe negare,
    Tamquam non liceat: nulla puella negat.
Casta igitur nulla est? sunt castae mille: quid ergo
    Casta facit? non dat, non tamen illa negat.

When Ammianus' father breathed
His last, his son, hovering in hope,
Found that the final will bequeathed
Him nothing but a length of rope.
Though none of us dreamed he could regret
The old man's death, he's most upset.

James Michie

Throughout the city,
Safronius Rufus,
I've long inquired
if any girl says no.
No girl says no.

As though it were not right,
as though it were sin to say no,
as though it were not allowed,
no girl says no.

Then are none chaste?
A thousand are chaste.
Then what does chastity do?
She neither yields
nor yet says no.

W. G. Shepherd

IV.84

Non est in populo nec urbe tota,
A se Thaida qui probet fututam,
Cum multi cupiant rogentque multi.
Tam casta est, rogo, Thais? Immo fellat.

IV.85

Nos bibimus vitro, tu murra, Pontice. Quare?
  Prodat perspicuus ne duo vina calix.

IV.86

Si vis auribus Atticis probari,
Exhortor moneoque te, libelle,
Ut docto placeas Apollinari.
Nil exactius eruditiusque est,
Sed nec candidius benigniusque:
Si te pectore, si tenebit ore,
Nec rhonchos metues maligniorum,
Nec scombris tunicas dabis molestas.
Si damnaverit, ad salariorum
Curras scrinia protinus licebit,
Inversa pueris arande charta.

No one in town can truly say
He's had Miss Thais in the hay.
Many ask, and no one's had the luck?
No. Unless you're asking, Does she suck?

Frederic Raphael and Kenneth McLeish

We drink from glasses, you from porphyry.
Ponticus, why do you like an opaque cup?
Transparency might make you blush
Seeing you serve yourself the vintage stuff.

Richard O'Connell

Attic ears for approbation,
Little book, I urge; commend
Tickling *Apollinaris'* taste.
None more erudite, more scrupulous,
None more candid, nor more helpful.
Should his heart, lips retain your lines
You'll not fear where Envy sneers, ne'er
Make *limp wrapping for mackerel.*
Should he condemn—hie to the salt-
fish stalls—scratch-paper for boys,
Your backsides scoring with their quills!

Peter Whigham

IV.87

Infantem secum semper tua Bassa, Fabulle,
    Conlocat et lusus deliciasque vocat,
Et, quo mireris magis, infantaria non est.
    Ergo quid in causa est? Pedere Bassa solet.

IV.88

Nulla remisisti parvo pro munere dona,
    Et iam Saturni quinque fuere dies.
Ergo nec argenti sex scripula Septiciani
    Missa nec a querulo mappa cliente fuit,
Antipolitani nec quae de sanguine thynni
    Testa rubet, nec quae cottana parva gerit,
Nec rugosarum vimen breve Picenarum,
    Dicere te posses ut meminisse mei?
Decipies alios verbis voltuque benigno,
    Nam mihi iam notus dissimulator eris.

Your Bassa always has a kid around,
Fabullus; calls it little darling and sweetheart.
Yet, amazingly, she dislikes them all, I've found.
Why does she do this then? She tends to fart.

J. P. Sullivan

My gift was small, but you returned me none,
And now five Saturnalian days are done.
Six silver scruples would have been enough—
Even of Septician plate—or piece of stuff
Given by an ill-pleased guest, or even a jar
Of bleeding tuna-pickle from afar,
Antibes-brand; or Syrian figs though tiny
Would have been *something*, and, yes, even the briny
Wrinkled Picenian olives in a punnet
Would have been welcome—but you've gone and done it!
Others may think your words and smiles mean well,
To me you're just a fake-bag—I can tell!

Olive Pitt-Kethley

BOOK V

(A.D. 90 AUTUMN)

V.1

Hoc tibi, Palladiae seu collibus uteris Albae,
  Caesar, et hinc Triviam prospicis, inde Thetin,
Seu tua veridicae discunt responsa sorores,
  Plana suburbani qua cubat unda freti,
Seu placet Aeneae nutrix, seu filia Solis,
  Sive salutiferis candidus Anxur aquis,
Mittimus, o rerum felix tutela salusque,
  Sospite quo gratum credimus esse Iovem.
Tu tantum accipias: ego te legisse putabo
  Et tumidus Galla credulitate fruar.

V.9

Languebam: sed tu comitatus protinus ad me
  Venisti centum, Symmache, discipulis.
Centum me tetigere manus aquilone gelatae:
  Non habui febrem, Symmache, nunc habeo.

Caesar, contented on the Alban Mount,
    Looking to Diana's Mirror or the sea's—
Or giving oracles to the truthful sisters
    Where the wave lies by Anzio at ease—
Lulled by Gaeta or on Circe's hill
    Or in white Terracina's healthy spring—
I send you this, Protector of our health:
    Whose safety shows the thanks of Heaven's king.
Just keep the book: my Gallic heart will credit,
In blissful ignorance, that you have read it.

                                        Alistair Elliot

A slight cold or a touch of flu,
but when THE SPECIALIST and all his crew
of a 100 students once are through,
and every inch of me's been handled twice
by a hundred medics' hands as cold as ice,
the pneumonia I didn't have I DO!

                                        Tony Harrison

V.10

"Esse quid hoc dicam, vivis quod fama negatur
    Et sua quod rarus tempora lector amat?"
Hi sunt invidiae nimirum, Regule, mores,
    Praeferat antiquos semper ut illa novis.
Sic veterem ingrati Pompei quaerimus umbram,
    Sic laudant Catuli vilia templa senes;
Ennius est lectus salvo tibi, Roma, Marone,
    Et sua riserunt saecula Maeoniden,
Rara coronato plausere theatra Menandro,
    Norat Nasonem sola Corinna suum.
Vos tamen o nostri ne festinate libelli:
    Si post fata venit gloria, non propero.

V.17

Dum proavos atavosque refers et nomina magna,
    Dum tibi noster eques sordida condicio est,
Dum te posse negas nisi lato, Gellia, clavo
    Nubere, nupsisti, Gellia, cistibero.

Why is it modern books are little read,
And no-one's famous till he's safely dead?
It must be envy, Regulus, when men praise
Old authors more than new. Thus, nowadays
Pompey's old Walk is sorely missed by us,
Our elders love that "temple" of Catulus.
Great Homer was a laugh to his own age,
Few praised Menander's glories on the stage,
Rome still reads Ennius—Virgil's left alone,
Ovid is only by Corinna known.
Then be content, my books, to be slow-paced;
Death before glory means—no need for haste.

                                        Olive Pitt-Kethley

For rank, descent and title famed,
To gentry Gellia showed her hauteur;
She'd wed only a duke, she claimed—
But then she ran off with a porter.

                                        J. P. Sullivan

v.18

Quod tibi Decembri mense, quo volant mappae
Gracilesque ligulae cereique chartaeque
Et acuta senibus testa cum Damascenis,
Praeter libellos vernulas nihil misi,
Fortasse avarus videar aut inhumanus.
Odi dolosas munerum et malas artes:
Imitantur hamos dona: namque quis nescit,
Avidum vorata decipi scarum musca?
Quotiens amico diviti nihil donat,
O Quintiane, liberalis est pauper.

Because in the month of December,
when napkins, delicate spoons, waxed spills
and pointed crocks of dried damsons fly,

I have sent you nothing
(except my home-grown booklets)
perhaps I seem stingy or impolite.

I dislike
the cunning and noxious arts of giving.
Presents resemble hooks.

Who does not know
That the greedy trout is betrayed
by the fly he has gulped?

The poor man is generous,
Quintianus, to his rich friend
whenever he gives him nothing.

W. G. Shepherd

V.19

Si qua fides veris, praeferri, maxime Caesar,
  Temporibus possunt saecula nulla tuis.
Quando magis dignos licuit spectare triumphos?
  Quando Palatini plus meruere dei?
Pulchrior et maior quo sub duce Martia Roma?
  Sub quo libertas principe tanta fuit?
Est tamen hoc vitium, sed non leve, sit licet unum,
  Quod colit ingratas pauper amicitias.
Quis largitur opes veteri fidoque sodali,
  Aut quem prosequitur non alienus eques?
Saturnaliciae ligulam misisse selibrae
  Flammarisve togae scripula tota decem
Luxuria est, tumidique vocant haec munera reges:
  Qui crepet aureolos, forsitan unus erit.
Quatenus hi non sunt, esto tu, Caesar, amicus:
  Nulla ducis virtus dulcior esse potest.
Iam dudum tacito rides, Germanice, naso,
  Utile quod nobis do tibi consilium.

If truth be told, great Caesar, then your age
Outrivals all the best on history's page.
When were our shores graced with such well-earned bays?
When did the Palatine win louder praise?
When was our Rome so fair and great to see?
What other time basked in such liberty?
But we lay one great blemish at its door;
Never were friends less generous to the poor.
Who showers his gifts upon a trusty friend?
When does a knight only for love attend?
To send a half-pound spoon as Christmas fee
Or half-crown coat is prodigality.
Our purse-proud patrons praise this bounty mean;
Who prate of gold are "few and far between."
Since all men fail, Caesar, to you I turn;
No greater laurels could a sovereign earn.
I see you smile with an indulgent wink;
This counsel's for myself, not you, I think.

                    A. L. Francis and H. F. Tatum

V.20

Si tecum mihi, care Martialis,
Securis liceat frui diebus,
Si disponere tempus otiosum
Et verae pariter vacare vitae:
Nec nos atria, nec domos potentum,
Nec litis tetricas forumque triste
Nossemus, nec imagines superbas;
Sed gestatio, fabulae, libelli,
Campus, porticus, umbra, virgo, thermae,
Haec essent loca semper, hi labores.
Nunc vivit necuter sibi, bonosque
Soles effugere atque abire sentit,
Qui nobis pereunt et inputantur.
Quisquam vivere cum sciat, moratur?

V.21

Quintum pro Decimo, pro Crasso, Regule, Macrum
  Ante salutabat rhetor Apollodotus.
Nunc utrumque suo resalutat nomine. Quantum
  Cura laborque potest! Scripsit et edidicit.

Were lives of ease, dear Namesake, ours
we'ld so dispose our carefree days
Life should be for living, free from
Anterooms of dominant men,
From forum pressures, legal strains,
From portrait galleries of the great;
For us, the boulevards . . . bookstores . . .
Esplanades . . . shade & *Tiberside* . . .
Portici . . . baths cold & thermal.
There we'ld linger, there we'ld labor.

Now, twin lives are not their own.
Our good suns flee & disappear,
Debited, as they die, to us.

Who hesitates that's learned to live?

Peter Whigham

No name of old could he recall,
    But always mixed them thus,
A Mr. Gross was Mr. Small,
    And Quintus Decimus;

But now his greetings are correct,
    Each name he rightly quotes;
How much can care and toil effect,
    He learned them from his notes!

J. A. Pott

V.24

Hermes Martia saeculi voluptas,
Hermes omnibus eruditus armis,
Hermes et gladiator et magister,
Hermes turba sui tremorque ludi,
Hermes, quem timet Helius, sed unum,
Hermes, cui cadit Advolans, sed uni,
Hermes vincere nec ferire doctus,
Hermes subpositicius sibi ipse,
Hermes divitiae locariorum,
Hermes cura laborque ludiarum,
Hermes belligera superbus hasta,
Hermes aequoreo minax tridente,
Hermes casside languida timendus,
Hermes gloria Martis universi,
Hermes omnia solus et ter unus.

HERMES the Martial darling of our day,
Hermes well-skilled in every kind of fray,
Hermes a fighter-teacher, both in one,
Hermes whom Helius fears and fears alone,
Hermes before whom Advolans falls mute,
Hermes himself his only substitute,
Hermes to whom his frightened pupils bow,
Hermes who wins nor needs to strike a blow,
Hermes from whom the theatre wealth derives,
Hermes the bane of gladiators' wives,
Hermes the joy of lady-connoisseurs,
Hermes whose spear the victory ensures,
Hermes terrific with his drooping crest,
Hermes whose trident lays the foe to rest,
Hermes who does each kind of fighting grace,
Hermes in all unique, the triple ace.

F. A. Wright

V.34

Hanc tibi, Fronto pater, genetrix Flaccilla, puellam
    Oscula commendo deliciasque meas,
Parvola ne nigras horrescat Erotion umbras
    Oraque Tartarei prodigiosa canis.
Inpletura fuit sextae modo frigora brumae,
    Vixisset totidem ni minus illa dies.
Inter tam veteres ludat lasciva patronos
    Et nomen blaeso garriat ore meum.
Mollia non rigidus caespes tegat ossa, nec illi,
    Terra, gravis fueris: non fuit illa tibi.

v.36

Laudatus nostro quidam, Faustine, libello
    Dissimulat, quasi nil debeat: inposuit.

Fronto, Father, Flacilla, Mother, extend
  your protection from the Stygian shadows.
The small Erotion (my household Iris)
  has changed my house for yours. See that the hell-
hound's horrid jaws don't scare her, who was no
  more than six years old (less six days) on the
Winter day she died. She'll play beside you
  gossiping about me in child's language.
Weigh lightly on her small bones, gentle earth,
  as she, when living, lightly trod on you.

Peter Whigham

A man I published in a little book
Acts like he owes me nothing.

He's a crook.

Richard O'Connell

V.37

Puella senibus dulcior mihi cycnis,
Agna Galaesi mollior Phalantini,
Concha Lucrini delicatior stagni,
Cui nec lapillos praeferas Erythraeos,
Nec modo politum pecudis Indicae dentem
Nivesque primas liliumque non tactum;
Quae crine vicit Baetici gregis vellus
Rhenique nodos aureamque nitelam;
Fragravit ore, quod rosarium Paesti,
Quod Atticarum prima mella cerarum,
Quod sucinorum rapta de manu glaeba;
Cui conparatus indecens erat pavo,
Inamabilis sciurus et frequens phoenix:
Adhuc recenti tepet Erotion busto,
Quam pessimorum lex amara fatorum
Sexta peregit hieme, nec tamen tota,
Nostros amores gaudiumque lususque—
Et esse tristem me meus vetat Paetus,
Pectusque pulsans pariter et comam vellens:
"Deflere non te vernulae pudet mortem?
Ego coniugem" inquit "extuli, et tamen vivo,
Notam, superbam, nobilem, locupletem."
Quid esse nostro fortius potest Paeto?
Ducentiens accepit, et tamen vivit.

My girl, sweeter voiced than slim-necked swans,
Fine against skin as Phalanthian fleece,
Smoother than blue-veined shell-hollow,
fished from Lucrinian pools, for her, forget
ivory new-gleaming, first snow, purest lily.
Brighter her hair than golden wool,
than knotted tresses of Rhine nymphs.
Her breath the scent of summer rose, young
honey fresh from Attic comb, amber
snatched from palm, still warm. By her
the peacock is a bawd, the squirrel
malicious, phoenix commonplace.
Warm she lies on a smouldering bier,
Erotion, not quite six years old.
Fate's bitter law snatched her from me.
My love, my joy, delight gone all away.
And my friend Paetus won't permit my tears.
Beating his breast, tearing his hair, bellowing,
"Have you no shame to mourn a common slave?
I've lost a wife," he says, "and yet I live,
a woman well-known, well-born, well-endowed."
You deserve a medal, Paetus, for she left
you twenty million, yet you live bereft.

Helen Deutsch

V.41

Spadone cum sis eviratior fluxo,
Et concubino mollior Celaenaeo,
Quem sectus ululat matris entheae Gallus,
Theatra loqueris et gradus et edicta
Trabeasque et Idus fibulasque censusque,
Et pumicata pauperes manu monstras.
Sedere in equitum liceat an tibi scamnis
Videbo, Didyme: non licet maritorum.

V.42

Callidus effracta nummos fur auferet arca,
    Prosternet patrios impia flamma lares:
Debitor usuram pariter sortemque negabit,
    Non reddet sterilis semina iacta seges:
Dispensatorem fallax spoliabit amica,
    Mercibus extructas obruet unda rates.
Extra fortunam est quidquid donatur amicis:
    Quas dederis, solas semper habebis opes.

V.43

Thais habet nigros, niveos Laecania dentes.
    Quae ratio est? Emptos haec habet, illa suos.

You've less balls than the loose eunuch; you're more
Unmanly than that Phrygian boy-whore
Cried by the ecstatic Mother's gelded priests,
Yet you talk theatres, places, the Ides' feasts,
Clasps, ceremonial robes, property, and
Point out the needy with your pumiced hand.
If you can use a knight's seat at the play,
I'll see, Didymus; a husband's though—no way!

Fiona Pitt-Kethley

Deft thieves can break your locks and carry off
your savings, fire consume your home,
debtors default on principal and interest, failed crops
return not even the seed you'd sown,
cheating women run up your charge accounts,
storm overwhelm ships freighted with all your goods—
fortune can't take away what you give friends:
that wealth stays yours forever.

Jim Powell

Thais has black teeth, Laecania's are white because
she bought 'em last night.

Ezra Pound

v.46

Basia dum nolo nisi quae luctantia carpsi,
    Et placet ira mihi plus tua, quam facies,
Ut te saepe rogem, caedo, Diadumene, saepe:
    Consequor hoc, ut me nec timeas nec ames.

v.55

Dic mihi, quem portas, volucrum regina? "Tonantem."
    Nulla manu quare fulmina gestat? "Amat."
Quo calet igne deus? "Pueri." Cur mitis aperto
    Respicis ore Iovem? "De Ganymede loquor." *

---

* Martial is describing, as often, a statue, here of Jupiter flying on his eagle.

Reluctant kisses are the kind
   I like the best;
More than your face your sulky mind
   Adds to my zest;
That's why you're often whipped, my dear,
   So I must sue;
What's the result? I rouse no fear
   Or love in you.

          Brian Hill

Tell me, fierce eagle, through the air
Whom do your mighty pinions bear?
   "I carry Jove omnipotent."
Then why no longer in his hand
Does the god grasp a flaming brand?
   "He is in love—his thunder's spent."
For whom, fierce eagle, is great Jove
Fired with the leaping flames of love?
   "For a fair boy his heart does bleed."
And why so mildly do you turn
On Jove your eyes that used to burn?
   "I speak to him of Ganymede."

          Brian Hill

v.58

Cras te victurum, cras dicis, Postume, semper.
  Dic mihi, cras istud, Postume, quando venit?
Quam longe cras istud, ubi est? aut unde petendum?
  Numquid apud Parthos Armeniosque latet?
Iam cras istud habet Priami vel Nestoris annos.
  Cras istud quanti, dic mihi, possit emi?
Cras vives? hodie iam vivere, Postume, serum est:
  Ille sapit, quisquis, Postume, vixit heri.

You say, *Postumus*, you'll live "tomorrow."

   Postumus, tell me, when comes "tomorrow"?

Is't far that "morrow"? Where? In what place found?

—Not lurking 'mid *Armenians* or *Parthians*?

Their "morrows" now wear *Priam's*, *Nestor's* years.

   At what cost, tell me, is that "morrow" bought?

"Tomorrow"?—*Postumus*, today's too late.

   The wise man, *Postumus*, lived yesterday.

Peter Whigham

v.61

Crispulus iste quis est, uxori semper adhaeret
    Qui, Mariane, tuae? crispulus iste quis est?
Nescio quid dominae teneram qui garrit in aurem
    Et sellam cubito dexteriore premit?
Per cuius digitos currit levis anulus omnes,
    Crura gerit nullo qui violata pilo?
Nil mihi respondes? "Uxoris res agit" inquis
    "Iste meae." Sane certus et asper homo est,
Procuratorem voltu qui praeferat ipso:
    Acrior hoc Chius non erit Aufidius.
O quam dignus eras alapis, Mariane, Latini:
    Te successurum credo ego Panniculo.
Res uxoris agit? res ullas crispulus iste?
    Res non uxoris, res agit iste tuas.

v.73

Non donem tibi cur meos libellos
Oranti totiens et exigenti,
Miraris, Theodore? Magna causa est:
Dones tu mihi ne tuos libellos.

This curly fellow who's always hanging about
your wife, Marianus . . . Who is
this Curly? Who prattles petits riens
in the mistress' indulgent ear (leaning his elbow
upon her chair)? Whose every finger
is coursed about by a ring? Who disposes legs
inviolate by a single hair? You make
me no reply? "Oh, him?" you say.
"He does things for my wife." Why, yes—
he's a trusty, sterling chap, and his very face
advertises efficiency, and Lotharius himself
will prove no cuter than him! O Marianus,
you deserve the thumps of Clown,
I do believe you'll succeed to Buffoon . . .
Does things for your wife? Does Curly
do anything? Then doing
things for your wife, he does
your thing.

W. G. Shepherd

You ask for my verse, so here. This evens scores:
I had kept mine in hopes you would keep yours.

James M. Young

v.74

Pompeios iuvenes Asia atque Europa, sed ipsum
   Terra tegit Libyes, si tamen ulla tegit.
Quid mirum toto si spargitur orbe? Iacere
   Uno non poterat tanta ruina loco.

v.76

Profecit poto Mithridates saepe veneno,
   Toxica ne possent saeva nocere sibi.
Tu quoque cavisti cenando tam male semper,
   Ne posses umquam, Cinna, perire fame.

The East and West yield Pompey's children graves:
His home is Libya or the salt sea waves:
Three continents must fence such ruins round.
This wreck could not be gathered in one mound.

A. L. Francis and H. F. Tatum

Drug-proof old Mithridates grew
    By frequent poisonous potation.
So with spare diet, Cinna, you
    Ensure yourself against starvation.

W. T. Webb

v.78

Si tristi domicenio laboras,
Torani, potes esurire mecum.
Non deerunt tibi, si soles προπίνειν,
Viles Cappadocae gravesque porri,
Divisis cybium latebit ovis.
Ponetur digitis tenendus ustis
Nigra coliculus virens patella,
Algentem modo qui reliquit hortum,
Et pultem niveam premens botellus,
Et pallens faba cum rubente lardo.
Mensae munera si voles secundae,
Marcentes tibi porrigentur uvae
Et nomen pira quae ferunt Syrorum,
Et quas docta Neapolis creavit,
Lento castaneae vapore tostae:
Vinum tu facies bonum bibendo.
Post haec omnia forte si movebit
Bacchus quam solet esuritionem,
Succurrent tibi nobiles olivae,
Piceni modo quas tulere rami,
Et fervens cicer et tepens lupinus.
Parva est cenula—quis potest negare?—
Sed finges nihil audiesve fictum
Et voltu placidus tuo recumbes;
Nec crassum dominus leget volumen,
Nec de Gadibus inprobis puellae

My lack of food is yours to share
Should dining home look desultory.
A pungent leek, a devilled egg
(With tuna stuffed), iceberg lettuce—
These for antipasto shall be yours.
Served on blackened pewter there'll be
Bright green broccoli fresh from garden,
Piping hot for hasty fingers,
Sausage on polenta, speck (pink),
Fave (pallid). . . . For second course,
Pears (labelled "Syrian"), raisins,
Chestnuts, Naples sagely ripened,
Roasting on slow-burning embers.
The wine, in drinking, you'll make good.
After such fare, should Bacchus prick
Hunger further, finest olives
From Picenian groves, hot chick-peas,
simm'ring lupins shall assuage
Your need. My board is spare. For sure.
But you'll not speak—not hear—false words,
Nor look false looks, relaxed, stretched out. . . .
No host declaiming lengthy poems,
No girls from sinful Gades grinding
With endless suggestivity sex-
y thighs in nuances of lust.
Instead, small Condylus 'll flute us

Vibrabunt sine fine prurientes
Lascivos docili tremore lumbos;
Sed quod non grave sit nec infacetum,
Parvi tibia condyli sonabit.
Haec est cenula. Claudiam sequeris.*
Quam nobis cupis esse tu priorem?

v.79

Undecies una surrexti, Zoile, cena,
    Et mutata tibi est synthesis undecies,
Sudor inhaereret madida ne veste retentus
    Et laxam tenuis laederet aura cutem.
Quare ego non sudo, qui tecum, Zoile, ceno?
    Frigus enim magnum synthesis una facit.

v.83

Insequeris, fugio; fugis, insequor; haec mihi mens est.
    Velle tuum nolo, Dindyme, nolle volo.

* The translator has adopted here Gruter's *Condyli* and Allan Kershaw's *Haec est cenula. "Cluditur," requiris?* instead of the printed text.

Melodies not crass nor precious.
You ask if this is all I offer;
"What more," I answer, "would you seek?"

Peter Whigham

Eleven times last night you changed—
From soup to nuts, eleven shirts.
"I *daren't* sweat. Damp shirt . . . draughts . . .
Open pores . . . I have to be *so* careful . . ."
Well, I shared your table. Did *I* sweat?
With just one shirt, I keep my bloody cool.

Frederic Raphael and Kenneth McLeish

I run, you chase; you chase, I run.
I love what's cold: what's hot I shun.

Peter Whigham

v.84

Iam tristis nucibus puer relictis
Clamoso revocatur a magistro,
Et blando male proditus fritillo,
Arcana modo raptus e popina,
Aedilem rogat udus aleator.
Saturnalia transiere tota,
Nec munuscula parva nec minora
Misisti mihi, Galla, quam solebas.
Sane sic abeat meus December:
Scis certe, puto, vestra iam venire
Saturnalia, Martias Kalendas;
Tunc reddam tibi, Galla, quod dedisti.

Now glumly pocketing their toys
Schoolkids heed the master's voice.

Sweet sounds of dice on countertops
Finger drunk gamblers to the cops
Who roust them from obscure drink shops.

Now days of Saturnalia end
And midget gifts you once would send
It seems are also at an end.

Sure, let my gift-days giftless run.
I know you know that March will come—
Matronalia. . . . *Then* I'll bestow,
Galla, on you my *quid pro quo*.

Peter Whigham

BOOK VI

(A.D. 91 SUMMER OR AUTUMN)

VI.6

Comoedi tres sunt, sed amat tua Paula, Luperce,
    Quattuor: et κωφὸν Paula πρόσωπον amat.

VI.15

Dum Phaethontea formica vagatur in umbra,
    Inplicuit tenuem sucina gutta feram.
Sic modo quae fuerat vita contempta manente,
    Funeribus facta est nunc pretiosa suis.

PAULA

She doesn't feel 3
parts in Comedy
quite do.

4's more & merrier!
She hopes the spear-carrier
comes on too!

Tony Harrison

An ant, disporting in a poplar's shade,
   Has got imprisoned in a drop of amber.
The tiny creature, scorned through all its days,
   Has become precious in its funeral chamber.

John Adlard

VI.19

Non de vi neque caede nec veneno,
Sed lis est mihi de tribus capellis:
Vicini queror has abesse furto.
Hoc iudex sibi postulat probari:
Tu Cannas Mithridaticumque bellum
Et periuria Punici furoris
Et Sullas Mariosque Muciosque
Magna voce sonas manuque tota.
Iam dic, Postume, de tribus capellis.

VI.23

Stare iubes nostrum semper tibi, Lesbia, penem:
    Crede mihi, non est mentula, quod digitus.
Tu licet et manibus blandis et vocibus instes,
    Te contra facies imperiosa tua est.

It's not a case of poisoned cup,
　　Assault, or slitting throats;
I've had to have my neighbour up
　　For stealing my three goats.

You dwell on Punic faith and fury,
　　Pontic wars, and Cannaes,
But this they're asking on the jury,
　　"Prove he stole the nannies."

And now with gestures various
　　You've told in ringing notes
Of Sulla, Mucius, Marius,
　　Please mention my three goats.

T. W. Melluish

Lesbia, you want my prick ever-ready for your enjoyment.
Believe me, it's not a finger, to be raised whenever you care.
In vain you put your hands and your voice to this
　　employment;
Their work's undone by your imperious stare.

John Adlard

VI.26

Periclitatur capite Sotades noster.
Reum putatis esse Sotaden? non est.
Arrigere desit posse Sotades: lingit.

VI.27

Bis vicine Nepos—nam tu quoque proxima Florae
    Incolis et veteres tu quoque Ficelias—
Est tibi, quae patria signatur imagine voltus,
    Testis maternae nata pudicitiae.
Tu tamen annoso nimium ne parce Falerno,
    Et potius plenos aere relinque cados.
Sit pia, sit locuples, sed potet filia mustum:
    Amphora cum domina nunc nova fiet anus.
Caecuba non solos vindemia nutriat orbos:
    Possunt et patres vivere, crede mihi.

Don't think it's a capital charge, but Sotades' head ✳
May roll. Alas, he can't get his prick to stand
And has to use his tongue instead.

John Adlard

O Nepos, twice my neighbour (since at home
We're door by door by Flora's temple dome,
And in the country, still conjoined by fate,
Behold our villas, standing gate by gate!)
Thou hast a daughter, dearer far than life,
Thy image and the image of thy wife;
But why for her neglect the flowing can
And lose the prime of thy Falernian?
Hoard casks of money, if to hoard be thine;
But let the daughter drink a younger wine!
Let her go rich and wise, in silk and fur;
Lay down a bin that shall grow old with her;
But thou, meantime, the while the batch is sound,
With pleased companions pass the bowl around:
Nor let the childless only taste delights,
For Fathers also may enjoy their nights.

Robert Louis Stevenson

VI.28

Libertus Melioris ille notus,
Tota qui cecidit dolente Roma,
Cari deliciae breves patroni,
Hoc sub marmore Glaucias humatus
Iuncto Flaminiae iacet sepulchro:
Castus moribus, integer pudore,
Velox ingenio, decore felix.
Bis senis modo messibus peractis
Vix unum puer adplicabat annum.
Qui fles talia, nil fleas, viator.

VI.29

Non de plebe domus nec avarae verna catastae,
    Sed domini sancto dignus amore puer,
Munera cum posset nondum sentire patroni,
    Glaucia libertus iam Melioris erat.
Moribus hoc formaeque datum: quis blandior illo?
    Aut quis Apollineo pulchrior ore fuit?
Inmodicis brevis est aetas et rara senectus.
    Quidquid ames, cupias non placuisse nimis.

Here sleeps beneath this marble urn
A youth whose death all Rome did mourn;
His lord's short-lived delight and joy,
So chaste, so comely was this boy,
So quick of wit, so innocent,
Scarce thirteen summers had he spent.
O stranger mourning at this grave,
May you no other sorrow have!

Brian Hill

Here Glaucia lies, a slave-boy never led
Back from the auction-block; but pure, home-bred,
Worthy his master's love, who made him free;
For none could be more honey-sweet than he,
Wistful and lovely as the fair Apollo.
Such the Gods call when young. Alas! they follow.
Reader, whatever you may love, I pray,
Less perfect than this boy, may longer stay.

Anthony Reid

VI.33

Nil miserabilius, Matho, pedicone Sabello
    Vidisti, quo nil laetius ante fuit.
Furta, fugae, mortes servorum, incendia, luctus
    Adfligunt hominem, iam miser et futuit.

VI.34

Basia da nobis, Diadumene, pressa. "Quot?" inquis.
    Oceani fluctus me numerare iubes
Et maris Aegaei sparsas per litora conchas
    Et quae Cecropio monte vagantur apes,
Quaeque sonant pleno vocesque manusque theatro,
    Cum populus subiti Caesaris ora videt.
Nolo quot arguto dedit exorata Catullo
    Lesbia: pauca cupit, qui numerare potest.

You never saw a man in more despair
Than is Sabellus, once so debonair;
Thefts, fires, deaths, truant slaves: by these deranged,
Even his sexual appetites have changed;
His wretchedness is such that he's beginning,
It's true I swear, to turn to normal sinning.

Brian Hill

Perversion's grown so rife
Kinky Sabellus fucks his wife.

Richard O'Connell

"Kiss me again, sweet boy. Hug me, and squeeze."
    "How many times?" you ask, and I reply:
"As many as the waves, the shells, the bees,
    Or clapping hands when Caesar passes by;
More than Catullus gained. He gets too few
Who knows the number of them, kissing you."

Anthony Reid

VI.36

Mentula tam magna est, quantus tibi, Papyle, nasus,
    Ut possis, quotiens arrigis, olfacere.

VI.40

Femina praeferri potuit tibi nulla, Lycori:
    Praeferri Glycerae femina nulla potest.
Haec erit hoc quod tu: tu non potes esse quod haec est.
    Tempora quid faciunt! hanc volo, te volui.

His tool was large and so was his nose,
Papylus could smell it whenever it rose.

Fiona Pitt-Kethley

Time makes enormous differences
between the past and present tenses,
the long way that I did is from I do.

I *love* Glycera, Lycoris. I love*d* you.

Tony Harrison

VI.42

Etrusci nisi thermulis lavaris,
Inlotus morieris, Oppiane.
Nullae sic tibi blandientur undae,
Nec fontes Aponi rudes puellis,
Non mollis Sinuessa fervidique
Fluctus Passeris aut superbus Anxur,
Non Phoebi vada principesque Baiae.
Nusquam tam nitidum vacat serenum:
Lux ipsa est ibi longior, diesque
Nullo tardius a loco recedit.
Illic Taygeti virent metalla
Et certant vario decore saxa,
Quae Phryx et Libys altius cecidit,
Siccos pinguis onyx anhelat aestus
Et flamma tenui calent ophitae:
Ritus si placeant tibi Laconum,
Contentus potes arido vapore
Cruda Virgine Marciave mergi;
Quae tam candida, tam serena lucet,
Ut nullas ibi suspiceris undas
Et credas vacuam nitere lygdon.
Non adtendis, et aure me supina
Iam dudum quasi neglegenter audis,
Inlotus morieris, Oppiane.

If, Oppianus, you're not tempted by
Etruscus' baths, unbathed you'll surely die.
No other waters offer such allure,
Not even Aponus, which young girls abjure,
Phoebus, mild Sinuessa, Passer's steams,
Anxur the splendid, Baiae's peerless streams.
There, over all a stainless radiance plays,
And the long daylight endlessly delays.
Purple-streaked Phrygian, yellow Libyan, green
Laconian marble—all to advantage seen;
The sweating onyx with the heat suspires,
And the rich snakestone glows with subtle fires.
Too hot? Then, should the Spartan method seem
More pleasing, plunge into the natural stream
Of Marcia, or the Virgin—baths so fair
One sees white marble not the water there.
You've hardly heard all this! You don't attend—
I really fear you'll die unbathed, my friend.

Olive Pitt-Kethley

VI.43

Dum tibi felices indulgent, Castrice, Baiae
   Canaque sulphureis nympha natatur aquis,
Me Nomentani confirmant otia ruris
   Et casa iugeribus non onerosa suis.
Hoc mihi Baiani soles mollisque Lucrinus,
   Hoc mihi sunt vestrae, Castrice, divitiae.
Quondam laudatas quocumque libebat ad undas
   Currere nec longas pertimuisse vias,
Nunc urbis vicina iuvant facilesque recessus,
   Et satis est, pigro si licet esse mihi.

VI.47

Nympha, mei Stellae quae fonte domestica puro
   Laberis et domini gemmea tecta subis,
Sive Numae coniunx Triviae te misit ab antris,
   Sive Camenarum de grege nona venis:
Exolvit votis hac se tibi virgine porca
   Marcus, furtivam quod bibit aeger aquam.
Tu contenta meo iam crimine gaudia fontis
   Da secura tui: sit mihi sana sitis.

For you, th' indulgent bliss that Baiae confers—
    the nymph's spray, the sulphurous wave;
For me, strength drawn from Nomentan retreat—
    a small house, its acres suited.
These, my Baian sun, my sensuous lake—
    the selfsame riches you enjoy.
Gone the days—racing to the last fashion-
    able spa—distance no object.
Now Rome's proximity is all I ask—
    and licensed indolence.

                    Peter Whigham

Nymph of the stream, whose limpid water laves,
As it glides in, my Stella's brilliant halls,
Sent by Egeria from the Trivian caves,
Or a ninth Muse perhaps, now Marcus calls
To make an offering of the pure young sow
Promised in sickness, when he drank by stealth
Your lovely waters. Nymph, absolve him now;
Lend him once more your joys, in perfect health.

                    Fiona Pitt-Kethley

VI.52

Hoc iacet in tumulo raptus puerilibus annis
    Pantagathus, domini cura dolorque sui,
Vix tangente vagos ferro resecare capillos
    Doctus et hirsutas excoluisse genas.
Sis licet, ut debes, tellus, placata levisque,
    Artificis levior non potes esse manu.

VI.57

Mentiris fictos unguento, Phoebe, capillos
    Et tegitur pictis sordida calva comis.
Tonsorem capiti non est adhibere necesse:
    Radere te melius spongia, Phoebe, potest.

Pantagathus lies here, so young a boy,
His master's grief, but once his greatest joy;
So perfectly he made unkempt hair sleek,
Gliding his razor gently on each cheek.
Earth lie your lightest on him, soft and bland,
You cannot match the lightness of his hand.

Anthony Reid

With fictive locks and scented glue
    You hide your dome: who's fooling who?
A haircut? That's a simple matter.
    No clippers, please; just soap and water.

Dudley Fitts

VI.59

Et dolet et queritur sibi non contingere frigus,
 Propter sescentas Baccara gausapinas,
Optat et obscuras luces ventosque nivesque,
 Odit et hibernos, si tepuere, dies.
Quid fecere mali nostrae tibi, saeve, lacernae,
 Tollere de scapulis quas levis aura potest?
Quanto simplicius, quanto est humanius illud,
 Mense vel Augusto sumere gausapinas!

She likes the Winter season
when there's lots of ice and snow
because it gives her reason
to hold a fashion show.

She loves the weather when it stinks
and no sooner does it freeze
than out come musquashes and minks
and chic *pendant-* and *après-skis.*

I don't flaunt $$$ on my back
or keep a wardrobe like a zoo,
only one threadbare anorak
the Winter blows right through,

so if you really want to be
more noticed in your clothes
and at the same time fair on me
please stay in when it snows,

but when I can sit out in my shorts
and sip a long iced drink,
then you dress up for Winter sports
and run around in mink.

                    Tony Harrison

VI.60

Laudat, amat, cantat nostros mea Roma libellos,
    Meque sinus omnes, me manus omnis habet.
Ecce rubet quidam, pallet, stupet, oscitat, odit.
    Hoc volo: nunc nobis carmina nostra placent.

VI.64

Cum sis nec rigida Fabiorum gente creatus
Nec qualem Curio, dum prandia portat aranti,
Hirsuta peperit rubicunda sub ilice coniunx,
Sed patris ad speculum tonsi matrisque togatae
Filius et possit sponsam te sponsa vocare:
Emendare meos, quos novit fama, libellos
Et tibi permittis felicis carpere nugas,—
Has, inquam, nugas, quibus aurem advertere totam
Non aspernantur proceres urbisque forique,
Quas et perpetui dignantur scrinia Sili
Et repetit totiens facundo Regulus ore,
Quique videt propius magni certamina Circi
Laudat Aventinae vicinus Sura Dianae,
Ipse etiam tanto dominus sub pondere rerum
Non dedignatur bis terque revolvere Caesar.
Sed tibi plus mentis, tibi cor limante Minerva
Acrius et tenues finxerunt pectus Athenae.
Ne valeam, si non multo sapit altius illud,

Rome praises, loves, and sings my little verses;
They're in all hands, all pockets, and all purses.
Look there! One blushes, pales, gasps, yawns, and curses.
That's what I want! I'm happy with my verses.

R. L. Barth

Though you're not of the hardy Fabian race,
Nor like the son the wife of Curius bore,
Halfway with dinner to the ploughing-place,
Beneath a shady oak—your father trims
His hair before the glass, your mother wears
The toga in your house, your spouse can call
You wife—you'd alter verse my fame declares
Well done, carp at my pleasant trifles which
The leading men do not disdain to hear.
Immortal Silius finds them worthy of
A place upon his shelves. My poems were
Recited frequently by Regulus
Who is so eloquent. A neighbour to
Diana on the Aventine, Sura
Commends my verse, (his house has the best view
Of Circus games). And Caesar, though he's got
The whole empire to run, thought reading it
Worthwhile—two or three times. But you're so bright,

Quod cum panticibus laxis et cum pede grandi
Et rubro pulmone vetus nasisque timendum
Omnia crudelis lanius per compita portat.
Audes praeterea, quos nullus noverit, in me
Scribere versiculos miseras et perdere chartas.
At si quid nostrae tibi bilis inusserit ardor,
Vivet et haerebit totoque legetur in orbe,
Stigmata nec vafra delebit Cinnamus arte.
Sed miserere tui, rabido nec perditus ore
Fumantem nasum vivi temptaveris ursi.
Sit placidus licet et lambat digitosque manusque,
Si dolor et bilis, si iusta coegerit ira,
Ursus erit: vacua dentes in pelle fatiges
Et tacitam quaeras, quam possis rodere, carnem.

VI.66

Famae non nimium bonae puellam,
Quales in media sedent Subura,
Vendebat modo praeco Gellianus.
Parvo cum pretio diu liceret,
Dum puram cupit adprobare cunctis,
Adtraxit prope se manu negantem
Et bis terque quaterque basiavit.
Quid profecerit osculo, requiris?
Sescentos modo qui dabat, negavit.

For Athens gave you sense, Minerva wit.
I'm hanged if there is not more taste in hearts
The cruel butcher carries where he goes,
With hoofs and bloody lights and guts galore,
Ancient, stinking, offensive to the nose.
Besides, you dare to scribble lines which none
Will read and waste your paper. But if I
Should brand you with my anger, it'll stick,
For all the city'll read it by and by,
And Cinnamus, though skilled, won't shift those stains.
Don't use your rabid mouth and try in vain
To harm a foaming bear's snout. For take care,
He may just lick your hands, but if wrath, pain
And righteous anger move, he'll be a bear.
Choose empty skins alone for your attack,
Look for some flesh to gnaw that can't bite back.

                                        Fiona Pitt-Kethley

Last week, the auctioneer was trying to sell
A girl whose reputation one could smell
From here to her street corner in the slums.
After some time, when only paltry sums
Were being offered, wishing to assure
The crowd that she was absolutely pure,
He pulled the unwilling "lot" across and smacked
Three or four kisses on her. Did this act
Make any difference to the price? It did.
The highest offerer withdrew his bid.

                                        James Michie

VI.68

Flete nefas vestrum, sed toto flete Lucrino,
    Naides, et luctus sentiat ipsa Thetis.
Inter Baianas raptus puer occidit undas
    Eutychos ille, tuum, Castrice, dulce latus.
Hic tibi curarum socius blandumque levamen,
    Hic amor, hic nostri vatis Alexis erat.
Numquid te vitreis nudum lasciva sub undis
    Vidit et Alcidae nympha remisit Hylan?
An dea femineum iam neglegit Hermaphroditum
    Amplexu teneri sollicitata viri?
Quidquid id est, subitae, quaecumque est causa rapinae,
    Sit, precor, et tellus mitis et unda tibi.

Ye river-nymphs bewail your crime until
Even the eyes of ancient Ocean fill!
For when your waters dragged down Eutychus
His other self you stole from Castricus,
His lovely friend, the comrade of his heart,
Consoler of his cares, his sweetest part.

Forgetting Hylas, when upon the stream
The nymph saw all his naked beauty gleam,
Did she to new love turn? Or Salmacis
Her wanton lover leave for his young kiss?
Whate'er the hand that brought swift death to him,
May earth and water softly lap each limb.

Brian Hill

VI.70

Sexagesima, Marciane, messis
Acta est et, puto, iam secunda Cottae,
Nec se taedia lectuli calentis
Expertum meminit die vel uno.
Ostendit digitum, sed inpudicum,
Alconti Dasioque Symmachoque.
At nostri bene computentur anni
Et quantum tetricae tulere febres
Aut languor gravis aut mali dolores,
A vita meliore separentur:
Infantes sumus, et senes videmur.
Aetatem Priamique Nestorisque
Longam qui putat esse, Marciane,
Multum decipiturque falliturque.
Non est vivere, sed valere vita est.

For Cotta the sixtieth harvest
is gathered and, I think, one more,
and he doesn't remember knowing
a single day of parching fatigue in bed:
he sticks his ribald finger out
at Drs. Symmachus, Dasius, Alcon.

For us, let the years be added with care,
and the amount sour fevers have docked
or heavy accidie, or grievous pain
be set apart from sounder life:
we are babes appearing as elders.

He who deems the age of Priam
and Nestor great, Marcianus,
is greatly deceived and mistaken:
to live is not just life, but health.

W. G. Shepherd

VI.71

Edere lascivos ad Baetica crusmata gestus
    Et Gaditanis ludere docta modis,
Tendere quae tremulum Pelian Hecubaeque maritum
    Posset ad Hectoreos sollicitare rogos,
Urit et excruciat dominum Telethusa priorem:
    Vendidit ancillam, nunc redimit dominam.

VI.79

Tristis es et felix. Sciat hoc Fortuna caveto:
    Ingratum dicet te, Lupe, si scierit.

VI.82

Quidam me modo, Rufe, diligenter
Inspectum, velut emptor aut lanista,
Cum vultu digitoque subnotasset,
"Tune es, tune" ait "ille Martialis,
Cuius nequitias iocosque novit,
Aurem qui modo non habet Batavam?"
Subrisi modice, levique nutu
Me quem dixerat esse non negavi.
"Cur ergo" inquit "habes malas lacernas?"
Respondi: "quia sum malus poeta."
Hoc ne saepius accidat poetae,
Mittas, Rufe, mihi bonas lacernas.

Skilled Telethusa plays her Cadiz games
To Spanish castanets; how she inflames,
She could, in palsied Pelias, have roused fire,
In Priam too, mourning by Hector's pyre—
Her previous master's kept upon the rack—
Sold as a maid, a mistress she's brought back.

Fiona Pitt-Kethley

Lucky yet sad? My friend, should Fortune find
You lacking gratitude, she'll change her mind.

Brian Hill

He scanned me closely, Rufus, just as
Slaves by trainers are e'er purchased—
Sizing me up with eye & thumb.
Then: "Are you Martial, you the one
Whose lewd wit delights all ears
Excepting those a Dutchman wears?"
A faint smile, an inclination,
acknowledging the imputation.
"Why then," he said, "the shabby clothes?"
"It's how a shabby poet goes."
To shield me, where your poet goes,
Send, Rufus, some not shabby clothes.

Peter Whigham

VI.85

Editur en sextus sine te mihi, Rufe Camoni,
    Nec te lectorem sperat, amice, liber:
Impia Cappadocum tellus et numine laevo
    Visa tibi cineres reddit et ossa patri.
Funde tuo lacrimas orbata Bononia Rufo,
    Et resonet tota planctus in Aemilia:
Heu qualis pietas, heu quam brevis occidit aetas!
    Viderat Alphei praemia quinta modo.
Pectore tu memori nostros evolvere lusus,
    Tu solitus totos, Rufe, tenere iocos,
Accipe cum fletu maesti breve carmen amici
    Atque haec absentis tura fuisse puta.

My sixth book is launched without you, friend,
Camonius Rufus, and has no hope that you will read it.

Visited Cappadocian country's unholy gods' will
Returns to your father ashes and bones.

Bononia, widowed of Rufus, pour out tears:
Let breast-beating cries resound throughout Aemilia.

Alas what filial love, alas how short a life is lost—
He had seen the Olympic prizes only five times.

You, from your remembering heart, were accustomed,
Rufus, to recite my bagatelles, retain whole scherzi.

Accept with his tears your grieving friend's short song,
Think it has been the incense of our parting.

                                    W. G. Shepherd

BOOK VII

(A.D. 92 DECEMBER)

VII.10

Pedicatur Eros, fellat Linus: Ole, quid ad te,
    De cute quid faciant ille vel ille sua?
Centenis futuit Matho milibus: Ole, quid ad te?
    Non tu propterea, sed Matho pauper erit.
In lucem cenat Sertorius: Ole, quid ad te,
    Cum liceat tota stertere nocte tibi?
Septingenta Tito debet Lupus: Ole, quid ad te?
    Assem ne dederis crediderisve Lupo.
Illud dissimulas, ad te quod pertinet, Ole,
    Quodque magis curae convenit esse tuae.
Pro togula debes: hoc ad te pertinet, Ole.
    Quadrantem nemo iam tibi credit: et hoc.
Uxor moecha tibi est: hoc ad te pertinet, Ole.
    Poscit iam dotem filia grandis: et hoc.
Dicere quindecies poteram, quod pertinet ad te:
    Sed quid agas, ad me pertinet, Ole, nihil.

Eros is buggered, Linus fellates—
   Olus, what's it to you
what use each may make of his own outside?
   Matho whores at a hundred thousand—
   Olus, what's it to you?
Not you but Matho will thereby be a pauper.
   Sertorius feasts till daybreak—
   Olus, what's it to you
since you may snore the whole night away?
   Lupus owes Titus point-seven-million—
   Olus, what's it to you?
Don't give or lend a penny to Lupus.

You pretend not to see what is
   your business, Olus,
what touches more your own concerns.
   You owe for your scanty toga—
   this is your business, Olus.
No one now will lend you a farthing—this too.
   Your wife's an adulterous tart—
   this is your business, Olus.
Your strapping daughter demands a dowry—this too.
   Another fifteen times I could tell you
   what is your business,
but what you do is no business, Olus, of mine.

                                W. G. Shepherd

VII.14

Accidit infandum nostrae scelus, Aule, puellae;
   Amisit lusus deliciasque suas:
Non quales teneri ploravit amica Catulli
   Lesbia, nequitiis passeris orba sui,
Vel Stellae cantata meo quas flevit Ianthis,
   Cuius in Elysio nigra columba volat:
Lux mea non capitur nugis neque moribus istis,
   Nec dominae pectus talia damna movent:
Bis denos puerum numerantem perdidit annos,
   Mentula cui nondum sesquipedalis erat.

VII.17

Ruris bibliotheca delicati,
Vicinam videt unde lector urbem,
Inter carmina sanctiora si quis
Lascivae fuerit locus Thaliae,
Hos nido licet inseras vel imo,
Septem quos tibi misimus libellos
Auctoris calamo sui notatos:
Haec illis pretium facit litura.
At tu munere dedicata parvo
Quae cantaberis orbe nota toto,
Pignus pectoris hoc mei tuere,
Iuli bibliotheca Martialis.

Aulus, my girlfriend's in a dreadful plight:
She's lost her plaything, her supreme delight;
No trivial thing, like Lesbia's sorry fix,
Losing that sparrow she'd taught naughty tricks;
Nor like Ianthis, mourning her dead dove
(Read Stella) which performed such feats of love.
My girl is not upset by mundane matters;
It's not for nothing that her heart's in tatters.
She's lost a boy of twice-six years. The clinch is:
He had a penis which was thrice-six inches.

Anthony Reid

O library of choice country house,
A place to gaze at Rome and browse,
Grant among your sober tomes
Room for my lascivious ones:
A meek nook let my Thalia find
Her sev'n slim vols, to you consigned,
Proofed by the pen that gave them birth—
Corrigenda that enhance their worth!
Since, choicest spot, these gifts I bring
Shall round the world your praises sing,
As proofs of heart embosom them,
O library of my Julius M.

Peter Whigham

VII.18

Cum tibi sit facies, de qua nec femina possit
    Dicere, cum corpus nulla litura notet,
Cur te tam rarus cupiat repetatque fututor,
    Miraris? Vitium est non leve, Galla, tibi:
Accessi quotiens ad opus mixtisque movemur
    Inguinibus, cunnus non tacet, ipsa taces.
Di facerent, ut tu loquereris et ille taceret:
    Offendor cunni garrulitate tui.
Pedere te mallem: namque hoc nec inutile dicit
    Symmachus et risum res movet ista simul:
Quis ridere potest fatui poppysmata cunni?
    Cum sonat hic, cui non mentula mensque cadit?
Dic aliquid saltem clamosoque obstrepe cunno,
    Et si adeo muta es, disce vel inde loqui.

Although your face no rival would criticize,
And there's no blemish on your unmarked thighs,
Why is it, you ask, no cocksman asks you twice?
Your beauty, Galla, 's marred by this one vice:
Whenever I get to work, our groins tight bound,
Your cunt makes all the noise, and you no sound.
God help you speak, and let your quim be mum.
Your cunt's so garrulous, I'm overcome.
I'd rather hear you fart. The doctors say
That's healthy; it's amusing, anyway.
But who's amused by clucks of a fatuous cunt?
Heart and hard on droop. It's an affront
I just can't stand. Drown out that cuntish squawk.
Or if you're truly dumb—teach it to talk!

                                   J. P. Sullivan

VII.19

Fragmentum quod vile putas et inutile lignum,
  Haec fuit ignoti prima carina maris.
Quam nec Cyaneae quondam potuere ruinae
  Frangere nec Scythici tristior ira freti,
Saecula vicerunt: sed quamvis cesserit annis,
  Sanctior est salva parva tabella rate.

This wooden fragment which you carelessly
    Pass by as of no great import, but cheap,
Is all that's left of that most famous ship,
    The first that dared to try the unknown deep.

This was the Argo, which the Clashing Rocks,
    The dread Symplegades, once failed to smash,
Which even the stormy Euxine's maddened waves,
    Hard though they struck, were powerless to crash.

Only the heavy weight of passing years
    Has conquered it. And only this remains:
A fragment, true, but far more precious now
    Than when, a ship, it leaped forth at the reins.

                                        Ralph Marcellino

VII.20

Nihil est miserius neque gulosius Santra.

Rectam vocatus cum cucurrit ad cenam,

Quam tot diebus noctibusque captavit,

Ter poscit apri glandulas, quater lumbum,

Et utramque coxam leporis et duos armos,

Nec erubescit peierare de turdo

Et ostreorum rapere lividos cirros.

Buccis placentae sordidam linit mappam;

Illic et uvae conlocantur ollares

Et Punicorum pauca grana malorum

Et excavatae pellis indecens volvae

Et lippa ficus debilisque boletus.

Sed mappa cum iam mille rumpitur furtis,

Rosos tepenti spondylos sinu condit

Et devorato capite turturem truncum.

Colligere longa turpe nec putat dextra

Analecta quidquid et canes reliquerunt.

Nec esculenta sufficit gulae praeda,

Mixto lagonam replet ad pedes vino.

Haec per ducentas cum domum tulit scalas

Seque obserata clusit anxius cella

Gulosus ille, postero die vendit.

What's grabbier than Santra, the walking doggy bag?
He gets his feet under the table, scans the menu—
Seven courses! Seven days and nights he fished
For an invite—eyes down and he's away:
Three pigs' kidneys; four pork chops;
Both rabbit's legs (oh *and* the arms);
He swears blind they forgot to serve
The thrush (pocketed), the oysters (whisked away);
Napkinned cheesecake oozes out,
Raisins, pomegranate pips,
A wrinkled, sucked sow's belly,
A (nibbled) fig, a mushroom (limp).
Why doesn't his napkin split with swag?
Because he saves the prawns and pigeon-breasts
To stuff his soggy shirt.
His crane arm hawks out scraps
The dogs disdain, and grabs.
For wine he keeps a jug of slops
Beside his foot, and fills it full.
Then home, up two hundred penthouse steps,
And double-lock the door (the thieves, my dear!).

Plans for tomorrow? A sale! A sale!

Frederic Raphael and Kenneth McLeish

VII.25

Dulcia cum tantum scribas epigrammata semper
    Et cerussata candidiora cute,
Nullaque mica salis nec amari fellis in illis
    Gutta sit, o demens, vis tamen illa legi!
Nec cibus ipse iuvat morsu fraudatus aceti,
    Nec grata est facies, cui gelasinus abest.
Infanti melimela dato fatuasque mariscas:
    Nam mihi, quae novit pungere, Chia sapit.

VII.30

Das Parthis, das Germanis, das, Caelia, Dacis,
    Nec Cilicum spernis Cappadocumque toros;
Et tibi de Pharia Memphiticus urbe fututor
    Navigat, a rubris et niger Indus aquis;
Nec recutitorum fugis inguina Iudaeorum,
    Nec te Sarmatico transit Alanus equo.
Qua ratione facis, cum sis Romana puella,
    Quod Romana tibi mentula nulla placet?

The epigrams you write are full of grace,
More dazzling than a white-enamelled face;
No grain of salt, no drop of bitter gall—
You're mad to think they will be read at all.
Sharp vinegar improves the appetite,
No face without a dimple will delight.
Give children figs and apples without zest—
For me strong figs of Chios taste the best.

Olive Pitt-Kethley

You grant your favours, Caelia, to all races—
Parthians, Germans, Dacians share your graces.
Cilicians, Cappadocians in your bed be,
And even a swarthy Indian from the Red Sea!
From Egypt's Memphis one sails to your door,
And Jews, though circumcised, you'll not ignore,
And that's not all! On his Sarmatian steed
No Scythian ever passed your door at speed.
You are a Roman girl, so tell me true,
Do Roman weapons have no charm for you?

Olive Pitt-Kethley

You'll fuck a Frog, a Kraut, a Jew,
        A Gippo, a Brit, a Pakki too;
Niggers and Russkis all go in your stew—
        But my prick's a Wop—Caelia, fuck you!

J. P. Sullivan

VII.39

Discursus varios vagumque mane
Et fastus et have potentiorum
Cum perferre patique iam negaret,
Coepit fingere Caelius podagram.
Quam dum volt nimis adprobare veram
Et sanas linit obligatque plantas
Inceditque gradu laborioso,
—Quantum cura potest et ars doloris!—
Desit fingere Caelius podagram.

VII.46

Commendare tuum dum vis mihi carmine munus
    Maeonioque cupis doctius ore loqui,
Excrucias multis pariter me teque diebus,
    Et tua de nostro, Prisce, Thalia tacet.
Divitibus poteris musas elegosque sonantes
    Mittere: pauperibus munera πεζά dato.

Having had enough of early rising
And running around, of patronizing
"Good-mornings" or "The great man's out,"
Caelius decided to have gout.
He smeared and bandaged both his feet
And in his eagerness to complete
The imposture hobbled about wincing.
Such power has art, so self-convincing
Was Caelius, that at last his act
Translated fiction into fact.

James Michie

Priscus, while you'd commend your gift in verse
With Homer's skill, knowing your Muse is terse,
You've harassed us for weeks now. She's still dumb;
And I think, "Will my present ever come?"
Send wealthy patrons high-flown elegies.
For poor men, gifts with simple prose will please.

R. L. Barth

VII.47

Doctorum Licini celeberrime Sura virorum,
  Cuius prisca gravis lingua reduxit avos,
Redderis—heu, quanto fatorum munere!—nobis,
  Gustata Lethes paene remissus aqua.
Perdiderant iam vota metum securaque flebat
  Tristitia, et lacrimis iamque peractus eras:
Non tulit invidiam taciti regnator Averni
  Et raptas Fatis reddidit ipse colus.
Scis igitur, quantas hominum mors falsa querellas
  Moverit, et frueris posteritate tua.
Vive velut rapto fugitivaque gaudia carpe:
  Perdiderit nullum vita reversa diem.

VII.48

Cum mensas habeat fere trecentas,
Pro mensis habet Annius ministros:
Transcurrunt gabatae volantque lances.
Has vobis epulas habete, lauti:
Nos offendimur ambulante cena.

Pre-eminent among scholars,
  whose accents speak of earlier days,
Sura is ours again (Fate smiles!), recalled
  with *Lethe's* waters all-but sipped. . . .
Our prayers lacked hope, resignedly
  we wept, and tears were tears of loss:
Dis (odium to avoid) restored
  th' unravelled distaff to the Fates.
Knowing the grief your false death caused,
  you've reaped, posthumously, your own fame.
Live snatched from death; seize fleet delight;
  waste not one day of life won back.

Peter Whigham

Three hundred tables—no waiting?
That's just the problem: every dish
A blur, a gobble.
If that's for you, *bon appétit!*
I never was a fast food freak.

Frederic Raphael and Kenneth McLeish

VII.53

Omnia misisti mihi Saturnalibus, Umber,
    Munera, contulerant quae tibi quinque dies:
Bis senos triplices et dentiscalpia septem;
    His comes accessit spongia, mappa, calix,
Semodiusque fabae cum vimine Picenarum,
    Et Laletanae nigra lagona sapae;
Parvaque cum canis venerunt cottana prunis
    Et Libycae fici pondere testa gravis.
Vix puto triginta nummorum tota fuisse
    Munera, quae grandes octo tulere Syri.
Quanto commodius nullo mihi ferre labore
    Argenti potuit pondera quinque puer!

Last Saturnalia, friend, I think
      You must have passed along
To me each little gift you got
      Yourself; now am I wrong?
Twelve tablets, seven toothpicks came;
      Sponge, napkin, cup not far
Behind, a half a peck of beans
      Some olives, a black jar
Of cheap new wine, some withered prunes,
      Some figlets (not too big),
And a monstrous heavy urn, filled up
      With the other kind of fig.
I'd say these gifts, in all, were worth
      30 sesterces or less,
But eight huge Syrian slaves were needed
      To carry the whole mess.

I have a better plan: next year
      When you're sending gifts to me
You'll find one boy could tote five pounds
      Of silver easily!

Dorothea Wender

VII.54

Semper mane mihi de me mera somnia narras,
  Quae moveant animum sollicitentque meum.
Iam prior ad faecem, sed et haec vindemia venit,
  Exorat noctes dum mihi saga tuas;
Consumpsi salsasque molas et turis acervos;
  Decrevere greges, dum cadit agna frequens;
Non porcus, non chortis aves, non ova supersunt.
  Aut vigila aut dormi, Nasidiane, tibi.

Mornings, you pour out dreams of me
    Recurrences that vex . . . alarm.
Two years' vintages have now been spilt,
    The wise crone "casting" dreams,
Casks of meal, incense, gone in smoke,
    Sheepfolds shrunk from frequent lambs felled.
I've no pig, hens, not one egg left.
    Stay up nights, friend, or dream solo.

Peter Whigham

VII.67

Pedicat pueros tribas Philaenis
Et tentigine saevior mariti
Undenas dolat in die puellas.
Harpasto quoque subligata ludit,
Et flavescit haphe, gravesque draucis
Halteras facili rotat lacerto,
Et putri lutulenta de palaestra
Uncti verbere vapulat magistri:
Nec cenat prius aut recumbit ante,
Quam septem vomuit meros deunces;
Ad quos fas sibi tunc putat redire,
Cum coloephia sedecim comedit.
Post haec omnia cum libidinatur,
Non fellat—putat hoc parum virile—,
Sed plane medias vorat puellas.
Di mentem tibi dent tuam, Philaeni,
Cunnum lingere quae putas virile.

Abhorrent of all natural joys,
  Philaenis sodomises boys,
And like a spouse whose wife's away
  She drains of spend twelve cunts a day.
With dress tucked up above her knees
  She hurls the heavy ball with ease,
And, smeared all o'er with oil and sand,
  She wields a dumb bell in each hand,
And when she quits the dirty floor,
  Still rank with grease, the jaded whore
Submits to the schoolmaster's whip
  For each small fault, each trifling slip:
Nor will she sit her down to dine
  Till she has spewed two quarts of wine:
And when she's eaten pounds of steak
  A gallon more her thirst will slake.
After all this, when fired by lust,
  For pricks alone she feels disgust,
These cannot e'en her lips entice,
  Forsooth it is a woman's vice!
But girls she'll gamahuche for hours,
  Their juicy quims she quite devours.
Oh, you that think your sex to cloak
  By kissing what you cannot poke,
May God grant that you, Philaenis,
  Will yet learn to suck a penis.

George Augustus Sala

VII.72

Gratus sic tibi, Paule, sit December,
Nec vani triplices, brevesque mappae
Nec turis veniant leves selibrae,
Sed lances ferat et scyphos avorum
Aut grandis reus aut potens amicus,
Seu quod te potius iuvat capitque;
Sic vincas Noviumque Publiumque
Mandris et vitreo latrone clusos;
Sic palmam tibi de trigone nudo
Unctae det favor arbiter coronae,
Nec laudet Polybi magis sinistras:
Si quisquam mea dixerit malignus
Atro carmina quae madent veneno,
Ut vocem mihi commodes patronam
Et quantum poteris, sed usque, clames:
"Non scripsit meus ista Martialis."

VII.83

Eutrapelus tonsor dum circuit ora Luperci
    Expingitque genas, altera barba subit.

Paulus, may December bring
You all the best of everything;
Hand-towels, short-weight frankincense,
Useless three-leafed tablets—hence!
No! gifts from friends or from the great,
Antique goblets, massy plate,
Or—which perhaps may please you more—
Novius or Publius to outscore
At Pawns and Robbers; or withstand
Polybus of the swift left-hand
When stripped for play—great praise to earn
From seasoned athletes. In return
Defend me with your voice of might
When I'm maligned as black with spite,
And shout till all the welkin rings;
"My Martial never wrote such things."

Fiona Pitt-Kethley

That barber's careful; his customer's
    The hairiest of men;
By the time he trims the sideburns
    The beard has grown again.

Dorothea Wender

VII.87

Si meus aurita gaudet lagalopece Flaccus,
    Si fruitur tristi Canius Aethiope;
Publius exiguae si flagrat amore catellae,
    Si Cronius similem cercopithecon amat;
Delectat Marium si perniciosus ichneumon,
    Pica salutatrix si tibi, Lause, placet;
Si gelidum collo nectit Glaucilla draconem,
    Luscinio tumulum si Telesilla dedit:
Blanda Cupidinei cur non amet ora Labycae,
    Qui videt haec dominis monstra placere suis?

VII.88

Fertur habere meos, si vera est fama, libellos
    Inter delicias pulchra Vienna suas:
Me legit omnis ibi senior iuvenisque puerque,
    Et coram tetrico casta puella viro.
Hoc ego maluerim, quam si mea carmina cantent
    Qui Nilum ex ipso protinus ore bibunt;
Quam meus Hispano si me Tagus impleat auro,
    Pascat et Hybla meas, pascat Hymettos apes.
Non nihil ergo sumus, nec blandae munere linguae
    Decipimur: credam iam, puto, Lause, tibi.

If my Flaccus delights in a lynx with long ears,
And Canius is fond of a saturnine Wog,
And Cronius is mad on a monkey, his double,
And Publius dotes on a dear little dog;
If Marius adores a bad rat from the Nile,
And a cold snake is worn as a scarf by Glaucilla,
And you, Lausus, talk to a chattering daw, while
Her nightingale's tomb comforts sad Telesilla—
Why shouldn't the Cupid-faced Labycus please
One who sees his friends fancy such monsters as these?

Olive Pitt-Kethley

My verse is found to be, or rumour lies,
Of fair Vienne the delight and prize.
By son and sire and grandsire I'm adored,
Conned by the chaste wife with her crusty lord.
'Tis better thus than if my books were read
By those who drink at Nilus' fountain-head,
Than if my Tagus drenched me with his ore,
Hybla, Hymettus gave my bees their store.
I'm something then, my faith is not amiss,
I must believe you, Lausus, after this.

A. L. Francis and H. F. Tatum

VII.89

I, felix rosa, mollibusque sertis
Nostri cinge comas Apollinaris.
Quas tu nectere candidas, sed olim—
Sic te semper amet Venus—memento.

VII.92

"Si quid opus fuerit, scis me non esse rogandum"
    Uno bis dicis, Baccara, terque die.
Appellat rigida tristis me voce Secundus:
    Audis, et nescis, Baccara, quid sit opus.
Pensio te coram petitur clareque palamque:
    Audis, et nescis, Baccara, quid sit opus.
Esse queror gelidasque mihi tritasque lacernas:
    Audis, et nescis, Baccara, quid sit opus.
Hoc opus est, subito fias ut sidere mutus,
    Dicere ne possis, Baccara: "Si quid opus."

Go, fortunate rose, with your soft petals touch
my favourite's head. Years hence, when the young hairs
have whitened, let roses clasp them still:
a memory of Venus in old age.

Peter Whigham

"When there is need, you do not have to plead!"
You say, Baccara, twice or thrice a day.
When hard Secundus whines to me to pay:
You hear, Baccara, and don't know my need.
I'm dunned before you in a public way:
You hear, Baccara, and don't know my need.
When I complain of my threadbare array:
You hear, Baccara, and don't know my need.
My need's some blow of fate, so you won't say
Your piece again, Baccara, "When there's need . . ."

Fiona Pitt-Kethley

BOOK VIII

(A.D. 94 AUTUMN)

VIII. PREFACE AND I

IMPERATORI DOMITIANO CAESARI AUGUSTO GER-
MANICO DACICO VALERIUS MARTIALIS S.

Omnes quidem libelli mei, domine, quibus tu famam, id est vitam, dedisti, tibi supplicant; et, puto, propter hoc legentur. Hic tamen, qui operis nostri octavus inscribitur, occasione pietatis frequentius fruitur. Minus itaque ingenio laborandum fuit, in cuius locum materia successerat: quam quidem subinde aliqua iocorum mixtura variare temptavimus, ne caelesti verecundiae tuae laudes suas, quae facilius te fatigare possint, quam nos satiare, omnis versus ingereret. Quamvis autem epigrammata a severissimis quoque et summae fortunae viris ita scripta sint, ut mimicam verborum licentiam adfectasse videantur, ego tamen illis non permisi tam lascive loqui quam solent. Cum pars libri et maior et melior ad maiestatem sacri nominis tui alligata sit, meminerit non nisi religiosa purificatione lustratos accedere ad templa debere. Quod ut custoditurum me lecturi sciant, in ipso libelli huius limine profiteri brevissimo placuit epigrammate.

Laurigeros domini, liber, intrature penates
  Disce verecundo sanctius ore loqui.
Nuda recede Venus; non est tuus iste libellus:
  Tu mihi, tu Pallas Caesariana, veni.

TO THE EMPEROR DOMITIANUS CAESAR AUGUSTUS GERMANICUS DACICUS VALERIUS MARTIALIS SENDS GREETINGS.

All my little books, my lord, to which you have granted fame, that is to say life, have humble requests for you; and it is, I believe, on this account that they will be read. This one, however, which is designated as the eighth book of my work, enjoys more frequent opportunities to show its loyalty and respect. And so my talent had to work less hard; the matter had taken over in its stead. Of course I have tried now and again to vary the material with an admixture of humour, so that every line would not heap its praises on your heaven-sent honour, although these can more easily weary you than pall on us. But, although epigrams have been written by the most respectable of men, and those in high places, epigrams that seem to strive for the verbal licence of the mime, I however have refused to allow them here their usual prurient language. Since part of the volume, the larger and the better part, is linked to the majesty of your sacred name, it should remember that only those cleansed by a religious purification ought to approach the temples. So that my future readers may know that I will preserve this principle, I thought it well to express it in a very short epigram at the very opening of this book.

Here, little book, is my lord's laurelled hall:
So clean up your language before you go call.
Venus, you're naked: stay away from my page;
Caesar's Pallas Minerva, now you take the stage!

J. P. Sullivan

VIII.12

Uxorem quare locupletem ducere nolim,
   Quaeritis? Uxori nubere nolo meae.
Inferior matrona suo sit, Prisce, marito:
   Non aliter fiunt femina virque pares.

VIII.20

Cum facias versus nulla non luce ducenos,
   Vare, nihil recitas. Non sapis, atque sapis.

VIII.23

Esse tibi videor saevus nimiumque gulosus,
   Qui propter cenam, Rustice, caedo cocum.
Si levis ista tibi flagrorum causa videtur,
   Ex qua vis causa vapulet ergo cocus?

VIII.27

Munera qui tibi dat locupleti, Gaure, senique,
   Si sapis et sentis, hoc tibi ait "Morere."

Why have I no desire to marry riches?
Because, my friend, I want to wear the breeches.
Wives should obey their husbands; only then
Can women share equality with men.

James Michie

Though Varus daily sits and writes—
Two hundred lines!—he neither tries
To publish verses nor recites.
He's not too witty, but he's wise.

R. L. Barth

I gave the cook a beating, not from spite
Or greed, you bumpkin, but to serve him right.
To whip for such a trifle! said your look;
Isn't it just desserts to baste a cook?

Olive Pitt-Kethley

If you were wise as well as rich and sickly,
You'd see that every gift means, "Please die quickly."

James Michie

VIII.28

Dic, toga, facundi gratum mihi munus amici,
    Esse velis cuius fama decusque gregis?
Apula Ledaei tibi floruit herba Phalanthi,
    Qua saturat Calabris culta Galaesus aquis?
An Tartesiacus stabuli nutritor Hiberi
    Baetis in Hesperia te quoque lavit ove?
An tua multifidum numeravit lana Timavum,
    Quem pius astrifero Cyllarus ore bibit?
Te nec Amyclaeo decuit livere veneno,
    Nec Miletos erat vellere digna tuo.
Lilia tu vincis nec adhuc delapsa ligustra,
    Et Tiburtino monte quod alget ebur;
Spartanus tibi cedet olor Paphiaeque columbae,
    Cedet Erythraeis eruta gemma vadis:
Sed licet haec primis nivibus sint aemula dona,
    Non sunt Parthenio candidiora suo.
Non ego praetulerim Babylonos picta superbae
    Texta, Samiramia quae variantur acu;
Non Athamanteo potius me mirer in auro,
    Aeolium dones si mihi, Phrixe, pecus.
O quantos risus pariter spectata movebit
    Cum Palatina nostra lacerna toga!

Speak Toga!—warm gift of a warm friend,
   from what flock sprung—its honor, renown?

Tarentum's grazing, sown of *Leda's* clan,
   where, from *Calabria, Galaesus* floods fields?

Or, feeding *Baetian* folds, the *Guadalquivir*
   sprinkling your fleece—still *Iberian* sheep?

Where *Castor's* faithful steed once drank—
   the *Istrian* delta—was your wool dipped there?

Laconian dyes did not become you.
   Caria was not fit to shear your fleece.

More white than lilies—privet still fresh,
   ivory that from *Tivoli* gleams.

The *Paphian Dove*, the *Swan of Sparta*, yield
   primacy—yields primacy the *Orient* Pearl.

Babylonian tapestries were not more dear
   stitched with the needle of *Semiramis*.

Athamantean gold, less cause for preening,
   should *Phryxus* loan me his *Aeolian* ram.

And yet—the mockery my old cloak evokes:
   foil for your imperial Toga!

                    Peter Whigham

VIII.33

De praetoricia folium mihi, Paule, corona
   Mittis et hoc phialae nomen habere iubes.
Hac fuerat nuper nebula tibi pegma perunctum,
   Pallida quam rubri diluit unda croci.
An magis astuti derasa est ungue ministri
   Brattea, de fulcro quam reor esse tuo?
Illa potest culicem longe sentire volantem
   Et minimi pinna papilionis agi;
Exiguae volitat suspensa vapore lucernae
   Et leviter fuso rumpitur icta mero.
Hoc linitur sputo Iani caryota Kalendis,
   Quam fert cum parco sordidus asse cliens.
Lenta minus gracili crescunt colocasia filo,
   Plena magis nimio lilia sole cadunt;
Nec vaga tam tenui discurrit aranea tela,
   Tam leve nec bombyx pendulus urget opus.
Crassior in facie vetulae stat creta Fabullae,
   Crassior offensae bulla tumescit aquae;
Fortior et tortos servat vesica capillos
   Et mutat Latias spuma Batava comas.
Hac cute Ledaeo vestitur pullus in ovo,
   Talia lunata splenia fronte sedent.
Quid tibi cum phiala, ligulam cum mittere possis,
   Mittere cum possis vel cocleare mihi,—
Magna nimis loquimur—cocleam cum mittere possis,
   Denique cum possis mittere, Paule, nihil?

You send a leaf, plucked from your praetor's crown,
    a bowl by decree.
Film from the lately frosted fingernails
    of your last mistress, chipped within minutes
or a flake, perhaps, scraped from a couch leg
    by a slave, astutely greedy.
Trembling at the flutter of a far-off gnat,
    transported by the tiniest butterfly,
at the heat of a single candle, it flies,
    melts into ecstasy at a wine-drop's splash.
Such a layer coats the trinket the shabby suppliant
    proffers with clinking coin.
Pliant beans stretch a stronger thread;
    Lilies, coarser, wilt in the strong sun.
The spider scuttles on a web less slender,
    pendulous silkworms ply heavier tasks,
old Fabula's chalky face cakes thicker,
    denser swell bubbles in tumbling water,
bladder-nets, Batavian pomade, better bind snaky locks.
Such skin clings to swan-egged chicks,
    or patches a crescented front.
Who need send a bowl, when table-spoons suit,
    a snail-pick is adequate,
when, dare I say it, a snail-shell suffices, when, dear Paullus,
    you can part with nothing?

            Helen Deutsch

VIII.40

Non horti neque palmitis beati,
Sed rari nemoris, Priape, custos,
Ex quo natus es et potes renasci,
Furaces, moneo, manus repellas
Et silvam domini focis reserves:
Si defecerit haec, et ipse lignum es.

VIII.44

Titulle, moneo, vive: semper hoc serum est;
Sub paedagogo coeperis licet, serum est.
At tu, miser Titulle, nec senex vivis,
Sed omne limen conteris salutator
Et mane sudas urbis osculis udus,
Foroque triplici sparsus ante equos omnis
Aedemque Martis et colosson Augusti
Curris per omnes tertiasque quintasque.
Rape, congere, aufer, posside: relinquendum est.
Superba densis arca palleat nummis,
Centum explicentur paginae Kalendarum,
Iurabit heres, te nihil reliquisse,
Supraque pluteum te iacente vel saxum,
Fartus papyro dum tibi torus crescit,
Flentes superbus basiabit eunuchos;
Tuoque tristis filius, velis nolis,
Cum concubino nocte dormiet prima.

No garden, *Priapus,* your ward,
Nor blest vineyard, but scantling copse
Whence wast hewn and could be re-hewn.
Take then your charge: "Repel thieves' fists,
For firewood keep your Master's wood,
Or your wood firewood too shall be."

Peter Whigham

Titullus, I warn you, *live.* (That's always late:
though your schoolmaster tells you first, it's late.)
For you, my wretched Titullus, don't live like Eld,
but wear down every doorstep with making calls;
and at dawn, wet with Town's kisses you sweat;
in all three Forums, mired before the equestrian
statues, the temple of Mars and Augustus' colossus,
you rush about throughout the hours of business.

Seize, hoard, extort, possess: it must be left. Let
your proud coffer gleam yellow with close-stacked coin,
a hundred pages of month-end debtors be opened—
your heir will state on oath you've left him nothing;
and when you lie on your board or your stone,
while stuffed with papyrus your pyre mounts up,
he'll condescend to kiss the crying eunuchs;
and will you or nill you your grieving son
will bed your catamite the very first night.

W. G. Shepherd

VIII.61

Livet Charinus, rumpitur, furit, plorat
Et quaerit altos, unde pendeat, ramos:
Non iam quod orbe cantor et legor toto,
Nec umbilicis quod decorus et cedro
Spargor per omnes Roma quas tenet gentes:
Sed quod sub urbe rus habemus aestivum
Vehimurque mulis non, ut ante, conductis.
Quid inprecabor, o Severe, liventi?
Hoc opto: mulas habeat et suburbanum.

VIII.62

Scribit in aversa Picens epigrammata charta,
    Et dolet, averso quod facit illa deo.

VIII.63

Thestylon Aulus amat, sed nec minus ardet Alexin,
    Forsitan et nostrum nunc Hyacinthon amat.
I nunc et dubita, vates an diligat ipsos,
    Delicias vatum cum meus Aulus amet.

Mr. Charinus is livid, is quite beside
Himself with rage; given to frequent sighs;
Eyes tall trees for future suicide.
    But it's not my reputation; the big literary prize,
    My international distribution, world-wide renown
    That he so strongly resents.
    I have my fans, who give me presents:
    A private car, a summer cottage near town.
Severus, suggest a curse for jealous obsessions.
Of course—the dubious joys of such possessions!

                                    J. P. Sullivan

Because the Muses turn their backsides on Aper
He writes his poems on toilet paper.

                Richard O'Connell

He loved Thestylus first, and then Alexis;
    My Hyacinth will soon attract his ploys.
He says he loves the poets, but annexes
    Their bed-companions—he loves poets' boys.

                Anthony Reid

VIII.68

Qui Corcyraei vidit pomaria regis,
    Rus, Entelle, tuae praeferet ille domus.
Invida purpureos urat ne bruma racemos
    Et gelidum Bacchi munera frigus edat,
Condita perspicua vivit vindemia gemma,
    Et tegitur felix nec tamen uva latet:
Femineum lucet sic per bombycina corpus,
    Calculus in nitida sic numeratur aqua.
Quid non ingenio voluit natura licere?
    Autumnum sterilis ferre iubetur hiems.

VIII.69

Miraris veteres, Vacerra, solos,
Nec laudas nisi mortuos poetas.
Ignoscas petimus, Vacerra: tanti
Non est, ut placeam tibi, perire.

Your country-house—its garden—far outstrips
  the orchards of *Alcinous*.
Vexed winter cannot nip your purpling grape,
  nor frost tipple *Bacchus'* gifts.
Treasured 'neath transparent glass the vine-crop
  protects, while it displays, itself.
A woman's body dawns through silken clothes.
  Smallest stones are clear in clearest streams.
At mankind's skill Nature yields, conjuring
  sterile winter issue autumn's fruits.

Peter Whigham

You puff the poets of other days,
  The living you deplore.
Spare me the accolade: your praise
  Is not worth dying for.

Dudley Fitts

VIII.71

Quattuor argenti libras mihi tempore brumae
    Misisti ante annos, Postumiane, decem,
Speranti plures—nam stare aut crescere debent
    Munera—venerunt plusve minusve duae;
Tertius et quartus multo inferiora tulerunt;
    Libra fuit quinto Septiciana quidem;
Besalem ad scutulam sexto pervenimus anno;
    Post hunc in cotula rasa selibra data est;
Octavus ligulam misit sextante minorem;
    Nonus acu levius vix cocleare tulit.
Quod mittat nobis decumus iam non habet annus:
    Quattuor ad libras, Postumiane, redi.

VIII.73

Instanti, quo nec sincerior alter habetur
    Pectore nec nivea simplicitate prior,
Si dare vis nostrae vires animosque Thaliae
    Et victura petis carmina, da quod amem.
Cynthia te vatem fecit, lascive Properti;
    Ingenium Galli pulchra Lycoris erat;
Fama est arguti Nemesis formosa Tibulli;
    Lesbia dictavit, docte Catulle, tibi:
Non me Paeligni nec spernet Mantua vatem,
    Si qua Corinna mihi, si quis Alexis erit.

You sent me, through the Saturnalian snow,
Four pounds of silver plate, ten years ago.
Hoping for more next year (for gifts must grow
Or stay the same), I got two pounds, or so.
The third and fourth, much less; the fifth, one pound,
A wartime pound at that, came wafting round.
The sixth year, just a little ten-ounce plate;
Then, a small goblet (half a pound); year eight,
A two-ounce jam-spoon; and year nine brought in,
Barely, a snail-pick lighter than a pin.
The tenth year's brought me nothing. Let's restore
The silver-pound age, and go back to four.

Alistair Elliot

If, *Instantius,* my open-hearted,
   clearly candid friend, you'ld propagate
With vigor, with *virtù,* my lyric *Muse,*
   draw lifelong song therefrom, grant *Martial* love.
Cynthia turned wild *Propertius* vatic;
   lovely *Lycoris* was the song in *Gallus;*
Fair *Nemesis,* the fame *Tibullus* sang;
   to you, *Catullus,* Lesbia gave *dictées.*
Sulmona, Mantua, should not scorn my *Muse,*
   were *Ovid's Corinne, Virgil's Alex,* mine.

Peter Whigham

VIII.76

"Dic verum mihi, Marce, dic amabo;
Nil est, quod magis audiam libenter."
Sic et cum recitas tuos libellos,
Et causam quotiens agis clientis,
Oras, Gallice, me rogasque semper.
Durum est me tibi, quod petis, negare.
Vero verius ergo quid sit, audi:
Verum, Gallice, non libenter audis.

VIII.77

Liber, amicorum dulcissima cura tuorum,
    Liber, in aeterna vivere digne rosa,
Si sapis, Assyrio semper tibi crinis amomo
    Splendeat et cingant florea serta caput;
Candida nigrescant vetulo crystalla Falerno
    Et caleat blando mollis amore torus.
Qui sic vel medio finitus vixit in aevo,
    Longior huic facta est quam data vita fuit.

"Please, Marcus, tell the truth," you say,
  "That's all I want to hear!"
If you read a poem or plead a case
  You din it in my ear:
"The truth, the honest truth!" you beg,
  It's damned hard to deny
Such a request. So here's the truth:
  You'd rather have me lie.

                    Dorothea Wender

O Liber, sweetest care
  Of all your friends' sweet cares,
  Who ought to live among the airs
And petals that immortal roses shed,
  Be wise and make your hair
  Glisten forever with Assyrian balm,
And bind continuous flowers round your head.

  Make the bright crystal dark
  With old Falernian wine;
  Make the soft couch where you recline
Warm with the counterblows of lovers' strife.
  One who has lived like this,
  Even if finished before half his time,
  Has made it longer than the given life.

                    Alistair Elliot

VIII.79

Omnes aut vetulas habes amicas
Aut turpes vetulisque foediores.
Has ducis comites trahisque tecum
Per convivia, porticus, theatra.
Sic formosa, Fabulla, sic puella es.

VIII.82

Dante tibi turba querulos, Auguste, libellos,
    Nos quoque quod domino carmina parva damus,
Posse deum rebus pariter Musisque vacare
    Scimus, et haec etiam serta placere tibi.
Fer vates, Auguste, tuos: nos gloria dulcis,
    Nos tua cura prior deliciaeque sumus.
Non quercus te sola decet nec laurea Phoebi:
    Fiat et ex hedera civica nostra tibi.

Her women friends are all old hags
Or, worse, hideous girls. She drags
Them with her everywhere she goes—
To parties, theatres, porticoes.
Clever Fabulla! Set among
Those foils you shine, even look young.

James Michie

Caesar, beleaguered by the selfish throng,
Accept this little tribute of my song.
For letters and affairs alike you've leisure,
We know; this humble wreath may give you pleasure.
Bear with your bard; we are your glory bright,
Your chiefest care and intimate delight.
You love not oak alone but Phoebus' bays:
Take then the civic garland of my lays.

A. L. Francis and H. F. Tatum

BOOK IX

IX.4

Aureolis futui cum possit Galla duobus
Et plus quam futui, si totidem addideris:
Aureolos a te cur accipit, Aeschyle, denos?
Non fellat tanti Galla. Quid ergo? Tacet.

IX.6

Dicere de Libycis reduci tibi gentibus, Afer,
Continuis volui quinque diebus Have:
"Non vacat" aut "dormit" dictum est bis terque reverso.
Iam satis est: non vis, Afer, havere: vale.

IX.8

Nil tibi legavit Fabius, Bithynice, cui tu
Annua, si memini, milia sena dabas.
Plus nulli dedit ille: queri, Bithynice, noli:
Annua legavit milia sena tibi.

Two bits of gold will open Galla's cunny,
And four will get you a lot more. Then why
Give her ten, Aeschylus? Much less will buy
Fellatio. What is this? Silence money.

                                        John Adlard

When, Afer, you returned from Libya home,
Five times I sought to welcome you to Rome.
"He's busy, he sleeps," five times I heard & fled:
You want no welcome: well, good-bye instead.

                            A. L. Francis and H. F. Tatum

You gave Bithynicus thousands yearly; still
He left you not a penny in his will.
But don't be sad; you really score—
You needn't send him money any more.

                                        J. P. Sullivan

IX.9

Cenes, Canthare, cum foris libenter,
Clamas et maledicis et minaris.
Deponas animos truces, monemus:
Liber non potes et gulosus esse.

IX.10

Nubere vis Prisco: non miror, Paula: sapisti.
Ducere te non vult Priscus: et ille sapit.

Although you're glad to be asked out,
Whenever you go, you bitch and shout
And bluster. You must stop being rude:
You can't enjoy free speech and food.

James Michie

You'd marry Priscus, Paula? Well, you're wise.
Priscus won't marry you? Well . . . he is wise.

W. G. Shepherd

IX.11

Nomen cum violis rosisque natum,
Quo pars optima nominatur anni,
Hyblam quod sapit Atticosque flores,
Quod nidos olet alitis superbae;
Nomen nectare dulcius beato,
Quo mallet Cybeles puer vocari
Et qui pocula temperat Tonanti,
Quod si Parrhasia sones in aula,
Respondent Veneres Cupidinesque;
Nomen nobile, molle, delicatum
Versu dicere non rudi volebam;
Sed tu syllaba contumax rebellas.
Dicunt Eiarinon tamen poetae,
Sed Graeci, quibus est nihil negatum
Et quos Ἆρες Ἄρες decet sonare:
Nobis non licet esse tam disertis,
Qui Musas colimus severiores.

IX.15

Inscripsit tumulis septem scelerata virorum
    SE FECISSE CHLOE: quid pote simplicius?

Name born with violets and roses;
Name from the best time in the year,
Tasting of Attic flowers and Hybla,
And scented like the phoenix' nest;
Name sweeter than celestial nectar,
That Attis and the boy who blends
His wine for Zeus wish they were called by,
That, ringing on the Palatine,
Brings Venuses and Cupids answering;
Name noble, soft and delicate,
I'd meant to put in polished verses—
But, stubborn syllable, you rebel.
Though poets do write Eiarinos,
They're Greek ones: they do anything.
They can pronounce the war-god Áres
And then Arés in the same breath.
We have no licence for such fluency:
Our Muses are of stricter stuff.

                              Alistair Elliot

Seven husbands' tombs
  Chloe chiseled thus:
CHLOE SET THIS UP.
  What's more obvious?

                    Richard Emil Braun

IX.20

Haec, quae tota patet tegiturque et marmore et auro,
    Infantis domini conscia terra fuit,
Felix o, quantis sonuit vagitibus et quas
    Vidit reptantis sustinuitque manus:
Hic steterat veneranda domus, quae praestitit orbi
    Quod Rhodos astrifero, quod pia Creta polo.
Curetes texere Iovem crepitantibus armis,
    Semiviri poterant qualia ferre Phryges:
At te protexit superum pater, et tibi, Caesar,
    Pro iaculo et parma fulmen et aegis erat.

IX.21

Artemidorus habet puerum sed vendidit agrum;
    Agrum pro puero Calliodorus habet.
Dic, uter ex istis melius rem gesserit, Aucte:
    Artemidorus amat, Calliodorus arat.

This construction site where the temples rise in gold and
  marble
Was birthplace to our infant Emperor.
How lucky to echo to his crying, to see and sustain
  Him crawling on hands and knees!
Here stood the worshipful house which bore our world's god
  Just as Rhodes and motherly Crete bore heaven's.
Clanging their weapons, the Curetes covered Jove's crying—
  Eunuchs, they raised what weapons they could.
But the father of the gods, Jove himself, bent over you,
  Caesar,
  His spear the lightning, and his shield the sky.

Patrick Diehl

Artemidorus sold his land to buy a boy
From Calliodorus. Both are happy now:
Both have fresh fields to plow.

Richard O'Connell

IX.25

Dantem vina tuum quotiens aspeximus Hyllum,
   Lumine nos, Afer, turbidiore notas.
Quod, rogo, quod scelus est, mollem spectare ministrum?
   Aspicimus solem, sidera, templa, deos.
Avertam vultus, tamquam mihi pocula Gorgon
   Porrigat atque oculos oraque nostra petat?
Trux erat Alcides, et Hylan spectare licebat;
   Ludere Mercurio cum Ganymede licet.
Si non vis teneros spectet conviva ministros,
   Phineas invites, Afer, et Oedipodas.

Whenever I dine at your flat,
   And glance at your lad with a smile,
Your face grows as black as my hat
   As you frown your distrust at my guile.

Good Lord! I may look at the sun
   Without being seized by desire;
What harm have I possibly done
   In admiring the boy you admire?

Do you want me to cover my face?
   Do you want me to turn him my shoulder
As though I saw there in his place
   A hump-backed and cross-eyed old scolder?

My advice to you then in this rhyme,
   If in glances such meanings you find,
Is—invite to your party next time
   Your guests from a School for the Blind.

Brian Hill

IX.27

Cum depilatos, Chreste, coleos portes
Et vulturino mentulam parem collo
Et prostitutis levius caput culis,
Nec vivat ullus in tuo pilus crure,
Purgentque saevae cana labra volsellae:
Curios, Camillos, Quintios, Numas, Ancos,
Et quidquid umquam legimus pilosorum
Loqueris sonasque grandibus minax verbis,
Et cum theatris saeculoque rixaris.
Occurrit aliquis inter ista si draucus,
Iam paedagogo liberatus et cuius
Refibulavit turgidum faber penem:
Nutu vocatum ducis, et pudet fari
Catoniana, Chreste, quod facis lingua.

IX.32

Hanc volo, quae facilis, quae palliolata vagatur,
    Hanc volo, quae puero iam dedit ante meo,
Hanc volo, quam redimit totam denarius alter,
    Hanc volo, quae pariter sufficit una tribus.
Poscentem nummos et grandia verba sonantem
    Possideat crassae mentula Burdigalae.

Chrestus, though not two hairs your scrotum deck,
    Though your prick's softer than the vulture's neck,
Though your mild face, effeminate, smooth and plump,
    Rivals the pathic's prostituted rump,
And girlish in your hairless thighs and hips,
    Art hides all trace of manhood on your lips;
You talk of deeds the great, and good, and bold
    Have done, with stern pomposity, and hold
Forth on the vices that corrupt the age;
    But while this virtuous war on vice you wage,
If some bright lad, who's just outgrown his school,
    While thoughts of freedom swell his youthful tool,
Come up, you lead aside the sprightly boy,
    And when replete of what you most enjoy,
Your Cato's tongue would never dare confess t' us,
    How very much you had behaved like Chrestus.

George Augustus Sala

This girl I want is easy, roams the town;
This girl I want has had my slave boy down.
This girl, for a dollar more, is mine entire,
Although this girl could slake three men's desire.
Let loud-mouthed whores who want to get rich quick
Impale themselves on some dull Frenchman's prick.

Mollie Barger

IX.33

Audieris in quo, Flacce, balneo plausum,
Maronis illic esse mentulam scito.

IX.52

Si credis mihi, Quinte, quod mereris,
Natales, Ovidi, tuas Aprilis
Ut nostras amo Martias Kalendas.
Felix utraque lux diesque nobis
Signandi melioribus lapillis!
Hic vitam tribuit, sed hic amicum.
Plus dant, Quinte, mihi tuae Kalendae.

If you're passing the baths and you hear,
From within, an uproarious cheer,
   You may safely conclude
   Maro's there, in the nude,
With that tool which has nowhere a peer.

                           Rolfe Humphries

Quintus, your April birthday here I toast
As I do mine in March; but yours the most,
For though mine gave me Life, is it not true
Yours gave me more? Your birthday gave me you.

                           Anthony Reid

IX.54

Si mihi Picena turdus palleret oliva,
    Tenderet aut nostras silva Sabina plagas,
Aut crescente levis traheretur harundine praeda
    Pinguis et inplicitas virga teneret aves:
Cara daret sollemne tibi cognatio munus,
    Nec frater nobis nec prior esset avus.
Nunc sturnos inopes fringuillarumque querellas
    Audit et arguto passere vernat ager;
Inde salutatus picae respondet arator,
    Hinc prope summa rapax miluus astra volat.
Mittimus ergo tibi parvae munuscula chortis:
    Qualia si recipis, saepe propinquus eris.

If I had hillside olives to fatten fieldfares
    or Sabine woods strung with gins
to cruelly carry hot bodies from the sky
    or could conduct like lightning
small morsels down on a stick, to walk
    grand garnerer of their flutterings,
crop on crop in my meadows of death:
    then I would send you these in token
of love, that you might bite their flesh
    as it were mine. Alas, my fields are asphalt
and listen only to the songs of starlings,
    the fidgeting of finches. The green
of tapered hedges hides the shrill sparrow,
    here the magpie suffers an air-change
to death's bird, while the banished kite
    haunts open fields, the only free man
in a heritage of dependence. Instead,
    I offer you the imagination of birds
whose hard eye drops on the brown earth
    without pardon: come to the start
of the world, we will deal with things cruelly
    as we have love and an inclination to.

                                    Peter Porter

IX.57

Nil est tritius Hedyli lacernis:
Non ansae veterum Corinthiorum,
Nec crus compede lubricum decenni,
Nec ruptae recutita colla mulae,
Nec quae Flaminiam secant salebrae,
Nec qui litoribus nitent lapilli,
Nec Tusca ligo vinea politus,
Nec pallens toga mortui tribulis,
Nec pigri rota quassa mulionis,
Nec rasum cavea latus visontis,
Nec dens iam senior ferocis apri.
Res una est tamen: ipse non negabit,
Culus tritior Hedyli lacernis.

IX.58

Nympha sacri regina lacus, cui grata Sabinus
    Et mansura pio munere templa dedit,
Sic montana tuos semper colat Umbria fontes,
    Nec tua Baianas Sassina malit aquas:
Excipe sollicitos placide, mea dona, libellos;
    Tu fueris Musis Pegasis unda meis.—
"Nympharum templis quisquis sua carmina donat,
    Quid fieri libris debeat, ipse monet."

What is rubbed smoother than Hedylus' cloak?
Not vase's rim or captive's iron-chafed shin;
Not mule's galled neck, nor sea-turned pebble shore;
Deep rutted road, nor hoe worked paper-thin,
Dead pauper's toga, nor the dragged cart's wheel,
Boar's tusk, nor cage-scraped ribs. Oh, but I swear
There is one thing—and this he won't deny—
More rubbed than all, his bum, and worse for wear.

Brian Hill

Queen of the sacred pool, sweet Nymph divine,
To whom Sabinus gives a grateful shrine,
A joy for ever, so may Umbria love you
Nor Sassina rate the Baian waves above you,
Accept my anxious verse with kindly smile;
You'll be my Hippocrene spring the while.
"Who to the Nymphs their verses dedicate
Give a shrewd forecast of their destined fate."

A. L. Francis and H. F. Tatum

IX.59

In Saeptis Mamurra diu multumque vagatus,
  Hic ubi Roma suas aurea vexat opes,
Inspexit molles pueros oculisque comedit,
  Non hos, quos primae prostituere casae,
Sed quos arcanae servant tabulata catastae
  Et quos non populus nec mea turba videt.
Inde satur mensas et opertos exuit orbes
  Expositumque alte pingue poposcit ebur,
Et testudineum mensus quater hexaclinon
  Ingemuit citro non satis esse suo.
Consuluit nares, an olerent aera Corinthon,
  Culpavit statuas et, Polyclite, tuas,
Et turbata brevi questus crystallina vitro
  Murrina signavit seposuitque decem.
Expendit veteres calathos et si qua fuerunt
  Pocula Mentorea nobilitata manu,
Et viridis picto gemmas numeravit in auro,
  Quidquid et a nivea grandius aure sonat.
Sardonychas vero mensa quaesivit in omni
  Et pretium magnis fecit iaspidibus.
Undecima lassus cum iam discederet hora,
  Asse duos calices emit et ipse tulit.

Mr. Flint goes up the West,
Walks for miles without a rest,
Where the gilded city squanders
All her money, there he wanders . . .
Views the tables in the shops,
Makes the men unwrap the tops,
Sees on high carved ivory legs,
Has them taken off the pegs.
Several times he measures well
A sofa made of tortoise-shell;
"No," he sighs to those in charge,
"My cedar table's just too large."
The bronzes, too, with knowing grin
He sniffs, to test their origin.
Statues then attract the fellow,
Carps at works by Donatello.
Then decries a crystal vase,
Shews a speck of glass that mars:
Picks a set of porcelain,
Sighs, and says, "I'll call again."
Feels an ancient piece of plate,
Tries a cup to test its weight,

IX.60

Seu tu Paestanis genita es seu Tiburis arvis,
    Seu rubuit tellus Tuscula flore tuo,
Seu Praenestino te vilica legit in horto,
    Seu modo Campani gloria ruris eras:
Pulchrior ut nostro videare corona Sabino,
    De Nomentano te putet esse meo.

Goblets, too, perhaps made grand
Once by Benvenuto's hand.
Emeralds that the craftsman mounts
On gold engraved he duly counts,
Every jewel large and clear
That tinkles from the snow-white ear.
On every jeweller's tray he fixes,
Hunts for perfect sardonyxes.
In the bidding then he cries
For jaspers of unusual size.
    And now when sinks the setting sun,
All wearied out, his shopping done,
Himself he takes it, in the end,
—Two penny mugs they would not send.

T. W. Melluish

Garland of roses, whether you come
From Tibur or from Tusculum,
Whether the earth you splashed with red
Was Paestum's or the flower-bed
Of some Praeneste farmer's wife
Who snipped you with her gardening-knife,
No matter in which countryside
You flew your flag before you died—
To lend my gift an added charm,
Let *him* believe you're from my farm.

James Michie

IX.67

Lascivam tota possedi nocte puellam,
 Cuius nequitias vincere nemo potest.
Fessus mille modis illud puerile poposci:
 Ante preces totas primaque verba dedit.
Inprobius quiddam ridensque rubensque rogavi:
 Pollicitast nulla luxuriosa mora.
Sed mihi pura fuit; tibi non erit, Aeschyle, si vis
 Accipere hoc munus condicione mala.

Last night the soft charms of an exquisite whore
   Fulfilled every whim of my mind,
Till, with fucking grown weary, I begged something more,
   One bliss that still lingered behind.
My prayer was accepted; the rose in the rear
   Was opened to me in a minute;
One rose still remained, which I asked of my dear,—
   'Twas her mouth and the tongue that lay in it.
She promised at once, what I asked her to do;
   Yet her lips were unsullied by me,
They'll not, my old friend, remain virgins for you,
   Whose penchant exceeds e'en her fee.

                    George Augustus Sala

IX.68

Quid tibi nobiscum est, ludi scelerate magister,
    Invisum pueris virginibusque caput?
Nondum cristati rupere silentia galli:
    Murmure iam saevo verberibusque tonas.
Tam grave percussis incudibus aera resultant,
    Causidicum medio cum faber aptat equo;
Mitior in magno clamor furit amphitheatro,
    Vincenti parmae cum sua turba favet.
Vicini somnum—non tota nocte—rogamus:
    Nam vigilare leve est, pervigilare grave est.
Discipulos dimitte tuos. Vis, garrule, quantum
    Accipis ut clames, accipere ut taceas?

IX.69

Cum futuis, Polycharme, soles in fine cacare.
    Cum pedicaris, quid, Polycharme, facis?

Why torment us, you villainous schoolmaster,
　　Detested creature to the girls and boys?
You thunder savage growl and blows still faster,
　　Before the crested cock breaks out with noise.
So harsh rings bronze upon the beaten swages
　　As craftsman fits a lawyer to a horse.
A gentler uproar in the Circus rages
　　When mobs their winning favorites endorse.
For sleep we neighbors plead—at least a token:
　　To be awakened surely can be borne,
To lie awake all night is pain unbroken.
　　Dismiss your pupils: babbler, do you scorn
That what you're paid to exercise your lung,
　　You get the same amount to hold your tongue?

Roy F. Butler

When you fuck, Polycharmus, you end by shitting,
When poked, Polycharmus, what'll be fitting?

Fiona Pitt-Kethley

IX.76

Haec sunt illa mei quae cernitis ora Camoni,
    Haec pueri facies primaque forma fuit.
Creverat hic vultus bis denis fortior annis,
    Gaudebatque suas pingere barba genas,
Et libata semel summos modo purpura cultros
    Sparserat: invidit de tribus una soror
Et festinatis incidit stamina pensis,
    Absentemque patri rettulit urna rogum.
Sed ne sola tamen puerum pictura loquatur,
    Haec erit in chartis maior imago meis.

IX.78

Funera post septem nupsit tibi Galla virorum,
    Picentine: sequi vult, puto, Galla viros.

This was the young Camonus; this his face,
This each lithe limb.
Not twice ten years in ever-changing race
Could alter him,
Save that the manlier his beauty shone,
Until old Time
Looked on him enviously and wished him gone
Still in his prime.
Cruel, to cut the thread of his young years
Not fully spun!
Cruel, to draw a parent's fruitless tears
For youth undone!
But, lest this portrait be his only shrine,
Here on my page
A sweeter picture shall be drawn to shine
With his image.

Brian Hill

Your Galla's buried seven; 'twas time the shrew
Died, Picentinus; so she married you.

A. L. Francis and H. F. Tatum

IX.81

Lector et auditor nostros probat, Aule, libellos,
    Sed quidam exactos esse poeta negat.
Non nimium curo: nam cenae fercula nostrae
    Malim convivis quam placuisse cocis.

IX.85

Languidior noster si quando est Paulus, Atili,
    Non se, convivas abstinet ille suos.
Tu languore quidem subito fictoque laboras,
    Sed mea porrexit sportula, Paule, pedes.

Reader and hearer, Aulus, love my stuff;
A certain poet says it's rather rough.
Well, I don't care. For dinners or for books
The guest's opinion matters, not the cook's.

A. L. Francis and H. F. Tatum

Atilius, when our Paulus ails he tends
To diet—well, not himself but all his friends.
Paulus, you're suddenly unwell, you *say*;
All I know is, my dinner's passed away.

Olive Pitt-Kethley

IX.92

Quae mala sint domini, quae servi commoda, nescis,
    Condyle, qui servum te gemis esse diu.
Dat tibi securos vilis tegeticula somnos,
    Pervigil in pluma Gaius, ecce, iacet.
Gaius a prima tremebundus luce salutat
    Tot dominos, at tu, Condyle, nec dominum.
"Quod debes, Gai, redde" inquit Phoebus et illinc
    Cinnamus: hoc dicit, Condyle, nemo tibi.
Tortorem metuis? podagra cheragraque secatur
    Gaius et mallet verbera mille pati.
Quod nec mane vomis nec cunnum, Condyle, lingis,
    Non mavis, quam ter Gaius esse tuus?

IX.96

Clinicus Herodes trullam subduxerat aegro:
    Deprensus dixit "Stulte, quid ergo bibis?"

Never the pros & cons of "slave," or "master,"
can you, mourning long servitude, discern.
The cheapest matting yields you dreamless sleep;
   Gaius's feather-bed keeps him awake.
From crack of dawn Gaius respectfully
   greets many masters; yours goes ungreeted.
"Pay day, Gaius, pay!" says Phoebus. "Pay! Pay!"
   chimes Cinnamus. What man speaks thus to you?
Screw & rack, you dread? Gaius' gout stabs so,
   he'ld far prefer the thumbscrew or the rack.
You've no hangover habit, oral sex:
   is not one life of yours worth three of his?

Peter Whigham

Herodes stole a cup from one of his patients. Caught,
He said: "What good's a drink to you, you idiot?"

Alistair Elliot

IX.101

Appia, quam simili venerandus in Hercule Caesar
   Consecrat, Ausoniae maxima fama viae,
Si cupis Alcidae cognoscere facta prioris,
   Disce: Libyn domuit, aurea poma tulit,
Peltatam Scythico discinxit Amazona nodo,
   Addidit Arcadio terga leonis apro,
Aeripedem silvis cervum, Stymphalidas astris
   Abstulit, a Stygia cum cane venit aqua,
Fecundam vetuit reparari mortibus hydram,
   Hesperias Tusco lavit in amne boves.
Haec minor Alcides: maior quae gesserit, audi,
   Sextus ab Albana quem colit arce lapis.
Adseruit possessa malis Palatia regnis,
   Prima suo gessit pro Iove bella puer;
Solus Iuleas cum iam retineret habenas,
   Tradidit inque suo tertius orbe fuit;
Cornua Sarmatici ter perfida contudit Histri,
   Sudantem Getica ter nive lavit equum;
Saepe recusatos parcus duxisse triumphos
   Victor Hyperboreo nomen ab orbe tulit;
Templa deis, mores populis dedit, otia ferro,
   Astra suis, caelo sidera, serta Iovi.
Herculeum tantis numen non sufficit actis:
   Tarpeio deus hic commodet ora patri.

Immortal Appius, upon whose road
Our sovereign Hercules new fame bestowed,
Would you his predecessor's worth compute,
He felled Antaeus, won the golden fruit,
The warrior maiden's girdle bore away,
The boar and lion flayed, foul birds from day
Cut off, from woods the brazen-footed deer,
And dragged the monster from the Stygian mere,
The Hydra's issue dried, that grew with slaughter,
And bathed his western herd in Tiber's water.
Thus far the less; now of the greater learn,
Whose altar-lamps by the sixth milestone burn.
The oppressor from the seat of power he threw
And sovereign Jove his young defender knew.
Sole lord, Iulus' mantle he laid down,
Third ruler in a world late all his own.
Three times he crushed the treacherous Danube's pride
And bathed his charger in its snow-fed tide.
Thrifty of triumphs, yet he won a name,
And from the northern world a conqueror came.
Shrines to the gods he gave and rest from wars,
To his folk virtue, fame to his own, new stars
To heaven; for Hercules a role too great,
That rather might beseem the Thunderer's state.

A. L. Francis and H. F. Tatum

BOOK X

(A.D. 98, SECOND EDITION)

X.I

Si nimius videor seraque coronide longus
    Esse liber, legito pauca: libellus ero.
Terque quaterque mihi finitur carmine parvo
    Pagina: fac tibi me quam cupis ipse brevem.

X.2

Festinata prior, decimi mihi cura libelli
    Elapsum manibus nunc revocavit opus.
Nota leges quaedam, sed lima rasa recenti;
    Pars nova maior erit: lector, utrique fave,
Lector, opes nostrae: quem cum mihi Roma dedisset,
    "Nil tibi quod demus maius habemus" ait.
"Pigra per hunc fugies ingratae flumina Lethes
    Et meliore tui parte superstes eris.
Marmora Messallae findit caprificus, et audax
    Dimidios Crispi mulio ridet equos:
At chartis nec furta nocent et saecula prosunt,
    Solaque non norunt haec monumenta mori."

My book too large? Some readers are afraid
If the last flourish is too long delayed.
My pages often with short verses close;
Abridge the book by reading only those.

Olive Pitt-Kethley

Slipshod writing, premature publication,
  brought Book X back for pumice work.
Much you'll recognise that's been refashioned;
  more that's new: smile, Reader, equally
On Each—Reader, Patron, willed to me by *Rome*
  saying: "No greater gift! Through him
You'll flee neglectful *Lethe's* stagnant flood—
  the better part of you survive.
Wild-fig rives the marble, heedless muleteers
  deride the busted steeds of bronze.
But verse no decrease knows, time adds to verse,
  deathless alone of monuments."

Peter Whigham

X.4

Qui legis Oedipoden caligantemque Thyesten,
  Colchidas et Scyllas, quid nisi monstra legis?
Quid tibi raptus Hylas, quid Parthenopaeus et Attis,
  Quid tibi dormitor proderit Endymion?
Exutusve puer pinnis labentibus? aut qui
  Odit amatrices Hermaphroditus aquas?
Quid te vana iuvant miserae ludibria chartae?
  Hoc lege, quod possit dicere vita "Meum est."
Non hic Centauros, non Gorgonas Harpyiasque
  Invenies: hominem pagina nostra sapit.
Sed non vis, Mamurra, tuos cognoscere mores
  Nec te scire: legas Aetia Callimachi.

X.7

Nympharum pater amniumque, Rhene,
Quicumque Odrysias bibunt pruinas,
Sic semper liquidis fruaris undis,
Nec te barbara contumeliosi
Calcatum rota conterat bubulci;
Sic et cornibus aureis receptis
Et Romanus eas utraque ripa:
Traianum populis suis et urbi,
Thybris te dominus rogat, remittas.

Read of Thyestes, Oedipus, dark suns,
  of Scyllas, Medeas—you read of freaks.
Hylas' rape . . . ? Attis . . . ? Parthenopaeus . . . ?
  Endymion's dreams changed your life? The Cretan
Glider moulting feathers . . . ? Hermaphroditus?
  averse to advances of Salmacian fount . . .
Why waste time on fantasy annals? Rather
  read my books, where Life cries: "This is me!"
No Centaurs here; you'll meet no Gorgons, Harpies.
  My page tastes of man. Yet you're incurious
To view your morals or yourself. Best stick
  to Callimachus—the *Mythic Origins*.

Peter Whigham

Father of nymphs, and all the springs
That drink the Thracian snow,
Old Rhine, in all your wanderings
Forever freely flow.

No boorish peasant with his team
Shall drive the lumbering wain,
Defaming thus your noble stream—
Now honour's come again.

The golden horns of victory raise,
On either bank be Rome!
And now your ruler, Tiber, prays,
Return our Trajan home!

Olive Pitt-Kethley

x.8

Nubere Paula cupit nobis, ego ducere Paulam
Nolo: anus est. Vellem, si magis esset anus.

x.9

Undenis pedibusque syllabisque
Et multo sale nec tamen protervo
Notus gentibus ille Martialis
Et notus populis—quid invidetis?—
Non sum Andraemone notior caballo.

x.10

Cum tu, laurigeris annum qui fascibus intras,
    Mane salutator limina mille teras,
Hic ego quid faciam? quid nobis, Paule, relinquis,
    Qui de plebe Numae densaque turba sumus?
Qui me respiciet, dominum regemque vocabo?
    Hoc tu—sed quanto blandius!—ipse facis.
Lecticam sellamve sequar? nec ferre recusas,
    Per medium pugnas et prior ire lutum.
Saepius adsurgam recitanti carmina? tu stas
    Et pariter geminas tendis in ora manus.
Quid faciet pauper, cui non licet esse clienti?
    Dimisit nostras purpura vestra togas.

Paula would wed: I pray to be exempted.
She's old. Were she but older, I'ld be tempted.

Peter Whigham

Martial, renowned throughout the world's domain,
The moral jester in Catullus' vein,
There is small ground for envy at my star;
The horse Andraemon is more famed by far.

A. L. Francis and H. F. Tatum

When you, whose brows the laurel wreaths adorn,
Beset a thousand thresholds every morn,
What shall I do? Paulus, what's left to me,
A man of common, vulgar quality?
I call my patron lord and master too;
The same, how much more daintily, do you.
I wait on chair or litter, you take hire
Yourself and fight for passage through the mire.
I rise when he recites; amazed you stand
And blow him favouring kisses with each hand.
God help the would-be client if he's poor!
Your purple robes have shown our gowns the door.

A. L. Francis and H. F. Tatum

X.13

Ducit ad auriferas quod me Salo Celtiber oras,
  Pendula quod patriae visere tecta libet,
Tu mihi simplicibus, Mani, dilectus ab annis
  Et praetextata cultus amicitia,
Tu facis; in terris quo non est alter Hiberis
  Dulcior et vero dignus amore magis.
Tecum ego vel sicci Gaetula mapalia Poeni
  Et poteram Scythicas hospes amare casas.
Si tibi mens eadem, si nostri mutua cura est,
  In quocumque loco Roma duobus erit.

X.14

Cum cathedrata litos portet tibi raeda ministros
  Et Libys in longo pulvere sudet eques,
Strataque non unas cingant triclinia Baias
  Et Thetis unguento palleat uncta tuo,
Candida Setini rumpant crystalla trientes,
  Dormiat in pluma nec meliore Venus:
Ad nocturna iaces fastosae limina moechae,
  Et madet, heu, lacrimis ianua surda tuis,
Urere nec miserum cessant suspiria pectus,
  Vis dicam, male sit cur tibi, Cotta? bene est.

What draws me back to Salo's goldwashed banks
and makes me long to see the houses overlooking
a certain Spanish hillside? Manius,
in simple boyhood I loved you there, and this
is your doing: no one in my native land's
dearer to me, no one more welcome to my love.
Beside you, I could learn to love a nomad
hut in Africa, call a Scythian hovel home.
If you still feel, still share my care for you,
wherever we're together—there is Rome.

                                          Jim Powell

Lolling in pampered ease your minions ride,
And in the coach's dusty trail outside
Comes the black equerry, sweating in the sun;
You've baths like Baiae's, Cotta—more than one
Long couch around—your sea-bath has grown dim
With poured-in perfumes; from your goblet's rim
The finest wine of Latium overflows;
Venus herself would envy your repose
In down so soft. And yet you choose to lie
At a proud harlot's door. Deaf to your cry,
Your tears, your burning sighs, she shuts you out . . .
You did need something to complain about.

                                          Olive Pitt-Kethley

X.16

Dotatae uxori cor harundine fixit acuta,
    Sed dum ludit Aper: ludere novit Aper.

X.17

Si donare vocas promittere nec dare, Gai,
    Vincam te donis muneribusque meis.
Accipe Callaicis quidquid fodit Astur in arvis,
    Aurea quidquid habet divitis unda Tagi,
Quidquid Erythraea niger invenit Indus in alga,
    Quidquid et in nidis unica servat avis,
Quidquid Agenoreo Tyros inproba cogit aheno:
    Quidquid habent omnes, accipe, quomodo das.

Aper the expert archer accidentally shot
His rich wife in the heart.

            He was lucky. She was not.

                Richard O'Connell

If, Gaius, you call it "giving" when
Kind words alone you offer,
I can surpass your bounty, then;
These gifts to you I proffer:

The wealth of the Asturian mines
In the Galician fields,
The ore that in the river shines—
That golden Tagus yields;

Pearls the dark Indian deems the best
Upon the Eastern strand,
The spices of the phoenix-nest,
Dyes from Agenor's land.

Gaius, my friend, for you it is,
The wealth of all men living
I freely give you all of this
—In your own style of giving.

                Fiona Pitt-Kethley

X.30

O temperatae dulce Formiae litus,
Vos, cum severi fugit oppidum Martis
Et inquietas fessus exuit curas,
Apollinaris omnibus locis praefert.
Non ille sanctae dulce Tibur uxoris,
Nec Tusculanos Algidosve secessus,
Praeneste nec sic Antiumque miratur;
Non blanda Circe Dardanisve Caieta
Desiderantur, nec Marica nec Liris,
Nec in Lucrina lota Salmacis vena.
Hic summa leni stringitur Thetis vento;
Nec languet aequor, viva sed quies ponti
Pictam phaselon adiuvante fert aura,
Sicut puellae non amantis aestatem
Mota salubre purpura venit frigus.
Nec saeta longo quaerit in mari praedam,
Sed a cubili lectuloque iactatam
Spectatus alte lineam trahit piscis.
Si quando Nereus sentit Aeoli regnum,
Ridet procellas tuta de suo mensa:
Piscina rhombum pascit et lupos vernas,
Natat ad magistrum delicata muraena,
Nomenculator mugilem citat notum,
Et adesse iussi prodeunt senes mulli.
Frui sed istis quando Roma permittit?
Quot Formianos inputat dies annus
Negotiosis rebus urbis haerenti?
O ianitores vilicique felices!
Dominis parantur ista, serviunt vobis.

O Formia, sweet good-natured coast!
When, shedding worries, he goes down
Fatigued from Mars' forbidding town,
Apollinaris loves you most.
You he regards more than his pure
Wife's favourite Tivoli, and more
Than Tusculum (without dispute)
And Alban Hills where villas hide,
Praeneste (on their northern side)
Or Anzio. Not even cute
Cape Circe and Aeneas' Nurse
Are missed so, nor Latinus' mother,
The nymph of Liris, nor the other,
Who splashes on the Lucrine shores.
Here a smooth wind strokes Thetis' skin;
The sea's not stagnant, but at peace,
Alive, and pushing with some breeze
A painted yacht across the scene,
As when a girl in heat-distress
Fans slow refreshment from her dress.
And anglers needn't seek their catch
That far off; still in bed, you watch
The fish draw down your horse-hair line.
The wave-god feels the wind-god's power
Sometimes, but at the dinner-hour
Your table laughs at storms—you dine.
For a pond feeds, in family waters,
Your pike's and turbots' sons and daughters;
The tender and luxurious eel

X.31

Addixti servum nummis here mille ducentis,
   Ut bene cenares, Calliodore, semel.
Nec bene cenasti: mullus tibi quattuor emptus
   Librarum cenae pompa caputque fuit.
Exclamare libet: "Non est hic, inprobe, non est
   Piscis: homo est; hominem, Calliodore, comes."

Swims round it by his master's heel;
The name-slave calls that fish you know;
And six old mullets rise and bow.
But when does Rome allow you here?
How many Formian days a year
Are counted out for city gents
Who live for making cents not sense?
O lucky guards at villa doors!
Bought for your masters, they are yours.

Alistair Elliot

Calliodorus, yesterday
You sold a slave, for which men pay
Twelve hundred silver pieces, so
That you could make a splendid show
And dine in style for once at least.
And the chief ornament of the feast?
A four pound mullet was the glory
And centre of your menu's story!
Calliodorus, let me say
You've not dined *well* at all, today.
'Twas not a fish upon the plate—
My friend, it was a Man you ate!

Olive Pitt-Kethley

X.32

Haec mihi quae colitur violis pictura rosisque,
    Quos referat voltus, Caediciane, rogas?
Talis erat Marcus mediis Antonius annis
    Primus: in hoc iuvenem se videt ore senex.
Ars utinam mores animumque effingere posset!
    Pulchrior in terris nulla tabella foret.

This portrait which I treasure so
Is Marcus painted long ago
When he was young and gay and fair,
Who now is old with silvered hair.

Would that the artist's brush could bind
In paint the beauties of his mind,
For then, I swear, the world to-day
No rarer picture could display.

Brian Hill

X.35

Omnes Sulpiciam legant puellae,
Uni quae cupiunt viro placere;
Omnes Sulpiciam legant mariti,
Uni qui cupiunt placere nuptae.
Non haec Colchidos adserit furorem,
Diri prandia nec refert Thyestae;
Scyllam, Byblida nec fuisse credit:
Sed castos docet et probos amores,
Lusus, delicias facetiasque.
Cuius carmina qui bene aestimarit,
Nullam dixerit esse nequiorem,
Nullam dixerit esse sanctiorem.
Tales Egeriae iocos fuisse
Udo crediderim Numae sub antro.
Hac condiscipula vel hac magistra
Esses doctior et pudica, Sappho:
Sed tecum pariter simulque visam
Durus Sulpiciam Phaon amaret.
Frustra: namque ea nec Tonantis uxor
Nec Bacchi nec Apollinis puella
Erepto sibi viveret Caleno.

Who would please their husbands only
Let such ladies read Sulpicia,
Who would please their wives alone
Let such husbands read Sulpicia.
Medea's rage means naught to her,
Nor Thyestes' baneful banquet.
Scylla & the Font of Byblis
Never loomed on her horizon.
She writes of true & tender loves,
Their sports, delights & pleasantries.
Read her verses as they merit:
None than her is more beguiling,
None than her as innocent.
Such, I've fancied was Egeria
Bantering love in Numa's cave.
Had as co-ed, teacher, Sappho
Had her, she'd more learned been—more chaste.
Had Phaon seen the two together,
Sulpicia 'tis he would have loved.
And loved in vain: for she, as spouse
Of Jove—as Bacchus' or Apollo's
Girl, could ne'er have loved or lived
                    —reft of Calenus.

Peter Whigham

X.36

Inproba Massiliae quidquid fumaria cogunt,
   Accipit aetatem quisquis ab igne cadus,
A te, Munna, venit: miseris tu mittis amicis
   Per freta, per longas toxica saeva vias;
Nec facili pretio, sed quo contenta Falerni
   Testa sit aut cellis Setia cara suis.
Non venias quare tam longo tempore Romam,
   Haec puto causa tibi est, ne tua vina bibas.

If the deplorable label says: *Marseilles Wine,*
   if, at the fire, the wine was smoked, not aged,
Munna sent it. You despatch by sea, overland,
   implacable toxins to your duped friends—
And not for little, but what from their dear cell-
   ars Setine or Falernian would cost.
The cause of your long holiday from Rome is clear:
   you cannot drink—nor yet refuse—your wines.

Peter Whigham

X.37

Iuris et aequarum cultor sanctissime legum,
  Veridico Latium qui regis ore forum,
Municipi, Materne, tuo veterique sodali
  Callaicum mandas siquid ad Oceanum—.
An Laurentino turpis in litore ranas
  Et satius tenues ducere credis acus,
Ad sua captivum quam saxa remittere mullum,
  Visus erit libris qui minor esse tribus?
Et fatuam summa cenare pelorida mensa
  Quosque tegit levi cortice concha brevis,
Ostrea Baianis quam non liventia testis,
  Quae domino pueri non prohibente vorent?
Hic olidam clamosus ages in retia volpem
  Mordebitque tuos sordida praeda canes:
Illic piscoso modo vix educta profundo
  Inpedient lepores umida lina meos.—
Dum loquor, ecce redit sporta piscator inani,
  Venator capta maele superbus adest:
Omnis ab urbano venit ad mare cena macello,
  Callaicum mandas siquid ad Oceanum—.

Pillar of Justice & Legislation,
   whose orat'ry in court holds sway,
Who shares (old friend) my *Bilbilis* with me,
   who from Tarragon's *coast requires*—

Or, is your preference from beaches here
   the rank frog, spindly stickleback?

(In *Spain*, netted mullet judged not three pounds,
   —back among the rocks we cast it.)

Or, for *entrée*, your choice th' insipid cock-
   le, bitty tight-shelled mussel?

(Oysters, divers promiscuously
   gobble—rare as any *Baiae* bears!)

Here, "Halloaing," net the stinking vixen—
   vile, verminlike 'twill rip your hounds.

(There, nets drip still from fish-filled deeps that
   field hares from my fields entangle.)

We talk . . . Your fisher passes, fishbox void . . .
   Comes ghillie, boasts one badger trapped . . .
Clearly, your beachhouse dinners hail from *Rome*,
   Who from Tarragon's *coast requires*—

Peter Whigham

x.38

O molles tibi quindecim, Calene,
Quos cum Sulpicia tua iugales
Indulsit deus et peregit annos!
O nox omnis et hora, quae notata est
Caris litoris Indici lapillis!
O quae proelia, quas utrimque pugnas
Felix lectulus et lucerna vidit
Nimbis ebria Nicerotianis!
Vixisti tribus, o Calene, lustris:
Aetas haec tibi tota conputatur
Et solos numeras dies mariti.
Ex illis tibi si diu rogatam
Lucem redderet Atropos vel unam,
Malles, quam Pyliam quater senectam.

x.40

Semper cum mihi diceretur esse
Secreto mea Polla cum cinaedo,
Inrupi, Lupe. Non erat cinaedus.

O sweet the years, Calenus, you
& your Sulpicia had handed
each, by the god, & made for you!

O nights & hours of each night, signed
with cherished stones from Indian coasts!

O battles, paired engagements, watched
by good-humored bed & lamp soused
with scents from Nicero's scent-shop!

Three lustres you have lived, your whole
life's computation, Calenus—
counting only the married days.

Of them, should Fate recall one longed-
for day, you'd sooner live that day
again, than four times Nestor's years.

Peter Whigham

The current rumor would indict
My Polla and a sodomite.
I caught them. Rumor wasn't right.

R. L. Barth

X.42

Tam dubia est lanugo tibi, tam mollis, ut illam
    Halitus et soles et levis aura terat.
Celantur simili ventura Cydonea lana,
    Pollice virgineo quae spoliata nitent.
Fortius inpressi quotiens tibi basia quinque,
    Barbatus labris, Dindyme, fio tuis.

X.44

Quinte Caledonios Ovidi visure Britannos
    Et viridem Tethyn Oceanumque patrem,
Ergo Numae colles et Nomentana relinquis
    Otia nec retinet rusque focusque senem?
Gaudia tu differs, at non et stamina differt
    Atropos atque omnis scribitur hora tibi.
Praestiteris caro—quis non hoc laudet?—amico,
    Ut potior vita sit tibi sancta fides;
Sed reddare tuis tandem mansure Sabinis
    Teque tuas numeres inter amicitias.

Irresolute the down upon your cheek,
  soft so sunlight or a breath of wind must
Bear it off. Cydonian quinces, under
  a young girl's fingers lose their feathery bloom
And gleam. Five hard kisses, Dindymus, I
  press on you. Bearded from your lips mine come.

Peter Whigham

Quintus Ovidius, called by Caledonia,
  by virid Tethys, by papa Ocean,
You'll leave these Numan hills, your Nomentan retreat,
  since fields & fireside cannot claim your years.
"Delights of rest can rest." But the spindles of the
  Fates rest not. Hour by hour is scribbled on your tab.
Your travelling companion will (as well he should)
  be edified: your pledge outweighed your life.
Come, Quintus, to your Sabine farm at last:
  let Quintus Quintus count as Quintus' friend.

Peter Whigham

X.45

Si quid lene mei dicunt et dulce libelli,
    Si quid honorificum pagina blanda sonat,
Hoc tu pingue putas et costam rodere mavis,
    Ilia Laurentis cum tibi demus apri.
Vaticana bibas, si delectaris aceto:
    Non facit ad stomachum nostra lagona tuum.

X.46

Omnia vis belle, Matho, dicere. Dic aliquando
    Et bene; dic neutrum; dic aliquando male.

The sweet & subtle flavor of my pamphlets,
   The flattering phrases dressed as eulogy,
You find insipid, preferring to gnaw spare ribs
   When offered choice loin-cut of Laurentian boar,
A taste for vinegar means Vatican's your wine:
   Ill on your stomach lies my amphora.

                                        Peter Whigham

"Omnia vult *belle* Matho dicere; dic aliquando
   Et *bene:* dic *neutrum:* dic aliquando *male.*"
The first is rather more than mortal can do;
   The second may be sadly done, or gaily;
The third is still more difficult to stand to;
   The fourth we hear, and see, and say too, daily:
The whole together is what I could wish
To serve in this conundrum of a dish.

                          George Gordon, Lord Byron
                          (*Don Juan,* Canto XV)

X.47

Vitam quae faciant beatiorem,
Iucundissime Martialis, haec sunt:
Res non parta labore, sed relicta;
Non ingratus ager, focus perennis;
Lis numquam, toga rara, mens quieta;
Vires ingenuae, salubre corpus;
Prudens simplicitas, pares amici;
Convictus facilis, sine arte mensa;
Nox non ebria, sed soluta curis;
Non tristis torus, et tamen pudicus;
Somnus, qui faciat breves tenebras:
Quod sis, esse velis nihilque malis;
Summum nec metuas diem nec optes.

My carefree Namesake, this the art
Shall lead thee to life's happier part:

A competence inherited, not won,
Productive acres & a constant home;

No courts, few formal days, your mind stable,
A native vigor in a healthy frame;

A tact in candor, friendships on a par,
Convivial courtesies, a plain table;

A night, not drunken, yet shall banish care,
A bed, not frigid, yet not one of shame;
A sleep that makes the dark hours shorter:

Prefer your state & hanker for none other,
Nor fear, nor seek to meet, your final hour.

Peter Whigham

x.48

Nuntiat octavam Phariae sua turba iuvencae,
  Et pilata redit iamque subitque cohors.
Temperat haec thermas, nimios prior hora vapores
  Halat, et inmodico sexta Nerone calet.
Stella, Nepos, Cani, Cerialis, Flacce, venitis?
  Septem sigma capit, sex sumus, adde Lupum.
Exoneraturas ventrem mihi vilica malvas
  Adtulit et varias, quas habet hortus, opes,
In quibus est lactuca sedens et tonsile porrum,
  Nec deest ructatrix menta nec herba salax;
Secta coronabunt rutatos ova lacertos,
  Et madidum thynni de sale sumen erit.
Gustus in his; una ponetur cenula mensa,
  Haedus, inhumani raptus ab ore lupi,
Et quae non egeant ferro structoris ofellae,
  Et faba fabrorum prototomique rudes;
Pullus ad haec cenisque tribus iam perna superstes
  Addetur. Saturis mitia poma dabo,
De Nomentana vinum sine faece lagona,
  Quae bis Frontino consule trima fuit.
Accedent sine felle ioci nec mane timenda
  Libertas et nil quod tacuisse velis:
De prasino conviva meus venetoque loquatur,
  Nec facient quemquam pocula nostra reum.

In acknowledgement, to B.J.

Two o'clock: the Egyptian priests have barred
   the temple gates, the Palace troop changed guard.
The baths are cooler now, that still breathed steam
   at one, and noon seemed hot as Nero's stream.
Cerialis, Stella, Canius, Flaccus, Nepos—
   with you we're six—my couch holds sev'n: add Lupus.
Okra (that purges) by my good dame got,
   expect, with riches from my garden plot.
Mint there'll be (for wind), leeks in slices,
   short-head lettuce, rocket (for what's nice is).
Scad, dressed with devilled eggs & sprigs of rue,
   sows' teats well sprinkled with a tunny stew.
These for tasters: the meal itself—one course,
   a kid made tender in some wild beast's jaws,
With morselled meats so carving is left out,
   & builders' beans & tender cabbage sprouts.
A chicken & a thrice-left-over ham
   as well. When filled, you've fruit & Nomentan—
Decanted from the flagon with no dreg,
   (Frontinus consul) three years in the keg.
And add to this, the jest that does not bite,
   a lack of fear of what you did last night,
Or said. Talk Green & Blue—the Circus show. . . .
   None from my Nomentan shall bad-mouthed go.

Peter Whigham

X.51

Sidera iam Tyrius Phrixei respicit agni
     Taurus, et alternum Castora fugit hiems;
Ridet ager, vestitur humus, vestitur et arbor,
     Ismarium paelex Attica plorat Ityn.
Quos, Faustine, dies, qualem tibi Roma Ravennam
     Abstulit! o soles, o tunicata quies!
O nemus, o fontes solidumque madentis harenae
     Litus et aequoreis splendidus Anxur aquis,
Et non unius spectator lectulus undae,
     Qui videt hinc puppes fluminis, inde maris!
Sed nec Marcelli Pompeianumque, nec illic
     Sunt triplices thermae, nec fora iuncta quater,
Nec Capitolini summum penetrale Tonantis,
     Quaeque nitent caelo proxima templa suo.
Dicere te lassum quotiens ego credo Quirino:
     "Quae tua sunt, tibi habe: quae mea, redde mihi."

X.53

Ille ego sum Scorpus, clamosi gloria Circi,
     Plausus, Roma, tui deliciaeque breves,
Invida quem Lachesis raptum trieteride nona,
     Dum numerat palmas, credidit esse senem.

The Tyrian Bull succeeds the Phryxian Ram,
　　sun in Gemini sends winter reeling,
Campania gleams in greening fields and woods,
　　Attic adultress sobs for Thracian child.
Ravenna days, Faustinus! Rome's stripped you
　　naked of those sunlit hours! Togaless times!
O groves! O fountains! That stretch of firm
　　wet sands. Anxur resplendent in the waves.
The couch with double view . . . this side watching
　　river shipping . . . there the ocean.
No Pompeian, no Marcellan theater,
　　no triple hot baths, nor four forum junction,
No Thunderer's heights upreared on Capitol,
　　no Flavian temples glimm'ring from their Heavens.
I've caught you, dog-tired, murmuring: "Quirinus,
　　you're welcome to what's yours; give back what's mine."

Peter Whigham

Rome, I am Scorpus, foremost in the race,
The short-lived darling of the populace;
Fate heard the long list of my victories told—
And cut me off thinking I must be old.

Brian Hill

X.55

Arrectum quotiens Marulla penem
Pensavit digitis diuque mensa est,
Libras, scripula sextulasque dicit;
Idem post opus et suas palaestras
Loro cum similis iacet remisso,
Quanto sit levior Marulla dicit.
Non ergo est manus ista, sed statera.

X.58

Anxuris aequorei placidos, Frontine, recessus
    Et propius Baias litoreamque domum,
Et quod inhumanae cancro fervente cicadae
    Non novere nemus, flumineosque lacus
Dum colui, doctas tecum celebrare vacabat
    Pieridas: nunc nos maxima Roma terit.
Hic mihi quando dies meus est? iactamur in alto
    Urbis, et in sterili vita labore perit,
Dura suburbani dum iugera pascimus agri
    Vicinosque tibi, sancte Quirine, lares.
Sed non solus amat qui nocte dieque frequentat
    Limina, nec vatem talia damna decent.
Per veneranda mihi Musarum sacra, per omnes
    Iuro deos: Et non officiosus amo.

Whenever she confronts erections
Her fingers heft and measure them.
She reads you off: feet, inches, ounces.
Then, after holds and falls and bounces,
When they hang slack as dangling reins,
She weighs how many drachms you've spent.
That's no hand: that's an instrument
For calculating meat-injections.

Alistair Elliot

When on the quiet headland at *Terracina*,
    or at *Baiae's* seaside villa,
On river-lakes, in groves where the grasshopper
    's no burden in the dog-days, then
Danced we attendance on the learn'd *Pierians*,
    —we whom *Rome* now pulverises.

When can I call a day my own? Plunged in town-
    living, toil lacking fruit, tilling
Hard suburban acres, with a second home,
    holy *Quirinus*, in your care.

Serenading does not make a lover, nor
    daily dalliance fit a poet.
By ev'ry God! The Sacred Nine! Love's no less
    love, that fails to dance attendance.

Peter Whigham

x.59

Consumpta est uno si lemmate pagina, transis,
    Et breviora tibi, non meliora placent.
Dives et ex omni posita est instructa macello
    Cena tibi, sed te mattea sola iuvat.
Non opus est nobis nimium lectore guloso;
    Hunc volo, non fiat qui sine pane satur.

x.61

Hic festinata requiescit Erotion umbra,
    Crimine quam fati sexta peremit hiems.
Quisquis eris nostri post me regnator agelli,
    Manibus exiguis annua iusta dato:
Sic lare perpetuo, sic turba sospite solus
    Flebilis in terra sit lapis iste tua.

If an epigram takes up a page, you skip it:
Art counts for nothing, you prefer the snippet.
The markets have been ransacked for you, reader,
Rich fare—and you want canapes instead!
I'm not concerned with the fastidious feeder:
Give me the man who likes his basic bread.

James Michie

Underneath this greedy stone,
Lies little sweet Erotion;
Whom the fates, with hearts as cold,
Nipt away at six years old.
Thou, whoever thou mayst be,
That hast this small field after me,
Let the yearly rites be paid
To her little slender shade;
So shall no disease or jar
Hurt thy house, or chill thy Lar;
But this tomb here be alone,
The only melancholy stone.

Leigh Hunt
(*The Indicator*, no. 3 [1819])

x.63

Marmora parva quidem, sed non cessura, viator,
   Mausoli saxis pyramidumque legis.
Bis mea Romano spectata est vita Tarento,
   Et nihil extremos perdidit ante rogos:
Quinque dedit pueros, totidem mihi Iuno puellas,
   Cluserunt omnes lumina nostra manus.
Contigit et thalami mihi gloria rara fuitque
   Una pudicitiae mentula nota meae.

The stone you read, it's true, is small.
But this rock, traveller, equals all
the Pyramids, Mausolus' stony pride.
At Tarentos, twice,
I watched, was watched, exemplified.
I never wavered. Then I died.
Five sons, five daughters, Juno's gift,
All closed my eyes. More than all this,
rare chastity my marriage graced:
One prick my modesty embraced.

                                 Helen Deutsch

x.65

Cum te municipem Corinthiorum
Iactes, Charmenion, negante nullo,
Cur frater tibi dicor, ex Hiberis
Et Celtis genitus Tagique civis?
An voltu similes videmur esse?
Tu flexa nitidus coma vagaris,
Hispanis ego contumax capillis;
Levis dropace tu cotidiano,
Hirsutis ego cruribus genisque;
Os blaesum tibi debilisque lingua est,
Nobis filia fortius loquetur:
Tam dispar aquilae columba non est,
Nec dorcas rigido fugax leoni.
Quare desine me vocare fratrem,
Ne te, Charmenion, vocem sororem.

Since you, Charmenion, come from Corinth
     And I from quite another
Part of the world, from Tagus, tell me
     Why do you call me "brother"?

You're Greek—my ancestors were Celts
     And Spaniards. Do we share
Some physical resemblances?
     Well, you have oily hair,

In ringlets—my stiff Spanish locks
     Are obstinately straight;
I'm shaggy-legged and bristle-cheeked—
     Daily you depilate

Your silky skin. Your voice is light;
     You lisp in a charming way—
My voice, as my loins can testify,
     Is gruff. And so I'll say:

We're less alike than eagles and doves,
     Or lions and does, so Mister,
Don't you call me "brother," or
     I'll have to call you "sister."

Dorothea Wender

x.66

Quis, rogo, tam durus, quis tam fuit ille superbus,
    Qui iussit fieri te, Theopompe, cocum?
Hanc aliquis faciem nigra violare culina
    Sustinet, has uncto polluit igne comas?
Quis potius cyathos aut quis crystalla tenebit?
    Qua sapient melius mixta Falerna manu?
Si tam sidereos manet exitus iste ministros,
    Iuppiter utatur iam Ganymede coco.

x.67

Pyrrhae filia, Nestoris noverca,
Quam vidit Niobe puella canam,
Laertes aviam senex vocavit,
Nutricem Priamus, socrum Thyestes,
Iam cornicibus omnibus superstes,
Hoc tandem sita prurit in sepulchro
Calvo Plutia cum Melanthione.

x.69

Custodes das, Polla, viro, non accipis ipsa.
    Hoc est uxorem ducere, Polla, virum.

Did he have eyes and, if so, did he look,
The fool who made fair Theopompus cook?
Could any man be mad enough to mar
Such lovely hair with kitchen soot and char?
What boy can take your place, and look divine
Pouring with graceful hand Falernian wine?
If perfect beauty was for this decreed,
Jove would have made a cook of Ganymede.

Anthony Reid

Daughter of Pyrrha; Nestor's stepmother,
Whom Niobe as a girl saw with white hair;
Who's been called Granny (by the old Laertes),
Nurse (by Priam), and Mother-in-Law (Thyestes);
Who's outlived all the tricentennial crows;
Buried at last, still itching in the tomb,
Plotia lies here, with bald Melanthion.

Alistair Elliot

You set spies on your husband, while you lead a free life:
That's taking, dear Polla, a husband to wife.

J. P. Sullivan

X.74

Iam parce lasso, Roma, gratulatori,
Lasso clienti. Quamdiu salutator
Anteambulones et togatulos inter
Centum merebor plumbeos die toto,
Cum Scorpus una quindecim graves hora
Ferventis auri victor auferat saccos?
Non ego meorum praemium libellorum
—Quid enim merentur?—Apulos velim campos:
Non Hybla, non me spicifer capit Nilus,
Nec quae paludes delicata Pomptinas
Ex arce clivi spectat uva Setini.
Quid concupiscam quaeris ergo? dormire.

Spare at length, Rome, a weary
Congratulator, a weary client. How long,
An ingratiator, shall I

In a whole day earn
Among the trotters-ahead, the fittingly clad,
A hundred counterfeit pence,

When in one hour victorious
Scorpus carries off fifteen heavy bags
Of seething gold?

I would not want Apulian
Plains as the price of my little books—
For what's their merit?

Neither Hybla nor arable Nile
Attracts me, nor the pampered Setine grape
Which from the slope's protection

Watches the Pomptine marshes.
You ask what I really long for?
Sleep . . .

W. G. Shepherd

X.78

Ibis litoreas, Macer, Salonas,
Ibit rara fides amorque recti
Et quae, cum comitem trahit pudorem,
Semper pauperior redit potestas:
Felix auriferae colone terrae,
Rectorem vacuo sinu remittes
Optabisque moras, et exeuntem
Udo Dalmata gaudio sequeris.
Nos Celtas, Macer, et truces Hiberos
Cum desiderio tui petemus.
Sed quaecumque tamen feretur illinc
Piscosi calamo Tagi notata,
Macrum pagina nostra nominabit:
Sic inter veteres legar poetas,
Nec multos mihi praeferas priores,
Uno sed tibi sim minor Catullo.

Off to the coastal capital
Of Dalmatia!—with rectitude,
Good faith, in your baggage, power
Bound to decorum, sure pledge
You'll return poorer than you left. . . .
Fortunate the colonial of gold-
laden country, who'll send Macer
Back with emptied purse, delaying—
O Dalmatian—the departure
Of one you'll speed with tearful toasts.
I, Martial, meanwhile head for Spain,
Land of truculent Iberians,
Where I'll miss my Macer dearly.
Whatever reaches you from there
(With reed from fish-brimmed Tagus writ!),
Know every page shall own your name,
That, reading me with oldtime poets,
You'll prize me more than most—second,
Martial, only to Catullus.

                    Peter Whigham

x.80

Plorat Eros, quotiens maculosae pocula murrae
    Inspicit aut pueros nobiliusve citrum,
Et gemitus imo ducit de pectore, quod non
    Tota miser coemat Saepta feratque domum.
Quam multi faciunt, quod Eros, sed lumine sicco!
    Pars maior lacrimas ridet et intus habet.

x.81

Cum duo venissent ad Phyllida mane fututum
    Et nudam cuperet sumere uterque prior,
Promisit pariter se Phyllis utrique daturam,
    Et dedit: ille pedem sustulit, hic tunicam.

Eros laments as often as he inspects
a superior citrus board or slave-boys
or cups of speckled murrine and heaves

Up groans from the pit of his chest
because the poor chap may not buy
The whole Saepta* and carry it home . . .

How many act like Eros!
But the greater part dry-eyed jeer
at his tears—and inwardly share them.

W. G. Shepherd

On Phyllis one morning a couple of bucks
Paid a lecherous call: they were looking for fucks.
But each wants to strip her and have the first thrust,
While Phyllis is eager to seem and be just.
So one lifts up her legs for the tool's firm caress,
As the other then lifts up the back of her dress.

J. P. Sullivan

* A smart, enclosed shopping center near the Campus Martius.

x.85

Iam senior Ladon Tiberinae nauta carinae
  Proxima dilectis rura paravit aquis.
Quae cum saepe vagus premeret torrentibus undis
  Thybris et hiberno rumperet arva lacu,
Emeritam puppem, ripa quae stabat in alta,
  Inplevit saxis obposuitque vadis.
Sic nimias avertit aquas. Quis credere posset?
  Auxilium domino mersa carina tulit.

x.90

Quid vellis vetulum, Ligeia, cunnum?
Quid busti cineres tui lacessis?
Tales munditiae decent puellas
—Nam tu iam nec anus potes videri—;
Istud, crede mihi, Ligeia, belle
Non mater facit Hectoris, sed uxor.
Erras, si tibi cunnus hic videtur,
Ad quem mentula pertinere desit.
Quare si pudor est, Ligeia, noli
Barbam vellere mortuo leoni.

The boatman Ladon chose in age to dwell
On land beside the stream he loved so well.
With frequent floods in winter Tiber raced,
Swilling the ploughed fields to a watery waste.
His superannuated boat sat high and dry—
He filled the ancient hulk with stones, thereby
Keeping the floods at bay. What a surprise!
A sunken ship made owner's fortune rise.

Olive Pitt-Kethley

Why pluck the bristles from your worn out cleft,
 Hoary and grizzled by time's onward march?
For wanton tricks you've no excuses left,
 Age should be all propriety and starch.
Let blooming girls their tender pussies trim,
 Those pouting buds expect some pleasure after;
My wife might charm me if she dressed her quim,
 But my grandmother would provoke my laughter.
That is no cunt at which a prick can stand,
 The whitened embers of young lust's spent force;
Then cast the tweezers from your palsied hand,
 Nor beard the once fierce lion's rotting corpse.

George Augustus Sala

X.92

Marri, quietae cultor et comes vitae,
Quo cive prisca gloriatur Atina,
Has tibi gemellas barbari decus luci
Commendo pinus ilicesque Faunorum
Et semidocta vilici manu structas
Tonantis aras horridique Silvani,
Quas pinxit agni saepe sanguis aut haedi,
Dominamque sancti virginem deam templi,
Et quem sororis hospitem vides castae,
Martem mearum principem Kalendarum,
Et delicatae laureum nemus Florae,
In quod Priapo persequente confugit.
Hoc omne agelli mite parvuli numen
Seu tu cruore sive ture placabis:
"Ubicumque vester Martialis est," dices,
"Hac, ecce, mecum dextera litat vobis
Absens sacerdos; vos putate praesentem
Et date duobus quidquid alter optabit."

X.95

Infantem tibi vir, tibi, Galla, remisit adulter.
    Hi, puto, non dubie se futuisse negant.

To *Marrus*, whom quietude beckons,
  antique *Atina's* cause of pride,
These twin pines gladdening this untilled glade,
  Martial commits, with *Fauns'* holm-oak,
With *Jove's*, rude *Silvanus'*, altar
  my factotum's unskilled hands once raised
(Oft imbrued with lamb or kid's blood),
  with virgin *Dian's* shrine, its queen,
And one his chaste sister harbors—
  Mars, dominant of my Kalends,
And the laurel grove where pretty
  Flora, sought by *Priapus*, hides.
My meagre fields' mild familiars
  with blood or incense fed.
Address: "Your *Martial* now, what place he be,
  with my right hand his offers this,
Absent celebrant; accept him present:
  on both what either asks bestow."

                                        Peter Whigham

Your husband's rejected your child; your lover has too:
Galla, they clearly deny laying a finger on you.

                                        J. P. Sullivan

X.96

Saepe loquar nimium gentes quod, Avite, remotas,
    Miraris, Latia factus in urbe senex,
Auriferumque Tagum sitiam patriumque Salonem
    Et repetam saturae sordida rura casae.
Illa placet tellus, in qua res parva beatum
    Me facit et tenues luxuriantur opes:
Pascitur hic, ibi pascit ager; tepet igne maligno
    Hic focus, ingenti lumine lucet ibi;
Hic pretiosa fames conturbatorque macellus,
    Mensa ibi divitiis ruris operta sui;
Quattuor hic aestate togae pluresve teruntur,
    Autumnis ibi me quattuor una tegit.
I, cole nunc reges, quidquid non praestat amicus
    Cum praestare tibi possit, Avite, locus.

X.97

Dum levis arsura struitur Libitina papyro,
    Dum murram et casias flebilis uxor emit,
Iam scrobe, iam lecto, iam pollinctore parato
    Heredem scripsit me Numa: convaluit.

Overfamiliar my theme to you, *Avitus*,
  marv'lling how one grown old in *Rome*
Should for golden *Tagus* long, his home *Salò*,
  the few fields . . . well-stocked cot remembered.
Dear land, where little shall suffice delight
  and modesty of means spells wealth.
These fields we feed, those feed us; these hearth-fires
  meanly flicker, those are ablaze.
Here, appetites are dear, markets ruinous;
  there, tables sag under their own produce.
Four togas, here, threadbare in one summer;
  there, one toga per four autumns.
Knock for preferment on these *Roman* doors . . . ?
  Spain can provide all here you lack.

Peter Whigham

The light-heaped pyre lay ready for the match,
Numa's wife, weeping, incense-bearing, hovered:
Grave, bier, undertaker . . . here's the catch—
He'd made me heir—but blast him, he recovered!

Stuart Piggott

x.98

Addat cum mihi Caecubum minister
Idaeo resolutior cinaedo,
Quo nec filia cultior nec uxor
Nec mater tua nec soror recumbit,
Vis spectem potius tuas lucernas
Aut citrum vetus Indicosque dentes?
Suspectus tibi ne tamen recumbam,
Praesta de grege sordidaque villa
Tonsos, horridulos, rudes, pusillos
Hircosi mihi filios subulci.
Perdet te dolor hic: habere, Publi,
Mores non potes hos et hos ministros.

The young wine-boy who tends my need
Is sexier than Ganymede.
Your daughter, mother, sister, wife
Lack all his elegance and life.
Lamps, antiques, stools with ivory trim
Don't hold my gaze. I look at him!

If you don't want to make me lust
Choose louts from out your farmyard dust:
Dull, short-haired, dirty, ugly ones,
Some stinking swineherd's puny sons.
But if you're jealous—we're not dim—
You can't be pure with boys like him!

Anthony Reid

X.103

Municipes Augusta mihi quos Bilbilis acri
    Monte creat, rapidis quem Salo cingit aquis,
Ecquid laeta iuvat vestri vos gloria vatis?
    Nam decus et nomen famaque vestra sumus,
Nec sua plus debet tenui Verona Catullo
    Meque velit dici non minus illa suum.
Quattuor accessit tricesima messibus aestas,
    Ut sine me Cereri rustica liba datis,
Moenia dum colimus dominae pulcherrima Romae:
    Mutavere meas Itala regna comas.
Excipitis placida reducem si mente, venimus;
    Aspera si geritis corda, redire licet.

Townsfolk born with me 'mid the sharp scarps
   of *Bilbilis Salò* swiftly circles,
Do you rejoice at my celebrity?
   My name's your honor, your repute.
Did learn'd *Gaius* bequeathe *Verona* more,
   that wills me now, as him, her own?
Four-&-thirty harvest-homes have passed since
   you & I gave cakes to *Ceres,*
Years yielded *Rome* in *Rome's* fair bailiwick—
   Italic climes my hair turns white.
Bid me but welcome and I'm thither bound:
   cold hearts—*Martial* heads back to *Rome.*

                    Peter Whigham

X.104

I nostro comes, i, libelle, Flavo
Longum per mare, sed faventis undae,
Et cursu facili tuisque ventis
Hispanae pete Tarraconis arces:
Illinc te rota tollet et citatus
Altam Bilbilin et tuum Salonem
Quinto forsitan essedo videbis.
Quid mandem tibi, quaeris? Ut sodales
Paucos, sed veteres et ante brumas
Triginta mihi quattuorque visos
Ipsa protinus a via salutes
Et nostrum admoneas subinde Flavum,
Iucundos mihi nec laboriosos
Secessus pretio paret salubri,
Qui pigrum faciant tuum parentem.
Haec sunt. Iam tumidus vocat magister
Castigatque moras, et aura portum
Laxavit melior: vale, libelle:
Navem, scis puto, non moratur unus.

"Go, little book with friend
Flavus, go! Your course set
Fair under wafting airs
Steer for the imperial
Steeps of *Spanish Tarragon*.
Thence, by coach-express,
Five stages at the most,
And you're where *Bilbilis*
Perches o'er fair *Salò*."
You ask: "What mandate's mine?"
And I: "Friends few but tried
Whom in the street you pass,
Whom thirty years have sunk
From sight, salute for me.
Besides, from time to time,
Remind our *Flavus* of
The happy hideaway
He's buying (modestly),
So light to manage, sloth
Must o'ertake your author.
So: th' exasperated
Ship's captain berates late-
Comers. *Bonne chance*, small book!
Tides, like Time, wait for none."

Peter Whigham

BOOK XI

(A.D. 96 DECEMBER)

XI.3

Non urbana mea tantum Pipleide gaudent
    Otia, nec vacuis auribus ista damus,
Sed meus in Geticis ad Martia signa pruinis
    A rigido teritur centurione liber,
Dicitur et nostros cantare Britannia versus.
    Quid prodest? Nescit sacculus ista meus.
At quam victuras poteramus pangere chartas
    Quantaque Pieria proelia flare tuba,
Cum pia reddiderint Augustum numina terris,
    Et Maecenatem si tibi, Roma, darent!

Not only leisured men enjoy my Muse;
Nor do I offer verse to vapid ear;
But on frost-blasted northermost frontiers,
By battle standards, my epigrams amuse
The harsh centurion; in Britain, too.
What profit? None; my purse remains threadbare.
But what deep, epic trumpets could I dare,
And what immortal poems carry through,
Seeing the gods returned Augustus home,
If they'd restore Maecenas, too, O Rome.

R. L. Barth

XI.7

Iam certe stupido non dices, Paula, marito,
    Ad moechum quotiens longius ire voles,
"Caesar in Albanum iussit me mane venire,
    Caesar Circeios." Iam stropha talis abit.
Penelopae licet esse tibi sub principe Nerva:
    Sed prohibet scabies ingeniumque vetus.
Infelix, quid ages? aegram simulabis amicam?
    Haerebit dominae vir comes ipse suae,
Ibit et ad fratrem tecum matremque patremque.
    Quas igitur fraudes ingeniosa paras?
Diceret hystericam se forsitan altera moecha
    In Sinuessano velle sedere lacu.
Quanto tu melius, quotiens placet ire fututum,
    Quae verum mavis dicere, Paula, viro!

Now no longer can you say
Paula, when you mean to stray,
"Caesar sent for me today."
Circeian villa, Alban too,
Are no alibi for you.
Nerva rules now; you must be,
Though would-be whore, Penelope.
A problem, this. If you pretend
To visit family or sick friend,
Your dim old husband sticks like glue—
"You're going out dear? I'll come too."
What on earth then can you say?
A lying whore would find a way,
In Sinuessa's springs redress
A bout of female nervousness.
But, Paula, you're no liar; you,
When off for an illicit screw,
Would first make sure your husband knew.

Olive Pitt-Kethley

XI.8

Lassa quod hesterni spirant opobalsama dracti,
   Ultima quod curvo quae cadit aura croco;
Poma quod hiberna maturescentia capsa,
   Arbore quod verna luxuriosus ager;
De Palatinis dominae quod Serica prelis,
   Sucina virginea quod regelata manu;
Amphora quod nigri, sed longe, fracta Falerni,
   Quod qui Sicanias detinet hortus apes;
Quod Cosmi redolent alabastra focique deorum,
   Quod modo divitibus lapsa corona comis:
Singula quid dicam? non sunt satis; omnia misce:
   Hoc fragrant pueri basia mane mei.
Scire cupis nomen? si propter basia, dicam.
   Iurasti: nimium scire, Sabine, cupis.

XI.13

Quisquis Flaminiam teris, viator,
Noli nobile praeterire marmor.
Urbis deliciae salesque Nili,
Ars et gratia, lusus et voluptas,
Romani decus et dolor theatri
Atque omnes Veneres Cupidinesque
Hoc sunt condita, quo Paris, sepulchro.

The breath of balm from foreign branches pressed;
The effluence that falling saffron brings;
The scent of apples ripening in a chest;
Or the rich foliage of a field in Spring;

Imperial silken robes from Palatine;
Or amber, warming in a virgin's hand;
The far-off smell of spilt Falernian wine;
A bee-loud garden in Sicilian land;

Odour, which spice and altar-incense send;
Or wreath of flowerets from a rich brow drawn;
Why speak of these? Words fail. Their perfect blend
Resemble my boy's kiss at early dawn.

You ask his name? Only to kiss him? Well!
You swear as much? Sabinus, I won't tell!

Anthony Reid

Traveller on the Flaminian Way,
Pause a little here, and stay
On this monument your eyes—
Here the actor, Paris, lies,
Delight of Rome, the wit of Nile,
All joy, all art, all grace, all style,
Of all the Roman theatre chief,
Its former joy and now its grief;
Nor for him only shed your tear—
Love and Desire lie with him here.

Olive Pitt-Kethley

XI.15

Sunt chartae mihi, quas Catonis uxor
Et quas horribiles legant Sabinae:
Hic totus volo rideat libellus
Et sit nequior omnibus libellis.
Qui vino madeat nec erubescat
Pingui sordidus esse Cosmiano,
Ludat cum pueris, amet puellas,
Nec per circuitus loquatur illam,
Ex qua nascimur, omnium parentem,
Quam sanctus Numa mentulam vocabat.
Versus hos tamen esse tu memento
Saturnalicios, Apollinaris:
Mores non habet hic meos libellus.

XI.16

Qui gravis es nimium, potes hinc iam, lector, abire
    Quo libet: urbanae scripsimus ista togae;
Iam mea Lampsacio lascivit pagina versu
    Et Tartesiaca concrepat aera manu.
O quotiens rigida pulsabis pallia vena,
    Sis gravior Curio Fabricioque licet!
Tu quoque nequitias nostri lususque libelli
    Uda, puella, leges, sis Patavina licet.
Erubuit posuitque meum Lucretia librum,
    Sed coram Bruto; Brute, recede: leget.

I've written what Cato's wife, what
Sabine vigilantes can peruse.
This, my laughing book from first
To last, black sheep of all my books.
I'll have you brimming wine, dripping
Cosmos' greasy decoctations. No
Verbal detours when we mention
Whence we spring, the common Father
Sacred Numa christened "cock" . . .
Remember, these are Martial's
Saturnalians, Apollinaris,
His book no way reflects his morals.

Peter Whigham

Let every prudish reader use his feet
And bugger off—I write for the elite.
My verses gambol with Priapic verve
As dancing harlots' patter starts a nerve.
Though stern as Curius or like Fabricius,
Your prick will stiffen and grow vicious.
Girls while they drink—even the chastest folk—
Will read each naughty word and dirty joke.
Lucretia blushes, throws away my book.
Her husband goes. She takes another look.

Anthony Reid

XI.18

Donasti, Lupe, rus sub urbe nobis;
Sed rus est mihi maius in fenestra.
Rus hoc dicere, rus potes vocare?
In quo ruta facit nemus Dianae,
Argutae tegit ala quod cicadae,
Quod formica die comedit uno,
Clusae cui folium rosae corona est;
In quo non magis invenitur herba,
Quam Cosmi folium piperve crudum;
In quo nec cucumis iacere rectus,
Nec serpens habitare tota possit.
Urucam male pascit hortus unam,
Consumpto moritur culex salicto,
Et talpa est mihi fossor atque arator.
Non boletus hiare, non mariscae
Ridere aut violae patere possunt.
Finis mus populatur et colono
Tamquam sus Calydonius timetur,
Et sublata volantis ungue Procnes
In nido seges est hirundinino;
Et cum stet sine falce mentulaque,
Non est dimidio locus Priapo.
Vix implet cocleam peracta messis,
Et mustum nuce condimus picata.
Errasti, Lupe, littera sed una:
Nam quo tempore praedium dedisti,
Mallem tu mihi prandium dedisses.

Lupe's gift—a "produce" villa:
My window-box produces more.
A "farm," you say . . . Call that a farm?
For Dian's grove, a sprig of rue
The rack'ty cricket's wing encloses,
Fodder to feed one ant per day:
A furled rose-leaf its *baldacchino*.
No herbage more than Cosmus for
His scent-shop needs, or pepper needs.
Here cucumber and garden snake
Find difficulty in lying straight.
The caterpillar pastures ill,
Gnat eats willow and expires.
Who but a mole my gardener is?
The mushroom, violet and fig
Can neither thrust, dilate, nor grin.
A fieldmouse plunders my terrain—
The boar of Calydon strikes again!
Wing'd Procne with her talons wrests
My harvest for her swallow's nest.
Priapus, lacking hook & prick,
Lacks too by half his bailiwick.
A snail's shell amply holds our yield,
A nut our wine, with resin sealed.
One letter changed, and all were neat—
That rather than this country *seat*
You'ld given me enough to *eat*.

Peter Whigham

XI.20

Caesaris Augusti lascivos, livide, versus
  Sex lege, qui tristis verba latina legis:
Quod futuit Glaphyran Antonius, hanc mihi poenam
  Fulvia constituit, se quoque uti futuam.
Fulviam ego ut futuam? quid si me Manius oret
  Pedicem, faciam? non puto, si sapiam.
"Aut futue, aut pugnemus" ait. Quid, quod mihi vita
  Carior est ipsa mentula? Signa canant!
Absolvis lepidos nimirum, Auguste, libellos,
  Qui scis Romana simplicitate loqui.

These hot six lines, you blue nose, great Augustus wrote,
Whereas plain, simple Latin is choking in your throat:
Antony is fucking Glaphyra, so Fulvia* brings suit—
Now I have to fuck her, and for her I don't give a hoot.
What, I fuck Fulvia? Suppose that Manius begged for my
    tool,
Would I bugger him? No, never! I don't think I'm quite
    such a fool.
"Fuck or fight!" she demands, but always dearer than
    breath
To me is my prick. Ho, trumpets, let's fight to the death.
Spicy little books, Augustus, I swear you'd never correct,
For you too could handle your Latin, however blunt and
    direct.

                                            J. P. Sullivan

* Antony's wife. The epigram attributed to Augustus purports to be written
before the bloody Perusine war of 41 B.C.

XI.21

Lydia tam laxa est, equitis quam culus aheni,
    Quam celer arguto qui sonat aere trochus,
Quam rota transmisso totiens inpacta petauro,
    Quam vetus a crassa calceus udus aqua,
Quam quae rara vagos expectant retia turdos,
    Quam Pompeiano vela negata noto,
Quam quae de pthisico lapsa est armilla cinaedo,
    Culcita Leuconico quam viduata suo,
Quam veteres bracae Brittonis pauperis, et quam
    Turpe Ravennatis guttur onocrotali.
Hanc in piscina dicor futuisse marina.
    Nescio; piscinam me futuisse puto.

Lydia is as wide and slack
As a bronze horse's cul-de-sac,
Or sounding hoop with copper rings,
Or board from which an athlete springs,
Or swollen shoe from muddy puddle,
Or net of thrushes in a huddle,
Or awning that won't stay outspread,
In Pompey's theatre, overhead,
Or bracelet that, at every cough,
From a consumptive poof slips off,
French cushion, where the stuffing leaks,
Poor Breton's knackered, baggy breeks,
Foul pelican-crop, Ravenna-bred!
Now there's a rumour—he who said
I had her in the fish-pond joked;
It was the pond itself I poked.

Olive Pitt-Kethley

XI.22

Mollia quod nivei duro teris ore Galaesi
  Basia, quod nudo cum Ganymede iaces,
(Quis negat?) hoc nimium est. Sed sit satis; inguina saltem
  Parce fututrici sollicitare manu.
Levibus in pueris plus haec, quam mentula, peccat,
  Et faciunt digiti praecipitantque virum:
Inde tragus celeresque pili mirandaque matri
  Barba, nec in clara balnea luce placent.
Divisit natura marem: pars una puellis,
  Una viris genita est. Utere parte tua.

XI.26

O mihi grata quies, o blanda, Telesphore, cura,
  Qualis in amplexu non fuit ante meo:
Basia da nobis vetulo, puer, uda Falerno,
  Pocula da labris facta minora tuis.
Addideris super haec Veneris si gaudia vera,
  Esse negem melius cum Ganymede Iovi.

Your rough mouth rubs Galaesus' tender lips.
Another naked youngster shares your kips.
Well, fair enough—but that's enough. Don't stand
And milk a boy's soft tool with lustful hand.
That harms young kids more than a questing prick.
From masturbation they mature too quick,
Smell goatish, shock their mums with sudden beard
And pubic hair. Bathers will think it weird.
Boys' pricks were made for girls, their bums for men.
Nature decreed it. Stick to your own den.

Anthony Reid

Cure of my unquietness,
    object of my sighs,
Than whom within my arms
    none now dearer lies;
Yield kisses of Falernian,
    shared lip yield to lip,
That from the reeking goblet
    Venus forth shall slip,
Then not Jove, nor Ganymede
    shall, as we, enjoy
Themselves my sweetest cock-
    tail-shaking wine-cup boy.

Peter Whigham

XI.28

Invasit medici Nasica phreneticus Eucti
Et percidit Hylan. Hic, puto, sanus erat.

XI.31

Atreus Caecilius cucurbitarum
Sic illas quasi filios Thyestae
In partes lacerat secatque mille.
Gustu protinus has edes in ipso,
Has prima feret alterave cena,
Has cena tibi tertia reponet,
Hinc seras epidipnidas parabit.
Hinc pistor fatuas facit placentas,
Hinc et multiplices struit tabellas
Et notas caryotidas theatris,
Hinc exit varium coco minutal,
Ut lentem positam fabamque credas;
Boletos imitatur et botellos,
Et caudam cybii brevesque maenas.
Hinc cellarius experitur artes,
Ut condat vario vafer sapore
In rutae folium Capelliana.
Sic inplet gabatas paropsidesque
Et leves scutulas cavasque lances.
Hoc lautum vocat, hoc putat venustum,
Unum ponere ferculis tot assem.

Nasica raped the doctor's pretty lad;
But then, they say, the fellow's raving mad.
  Mad? I maintain
  He's very sane.

Brian Hill

Gourds get a raw deal with Caecilius,
Cut, sliced and diced in little pieces—thus
Atreus made his nephews into martyrs.
You dine with him—he'll give you gourds for starters,
Gourds for the first, likewise the second course,
Then comes the third, and they turn up in force.
Even for dessert you cannot well escape,
The gourds come in confectionery shape—
A baker's feeble effort—dates as well,
Like those small gilded ones the theatres sell;
Then strange concoctions from behind the scenes,
Fine imitation mincemeats, lentils, beans,
Tunny's tail, salt-fish, will appear to greet us,
Black-pudding and the edible boletus.
The storekeeper has tried experiments
With leaves of rue and various flavouring scents
And made Capellian sweetmeats. Choice and rare
All looks, displayed in stylish manner there
On tiny saucer or great shining plate—
A lovely feast, laid out in splendid state;
But to the host—a lovelier thought than any—
To lay all this on, he's laid out one penny.

Olive Pitt-Kethley

XI.39

Cunarum fueras motor, Charideme, mearum
  Et pueri custos adsiduusque comes.
Iam mihi nigrescunt tonsa sudaria barba
  Et queritur labris puncta puella meis;
Sed tibi non crevi: te noster vilicus horret,
  Te dispensator, te domus ipsa pavet.
Ludere nec nobis, nec tu permittis amare;
  Nil mihi vis et vis cuncta licere tibi.
Corripis, observas, quereris, suspiria ducis,
  Et vix a ferulis temperat ira tua.
Si Tyrios sumpsi cultus unxive capillos,
  Exclamas "Numquam fecerat ista pater";
Et numeras nostros adstricta fronte trientes,
  Tamquam de cella sit cadus ille tua.
Desine; non possum libertum ferre Catonem.
  Esse virum iam me dicet amica tibi.

XI.40

Formosam Glyceran amat Lupercus
Et solus tenet imperatque solus.
Quam toto sibi mense non fututam
Cum tristis quereretur et roganti
Causam reddere vellet Aeliano,
Respondit, Glycerae dolere dentes.

You rocked my cradle, Charidemus, once,
And played the guardian to the schoolboy dunce,
But now my barber's towel's black with beard;
By tender lips are my rough kisses feared.
But to you I've never grown up: just another one
Of the slaves in the fear-ridden household you run.
You allow me no license for women or for sport:
You do what you like—I must do what I ought.
You chide and you spy, you sigh and complain;
Your anger keeps eying that juvenile cane.
If I smell of perfume, or dress up for a show,
You protest that my father would never act so.
With twitching brow, you count the cups I pour,
As though each drop came from your private store.
No more of it, ex-slave! You carp—I'll rage!
My mistress will tell you—I've now come of age.

                                                    J. P. Sullivan

He loves her, pretty Glycera;
No-one else owns or orders her.
But gloomily complaining he's
Not fucked her for a month or more,
He finds his friends begin to tease
And ask him what it's like to wank;
So he decided to be frank,
And told them Glycera's teeth were sore.

                                        Alistair Elliot

XI.43

Deprensum in puero tetricis me vocibus, uxor,
   Corripis et culum te quoque habere refers.
Dixit idem quotiens lascivo Iuno Tonanti!
   Ille tamen grandi cum Ganymede iacet.
Incurvabat Hylan posito Tirynthius arcu:
   Tu Megaran credis non habuisse natis?
Torquebat Phoebum Daphne fugitiva: sed illas
   Oebalius flammas iussit abire puer.
Briseis multum quamvis aversa iaceret,
   Aeacidae propior levis amicus erat.
Parce tuis igitur dare mascula nomina rebus,
   Teque puta cunnos, uxor, habere duos.

XI.45

Intrasti quotiens inscriptae limina cellae,
   Seu puer arrisit sive puella tibi,
Contentus non es foribus veloque seraque,
   Secretumque iubes grandius esse tibi:
Oblinitur minimae si qua est suspicio rimae
   Punctaque lasciva quae terebrantur acu.
Nemo est tam teneri tam sollicitique pudoris,
   Qui vel pedicat, Canthare, vel futuit.

"Bumming a boy again!" comes my wife's yell,
Demanding "Don't I have a rump as well?"
How many times did Juno ask Jove that,
When he and Ganymede played acrobat!
Hercules, bow-less, buggered Hylas' rear
Though his wife had a bottom, never fear.
The flight of Daphne drove great Phoebus mad
Until he made it with a shepherd lad.
Achilles' wife bent for him like a crescent,
Yet he preferred a young male adolescent.
Don't think, my wife, your arse is male (or fine as).
To me what you have is just two vaginas.

Anthony Reid

Inside that little private brothel-room,
     Marked with the name of smiling girl or boy,
Doors, bolts and curtains all serve to entomb,
     But more precautions still you must employ
To plaster up the chinks and cunning tears
     Made by *voyeurs*, peering outside the gates. ⸍
What vices are you hiding? No one cares
     Who's watching while he merely copulates.

Anthony Reid

XI.46

Iam nisi per somnum non arrigis et tibi, Mevi,
    Incipit in medios meiere verpa pedes,
Truditur et digitis pannucea mentula lassis
    Nec levat extinctum sollicitata caput.
Quid miseros frustra cunnos culosque lacessis?
    Summa petas: illic mentula vivit anus.

XI.47

Omnia femineis quare dilecta catervis
    Balnea devitat Lattara? Ne futuat.
Cur nec Pompeia lentus spatiatur in umbra,
    Nec petit Inachidos limina? Ne futuat.
Cur Lacedaemonio luteum ceromate corpus
    Perfundit gelida Virgine? Ne futuat.
Cum sic feminei generis contagia vitet,
    Cur lingit cunnum Lattara? Ne futuat.

Mevius, your tool won't stand erect, nor beat,
Nor shoot his urine further than your feet.
Not even masturbation makes him stand; he
Lies unawakened, flaccid, never randy.
Engaging butts or sluts is useless strife—
Go further up, and seek the kiss of life.

Anthony Reid

Does Lattara shun the baths where crowds
    Of women go? It's true.
And why is he so particular?
    —He does not wish to screw.

He never goes to Pompey's Porch
    As many others do,
Or Isis' shrine, where whores hang out,
    —He does not wish to screw.

Why does he take those long cold baths
    Anointed with Spartan goo,
In the waters of the Virgin? Why?
    —He does not wish to screw.

If he's so scared of women
    (That contaminating crew)
Why is he fond of cunnilingus?
    —He does not wish to screw.

Dorothea Wender

XI.51

Tanta est quae Titio columna pendet,
Quantam Lampsaciae colunt puellae.
Hic nullo comitante nec molesto
Thermis grandibus et suis lavatur.
Anguste Titius tamen lavatur.

XI.56

Quod nimium mortem, Chaeremon Stoice, laudas,
   Vis animum mirer suspiciamque tuum?
Hanc tibi virtutem fracta facit urceus ansa,
   Et tristis nullo qui tepet igne focus,
Et teges et cimex et nudi sponda grabati,
   Et brevis atque eadem nocte dieque toga.
O quam magnus homo es qui faece rubentis aceti
   Et stipula et nigro pane carere potes!
Leuconicis agedum tumeat tibi culcita lanis
   Constringatque tuos purpura pexa toros,
Dormiat et tecum qui cum modo Caecuba miscet
   Convivas roseo torserat ore puer:
O quam tu cupies ter vivere Nestoris annos
   Et nihil ex ulla perdere luce voles!
Rebus in angustis facile est contemnere vitam:
   Fortiter ille facit qui miser esse potest.

From Titius extends a beam
as long as the one
the girls of Lampsacus adore:
the giant bath-house Titius reserves
for his "private" ablutions
is stuffed to capacity,
empty of all except Titius.

Eugene O'Connor

Your Stoic commendations of the grave
   rouse neither wonder nor esteem.
'Tis virtue caused by mere cracked crockery,
   by a cheerless, chilled, fireless hearth,
By flea-ridden mattressing, bare bedframe,
   one all-purpose, skimpy toga.
A rare asceticism to renounce
   lees of cheap red wine, straw, black bread!
What with a mattress of Leucanian wool?
   What with thick-napped sofa draperies?
A cup-boy for your couch, whose Caecuban, whose
   pink mouth, makes havoc with your guests?
You'ld settle then for three times Nestor's years,
   and not mislay one day of them.
Straitened means invite to scorn of living:
   fortitude meets penury head on.

Peter Whigham

XI.57

Miraris, docto quod carmina mitto Severo,
  Ad cenam cum te, docte Severe, vocem?
Iuppiter ambrosia satur est et nectare vivit;
  Nos tamen exta Iovi cruda merumque damus.
Omnia cum tibi sint dono concessa deorum,
  Si quod habes non vis, ergo quid accipies?

XI.58

Cum me velle vides tentumque, Telesphore, sentis,
  Magna rogas—puta me velle negare: licet?—
Et nisi iuratus dixi "dabo", subtrahis illas,
  Permittunt in me quae tibi multa, natis.
Quid si me tonsor, cum stricta novacula supra est,
  Tunc libertatem divitiasque roget?
Promittam; neque enim rogat illo tempore tonsor,
  Latro rogat; res est imperiosa timor:
Sed fuerit curva cum tuta novacula theca,
  Frangam tonsori crura manusque simul.
At tibi nil faciam, sed lota mentula lana
  Λαικάζειν cupidae dicet avaritiae.

Do you marvel I send to laureate Severus verse
When I bid you, laureate Severus, to dinner?

Jupiter's glutted with ambrosia, lives on nectar,
Yet we offer to Jove raw entrails, unmixed wine.

All has been yielded to you by gift of the gods:
Unless you wish for what you have, what will you have?

W. G. Shepherd

When I am randy, boy, and hot to use you
You ask the earth, and know I can't refuse you.
If I won't swear to pay, what's sure to come?
You'll bugger off with your beguiling bum.
Suppose my barber-slave, with blade at throat,
Demanded wealth and freedom? Antidote—
I'd promise smartly. When a robber's near
(For such that barber is) one's numbed by fear.
But crisis over, razor back in case,
I'd beat the bastard up at no small pace.
Nix doing, kid! I'll find another fucker,
And my limp tool will not require your succour.

Anthony Reid

XI.59

Senos Charinus omnibus digitis gerit,
   Nec nocte ponit anulos,
Nec cum lavatur. Causa quae sit, quaeritis?
   Dactyliothecam non habet.

XI.61

Lingua maritus, moechus ore Nanneius,
Summemmianis inquinatior buccis;
Quem cum fenestra vidit a Suburana
Obscena nudum Leda, fornicem cludit
Mediumque mavult basiare, quam summum;
Modo qui per omnes viscerum tubos ibat
Et voce certa consciaque dicebat,
Puer an puella matris esset in ventre:
—Gaudete cunni; vestra namque res acta est—
Arrigere linguam non potest fututricem,
Nam dum tumenti mersus haeret in volva
Et vagientes intus audit infantes,
Partem gulosam solvit indecens morbus.
Nec purus esse nunc potest nec inpurus.

On ev'ry finger he's six rocks;
  Those rings he'll keep
  In bath or sleep.
The reason for the paradox:
He can't afford a jewel-box.

Roy F. Butler

Oh husband that ne'er became father,
  Oh lover whose sweetheart's a maid,
Who would delve love's soft acreage rather
  With aught save its natural spade,
More foul than the cheeks of a harlot
  With the slime of stale kisses o'erhung,
Oh potent, yet impotent varlet,
  That's man but only in tongue,
At whose coming the vilest whores hasten
  To shut and to bar up their den,
From lips that care only to fasten
  On what's shameful of women and men:
E'en the o'erburdened womb's gaping threshold
  By him is lasciviously sipped,

XI.62

Lesbia se iurat gratis numquam esse fututam,
Verum est. Cum futui vult, numerare solet.

And he'll guess, as he sucks the soft flesh fold,
  If a boy or a girl's to be slipped.
Oh tongue that was meant for a penis,
  Oh head that was meant for a tail,
No more shall ye riot, and Venus
  No more at your riots grow pale,
To thighs ye shall be no more mated,
  No more shall soft cunnies be rung
With agonies not to be sated
  By merely a tongue!
For while this most lustful of mortals
  His slavering member had glued
To a vivified womb's hanging portals,
  This terrible vengeance ensued:
The gods the closed fountain releasing
  Of the woman, there rolled down a flood,
Ropy, and clotted, unceasing,
  Of menstrual blood,
And he rose amid gasping and choking,
  And from his mouth hung
No longer a potent and poking
  But paralysed tongue.

                        George Augustus Sala

Lesbia swears she's never been fucked for free.
True, for when she wants it, she pays the fee.

                        Fiona Pitt-Kethley

XI.63

Spectas nos, Philomuse, cum lavamur,
Et quare mihi tam mutuniati
Sint leves pueri, subinde quaeris.
Dicam simpliciter tibi roganti:
Pedicant, Philomuse, curiosos.

XI.69

Amphitheatrales inter nutrita magistros
    Venatrix, silvis aspera, blanda domi,
Lydia dicebar, domino fidissima Dextro,
    Qui non Erigones mallet habere canem,
Nec qui Dictaea Cephalum de gente secutus
    Luciferae pariter venit ad astra deae.
Non me longa dies nec inutilis abstulit aetas,
    Qualia Dulichio fata fuere cani:
Fulmineo spumantis apri sum dente perempta,
    Quantus erat, Calydon, aut, Erymanthe, tuus.
Nec queror infernas quamvis cito rapta sub umbras:
    Non potui fato nobiliore mori.

Why are my bath-friends all boys in their 'teens,
    Well-endowed, young?
So Nosey-Parkers can learn what it means
    To be well-hung.

Anthony Reid

Bred by the rulers of the amphitheatre,
A ruthless hunter in the woods was I,
Yet mild at home, my Dexter's well-loved creature,
Here I, his faithful mastiff, Lydia, lie.
For him those famous hounds I far out-classed,
Erigone's own, or that of Dicte's race
Who followed Cephalus, and with him passed
Into the skies, by great Aurora's grace.
I was not doomed to die in sad old age,
Like faithful Argus, but was called at once,
Slain by the lightning tusk and foaming rage
Of a great boar, as huge as Calydon's,
Or Erymanthus, thine. So who'd waste breath
And mourn so swift an end, so rich a death!

Olive Pitt-Kethley

XI.70

Vendere, Tucca, potes centenis milibus emptos?
　Plorantis dominos vendere, Tucca, potes?
Nec te blanditiae, nec verba rudesve querellae,
　Nec te dente tuo saucia colla movent?
A facinus! tunica patet inguen utrimque levata,
　Inspiciturque tua mentula facta manu.
Si te delectat numerata pecunia, vende
　Argentum, mensas, murrina, rura, domum;
Vende senes servos, ignoscent, vende paternos:
　Ne pueros vendas, omnia vende, miser.
Luxuria est emere hos—quis enim dubitatve negatve?—,
　Sed multo maior vendere luxuria est.

XI.72

Drauci Natta sui vocat pipinnam,
Collatus cui Gallus est Priapus.

What, Tucca, sell the boys you bought for sex?
    Look at their tear-stained faces. Can you sell
When they caress you, pleading; both their necks
    Showing the teeth-marks of your love-bites? Well,
Lift their short tunics; see each penis bare,
    So often stroked and fondled by your hand.
If cash you *must* have—then sell silver-ware,
    Sell *aged* slaves, cups, porcelain, house or land;
Rather than part with these, sell anything.
    Buying the boys was madness, truth to tell—
No one can doubt it, and you've had your fling—
    But it's a greater madness still to sell.

                                    Anthony Reid

Natta calls "small" (beneath his lover's tunic)
A prick that makes Priapus seem a eunuch.

                                    Anthony Reid

XI.73

Venturum iuras semper mihi, Lygde, roganti
  Constituisque horam constituisque locum.
Cum frustra iacui longa prurigine tentus,
  Succurrit pro te saepe sinistra mihi.
Quid precer, o fallax, meritis et moribus istis?
  Umbellam luscae, Lygde, feras dominae.

XI.75

Theca tectus ahenea lavatur
Tecum, Caelia, servus; ut quid, oro,
Non sit cum citharoedus aut choraules?
Non vis, ut puto, mentulam videre.
Quare cum populo lavaris ergo?
Omnes an tibi nos sumus spadones?
Ergo, ne videaris invidere,
Servo, Caelia, fibulam remitte.

Whenever I say, "Please come," you always swear
You will, and you yourself fix when and where.
I'm there all right, but usually, after I've lain
Interminably frustrated, stiff with strain,
My left hand helps me out—sad substitute.
Lygdus, what curse can I devise to suit
A stander-up like you? May you be made
To carry a one-eyed harridan's sunshade!

James Michie

Your slave attends you at the baths
    Brass-ringed beneath his trunks. Pray why?
He's not a musician. Or would
    His genitals displayed cause pain?
Then why frequent the public baths?
    Or are we eunuchs in your sight?
Caelia, lest possessive you appear,
    Remove the trunks; unhook the ring.

Peter Whigham

XI.77

In omnibus Vacerra quod conclavibus
Consumit horas et die toto sedet,
Cenaturit Vacerra, non cacaturit.

XI.78

Utere femineis conplexibus, utere, Victor,
    Ignotumque sibi mentula discat opus.
Flammea texuntur sponsae, iam virgo paratur,
    Tondebit pueros iam nova nupta tuos.
Pedicare semel cupido dabit illa marito,
    Dum metuit teli vulnera prima novi:
Saepius hoc fieri nutrix materque vetabunt
    Et dicent "Uxor, non puer, ista tibi est."
Heu quantos aestus, quantos patiere labores,
    Si fuerit cunnus res peregrina tibi!
Ergo Suburanae tironem trade magistrae.
    Illa virum faciet; non bene virgo docet.

XI.85

Sidere percussa est subito tibi, Zoile, lingua,
    Dum lingis. Certe, Zoile, nunc futues.

For hours, for a whole day, he'll sit
On every public lavatory seat.
It's not because he needs a shit:
He wants to be asked out to eat.

James Michie

You must try embracing women, Victor; you must.
    Make your prick learn this unfamiliar lust.
The bridal veil's being woven, the girl prepared;
    Soon the new wife will make your boys short-haired.
She'll let the keen groom bugger her, just once,
    While she still fears the primal wound: her cunt's.
But nurse and mother will say you can't enjoy
    This oftener: "She's your wife, and not a boy."
Oh dear, what sweats and pains you're going to suffer
    If cunt's a stranger when you have to stuff her.
Get a Suburran tool-mistress for a spell—
    She'll prime your dunce. But virgins don't teach well.

Alistair Elliot

Paralysis engaged the tongue
    of Zoilus. I grieve to say,
as he was tasting beauty's bung.
    Now he must try the triter way.

Dudley Fitts

XI.87

Dives eras quondam: sed tunc pedico fuisti,
    Et tibi nulla diu femina nota fuit.
Nunc sectaris anus. O quantum cogit egestas!
    Illa fututorem te, Charideme, facit.

XI.89

Intactas quare mittis mihi, Polla, coronas?
    A te vexatas malo tenere rosas.

XI.91

Aeolidos Canace iacet hoc tumulata sepulchro,
    Ultima cui parvae septima venit hiems.
A scelus, a facinus! properas qui flere, viator,
    Non licet hic vitae de brevitate queri:
Tristius est leto leti genus: horrida vultus
    Abstulit et tenero sedit in ore lues,
Ipsaque crudeles ederunt oscula morbi,
    Nec data sunt nigris tota labella rogis.
Si tam praecipiti fuerant ventura volatu,
    Debuerant alia fata venire via.
Sed mors vocis iter properavit cludere blandae,
    Ne posset duras flectere lingua deas.

Once you were rich, and a gay life you led;
You took boys, never women, into your bed.
Now you're chasing old ladies, down on your luck,
So poverty finally forced you to fuck.

J. P. Sullivan

Dearest, send no fresh flowers! I love best
The roses that have died upon your breast.

Hubert Dynes Ellis

Buried in this tomb, Canace, Breath of Wind:
    her seventh year brought her here.
With ready tears you grieve, "What waste!"
    Grieve not for brevity of life:
Harsher than death, death's shape. Foul
    cancer ate her face, her tender mouth.
The blight consumed her kisses. Her lips
    half-gone before cremation. Death
Thus precipitately falling
    needs kinder course. Hurriedly it
Sealed her tongue's means of blandishment
    lest th' unbending Fates, at her breath, bend.

Peter Whigham

XI.93

Pierios vatis Theodori flamma penates
   Abstulit. Hoc Musis et tibi, Phoebe, placet?
O scelus, o magnum facinus crimenque deorum,
   Non arsit pariter quod domus et dominus!

XI.96

Marcia, non Rhenus, salit hic, Germane: quid obstas
   Et puerum prohibes divitis imbre lacus?
Barbare, non debet, submoto cive, ministro
   Captivam victrix unda levare sitim.

XI.97

Una nocte quater possum: sed quattuor annis
   Si possum, peream, te Telesilla semel.

Flames have gutted th' abode Pierian
  Of the wide-renowned poet Theodorus.
Didst thou permit this sacrilege, Apollo?
  Where were ye, Muses' Chorus?

Ay me, I fondly sigh, that was a crime,
  A wicked deed, a miserable disaster.
Ye gods are much to blame: ye burnt the house
  But failed to singe its master!

Dorothea Wender

German, this is our aqueduct
And not the Rhine. Barbarian clot,
How dare you elbow and obstruct
A thirsty boy from drinking? What!
Jostle a Roman from his place!
This is the conqueror's fountain, not
A trough for your defeated race.

James Michie

In one night I'm good for four,
Sometimes less and sometimes more,
But I'll be damned if I could screw
Once in four years, babe, with you.

D. Jon Grossman

XI.99

De cathedra quotiens surgis—iam saepe notavi—
  Pedicant miserae, Lesbia, te tunicae.
Quas cum conata es dextra, conata sinistra
  Vellere, cum lacrimis eximis et gemitu:
Sic constringuntur gemina Symplegade culi
  Et nimias intrant cyaneasque natis.
Emendare cupis vitium deforme? docebo:
  Lesbia, nec surgas censeo, nec sedeas.

XI.100

Habere amicam nolo, Flacce, subtilem,
Cuius lacertos anuli mei cingant,
Quae clune nudo radat et genu pungat,
Cui serra lumbis, cuspis eminet culo.
Sed idem amicam nolo mille librarum.
Carnarius sum, pinguiarius non sum.

XI.103

Tanta tibi est animi probitas orisque, Safroni,
  Ut mirer fieri te potuisse patrem.

Yours is a classic dilemma, Lesbia;
whenever you get up from your chair
your clothes treat you most indecently.
Tugging and talking, with right hand and left
you try to free the yards of cloth swept
up your fundament. Tears and groans
are raised to Heaven as the imperilled
threads are pulled to safety from
those deadly straits: the huge Symplegades
of your buttocks grip all that pass.
What should you do to avoid such
terrible embarrassment? Ask Uncle Val—
don't get up, girl, and don't sit down!

Peter Porter

Flaccus, I hate a scrawny girl
Who jabs you with a spearlike tail,
Knees like knives, skin and bone,
I'd sooner screw a skeleton.
No blubber either—tasty quail,
Mouth-watering filet, not whale.

Richard O'Connell

Safronius, you look so meek and mild
I can't imagine how you got your child.

James Michie

BOOK XII

XII. PREFACE

VALERIUS MARTIALIS PRISCO SUO S.

Scio me patrocinium debere contumacissimae trienni desidiae; quo absolvenda non esset inter illas quoque urbicas occupationes, quibus facilius consequimur, ut molesti potius, quam ut officiosi esse videamur; nedum in hac provinciali solitudine, ubi nisi etiam intemperanter studemus, et sine solacio et sine excusatione secessimus. Accipe ergo rationem. In qua hoc maximum et primum est, quod civitatis aures, quibus adsueveram, quaero et videor mihi in alieno foro litigare; si quid est enim, quod in libellis meis placeat, dictavit auditor: illam iudiciorum subtilitatem, illud materiarum ingenium, bibliothecas, theatra, convictus, in quibus studere se voluptates non sentiunt, ad summam omnium illa, quae delicati reliquimus, desideramus quasi destituti. Accedit his municipalium robigo dentium et iudici loco livor, et unus aut alter mali, in pusillo loco multi; adversus quod difficile est habere cotidie bonum stomachum: ne mireris igitur abiecta ab indignante quae a gestiente fieri solebant. Ne quid tamen et advenienti tibi ab urbe et exigenti negarem—cui non refero gratiam, si tantum ea praesto quae possum—imperavi mihi, quod indulgere consueram, et studui paucissimis diebus, ut familiarissimas mihi aures tuas exciperem adventoria sua. Tu velim ista, quae tantum apud te non periclitantur, diligenter aestimare et excutere non graveris; et, quod tibi difficillimum est, de nugis nostris iudices nitore seposito, ne Romam, si ita decreveris, non Hispaniensem librum mittamus, sed Hispanum.

VALERIUS MARTIALIS SENDS GREETINGS TO HIS FRIEND PRISCUS.

I realize I ought to offer an apology for my extremely wilful idleness over the last three years. Such idleness is not to be pardoned even amidst the demands on my time in Rome, when I manage more easily to be a nuisance rather than effective, and least of all in the seclusion of the provinces. Unless I follow intellectual pursuits even to excess, I have retired here without gratification or excuse. Understand my reasoning then. The first and most important point is this: I miss the public acceptance to which I had grown accustomed and I feel I am pleading a case in a strange court. Whatever was well received in my volumes, my audience dictated: that refinement of critical judgement, the inspiration of the material, the libraries, the theatres, the parties, where one's play unconsciously becomes work. In short, all those things which I so squeamishly abandoned I regret as though I had been robbed of them. In addition, there are the green fangs of my fellow townsmen and the envy that replaces judicious criticism. One or two people are malevolent, who are a lot in a tiny place. All this is difficult to stomach day in and day out. So you should not be surprised that what used to be done with enthusiasm has been rejected in indignation. However, since you're coming from Rome and are pressing me, I want to avoid disappointing you. And I'm not showing you my gratitude, if I produce only what I can. So I have ordered myself to do what I used to do for my own self-satisfaction, and I have worked at my desk on a very occasional day or so to greet your friendly ears with a special poem of welcome. It would please me if you, in whose hands alone they are in no danger, would be so kind as to carefully evaluate and scrutinize the writings, and pass judgment, very difficult though it is for you, on my trivial efforts, all the glamour aside, so that I won't be sending to Rome, if that is your decision, a volume not so much written in Spain as written in Spanish.

J. P. Sullivan

XII.I

Retia dum cessant latratoresque Molossi
    Et non invento silva quiescit apro,
Otia, Prisce, brevi poteris donare libello.
    Hora nec aestiva est nec tibi tota perit.

XII.2

Ad populos mitti qui nuper ab Urbe solebas,
    Ibis, io, Romam nunc peregrine liber
Auriferi de gente Tagi tetricique Salonis,
    Dat patrios amnes quos mihi terra potens.
Non tamen hospes eris, nec iam potes advena dici,
    Cuius habet fratres tot domus alta Remi.
Iure tuo veneranda novi pete limina templi,
    Reddita Pierio sunt ubi tecta choro.
Vel si malueris, prima gradiere Subura;
    Atria sunt illic consulis alta mei:
Laurigeros habitat facundus Stella penatis,
    Clarus Hyanteae Stella sititor aquae;
Fons ibi Castalius vitreo torrente superbit,
    Unde novem dominas saepe bibisse ferunt:
Ille dabit populo patribusque equitique legendum,
    Nec nimium siccis perleget ipse genis.
Quid titulum poscis? versus duo tresve legantur,
    Clamabunt omnes te, liber, esse meum.

Priscus take it easy,
put your feet up, relax.
Now woods are quiet
dogs rest enjoy the lull
read my book, stretch
as nets dry, idle.

W. S. Milne

Always you've been sent abroad from Rome, now
    booklet, from foreign parts you go to Rome
From folk by dour Salo, gold-yielding Tagus,
    this forceful landscape's patrimonial streams.
Foreign? Not you. Not even a stranger,
    who claims so many kinsfolk in tall Rome.
Head, as by right, for Augustus' Temple porch:
    The Pierian sanctuary has been rebuilt;
Alternatively, where Subura starts,
    where Stella's mansion stands—eloquent
Stella, your roof crowned with laurels, brilliant
    Stella, thirsting for the spring "Ianthe,"
Lucid Castalian fount superbly welling
    where gossip holds Nine ladies often drink.
He'll press you on patrician, pleb, knight,
    less than dry-eyed while he scans the scroll.
Who talks of titles? Two lines, three, they'll read
    and shout in unison, O book, you're mine!

Peter Whigham

XII.9

Palma regit nostros, mitissime Caesar, Hiberos,
   Et placido fruitur pax peregrina iugo.
Ergo agimus laeti tanto pro munere grates:
   Misisti mores in loca nostra tuos.

Kind Caesar, Palma rules my native Spain;
A willing captive, she has peace again.
With thanks we recognize your gracious hand
And greet your virtues in our native land.

A. L. Francis and H. F. Tatum

XII.18

Dum tu forsitan inquietus erras
Clamosa, Iuvenalis, in Subura,
Aut collem dominae teris Dianae;
Dum per limina te potentiorum
Sudatrix toga ventilat vagumque
Maior Caelius et minor fatigant:
Me multos repetita post Decembres
Accepit mea rusticumque fecit
Auro Bilbilis et superba ferro.
Hic pigri colimus labore dulci
Boterdum Plateamque—Celtiberis
Haec sunt nomina crassiora terris—:
Ingenti fruor inproboque somno,
Quem nec tertia saepe rumpit hora,
Et totum mihi nunc repono quidquid
Ter denos vigilaveram per annos.
Ignota est toga, sed datur petenti
Rūpta proxima vestis a cathedra.
Surgentem focus excipit superba
Vicini strue cultus iliceti,
Multa vilica quem coronat olla.
Venator sequitur, sed ille quem tu
Secreta cupias habere silva;
Dispensat pueris rogatque longos
Levis ponere vilicus capillos.
Sic me vivere, sic iuvat perire.

While unquiet, *Juvenal*, you haunt
The shrill *Subura*, or loiter
On *Dian's Aventine* . . . while your
Damp toga flaps round great men's doors . . .
While you grow worn with mounting now
The big, the little *Caelian*—I
These winters late, revisiting my
Bilbilis (replete with gold & iron)
Have been accepted . . . countryfied.
Here lazily are trips (sweet chores)
To *Plataea, Boterdus.* (Ah,
These *Celtiberian* vocables!)
. . . Indulging in inordinate
Amounts of sleep—past nine or ten.
That's paying myself back, in full,
For thirty years of lack of it.
Togas are unheard of . . . a quilt
From some disused sedan will serve.
Rising, I've a log fire greet me,
Fed handsomely from neighboring oak.
My maid drapes it with cooking pots.
The hunting boy comes in—he's one
Some bosky dell would set you lusting.
My steward gives the houseboys food,
Pleads: May he wear his long locks shorter?
These my aids to living, aids to death.

Peter Whigham

XII.20

Quare non habeat, Fabulle, quaeris
Uxorem Themison? habet sororem.

XII.21

Municipem rigidi quis te, Marcella, Salonis
  Et genitam nostris quis putet esse locis?
Tam rarum, tam dulce sapis. Palatia dicent,
  Audierint si te vel semel, esse suam;
Nulla nec in media certabit nata Subura
  Nec Capitolini collis alumna tibi;
Nec cito ridebit peregrini gloria partus,
  Romanam deceat quam magis esse nurum.
Tu desiderium dominae mihi mitius urbis
  Esse iubes: Romam tu mihi sola facis.

XII.23

Dentibus atque comis—nec te pudet—uteris emptis.
  Quid facies oculo, Laelia? non emitur.

Fabullus, do you want to know why Mr.
Themison has no wife? He has his sister.

Jim Powell

Who'ld guess Salo's rigors yours, Marcella,
    who'ld guess one place produced us both?
Your sophistication's too rare, too delicate.
    If the Palatine could hear you, it would claim you.
As thought from mid-Subura, or near
    the Capitoline: none there to match you.
No foreign beauty can take lightly, mock
    one better fitted as a Roman bride.
"Drop that nostalgia for Rome!" you often
    bid. Marcella, you are all the Rome I need.

Peter Whigham

You're not ashamed to use the teeth and hair you buy.
What'll you do, Laelia? One can't buy an eye.

Fiona Pitt-Kethley

XII.28

Hermogenes tantus mapparum, Pontice, fur est
    Quantus nummorum vix, puto, Massa fuit;
Tu licet observes dextram teneasque sinistram,
    Inveniet mappam qua ratione trahat:
Cervinus gelidum sorbet sic halitus anguem,
    Casuras alte sic rapit Iris aquas.
Nuper cum Myrino peteretur missio laeso,
    Subduxit mappas quattuor Hermogenes;
Cretatam praetor cum vellet mittere mappam,
    Praetori mappam surpuit Hermogenes.
Attulerat mappam nemo, dum furta timentur:
    Mantele a mensa surpuit Hermogenes.
Hoc quoque si deerit, medios discingere lectos
    Mensarumque pedes non timet Hermogenes.
Quamvis non modico caleant spectacula sole,
    Vela reducuntur, cum venit Hermogenes.
Festinant trepidi substringere carbasa nautae,
    Ad portum quotiens paruit Hermogenes.
Linigeri fugiunt calvi sistrataque turba,
    Inter adorantes cum stetit Hermogenes.
Ad cenam Hermogenes mappam non attulit unquam,
    A cena semper rettulit Hermogenes.

Massa stole money, but Hermogenes
Loved napkins and used tactics such as these:
Watch his right hand, Ponticus, hold his left—
Still of your napkin you would be bereft.
As the stag's breath draws out the clammy snake,
Or Iris, from rain about to fall will make
A sudden rainbow, such his artistry!
When wounded Myrinus asked for quarter, he
Stole some four napkins waved by the spectators,
And one used as a starting-flag—the praetor's.
Guests left their stuff at home for fear of theft
And found not even the tablecloth was left.
He'd even try, as far as he was able,
To unwind trimming from the couch or table.
When the arena sweltered in the sun,
Men dared not leave the awning, but would run
To save it when Hermogenes appeared.
He'd go down to the docks—the sailors feared
To see him there; they'd furl up every sail.
Bareheaded priests of Isis, too, would quail,
Their timbrels faltering, seeing their robes in danger.
For there, among the faithful, was—a stranger!
He never took a napkin out to dine;
The Son-of-Hermes brought home yours or mine.

                                        Olive Pitt-Kethley

XII.31

Hoc nemus, hi fontes, haec textilis umbra supini
    Palmitis, hoc riguae ductile flumen aquae,
Prataque nec bifero cessura rosaria Paesto,
    Quodque viret Iani mense nec alget holus,
Quaeque natat clusis anguilla domestica lymphis,
    Quaeque gerit similes candida turris aves,
Munera sunt dominae: post septima lustra reverso
    Has Marcella domos parvaque regna dedit.
Si mihi Nausicaa patrios concederet hortos,
    Alcinoo possem dicere "Malo meos."

This glade, these spring-waters, this laced shade
  of roving vine, irrigant winding stream,
Rose-beds fine as Paestum's, flow'ring twice,
  winter greens that sprout in winter's frosts,
Pet eels squiggling in th' aquarium,
  dovecote white as white doves it harbors—
Gifts of Marcella: I, back (long gone), these
  small domestic sovereignties receive.
Should Nausicaa her father's gardens proffer,
  "Alcinous, thanks," I'ld say, "I like mine best."

Peter Whigham

XII.32

O Iuliarum dedecus Kalendarum,
Vidi, Vacerra, sarcinas tuas, vidi;
Quas non retentas pensione pro bima
Portabat uxor rufa crinibus septem
Et cum sorore cana mater ingenti.
Furias putavi nocte Ditis emersas.
Has tu priores frigore et fame siccus
Et non recenti pallidus magis buxo
Irus tuorum temporum sequebaris.
Migrare clivom crederes Aricinum.
Ibat tripes grabatus et bipes mensa,
Et cum lucerna corneoque cratere
Matella curto rupta latere meiebat;
Foco virenti suberat amphorae cervix;
Fuisse gerres aut inutiles maenas
Odor inpudicus urcei fatebatur,
Qualis marinae vix sit aura piscinae.
Nec quadra deerat casei Tolosatis,
Quadrima nigri nec corona pulei
Calvaeque restes alioque cepisque,
Nec plena turpi matris olla resina,
Summemmianae qua pilantur uxores.
Quid quaeris aedes vilicosque derides,
Habitare gratis, o Vacerra, cum possis?
Haec sarcinarum pompa convenit ponti.

You blot upon a Summer's Quarter-Day,
Vacerra, you and yours are now away,
With two years rent unpaid, at last ejected,
Taking the traps the landlord, even, rejected.
First came your wife, with her seven reddish curls
—She did the carrying—then the other girls,
Your white-haired mother, and, last, to assist her,
The hulking creature that you call your sister.
I thought them Furies, risen from Down Below!
They forged ahead, you followed after, slow,
Cold, hungry, shrivelled, of faded boxwood-grain,
—The beggar, Irus, come to life again!
Aricia's hill, where beggars daily stand,
One would have thought was moving from the land!
A three-legg'd bed was first to greet the morn,
Then an oil-lamp, a mixing-bowl of horn,
Beside a table, with two legs gone missing;
A cracked old chamber-pot, that came out pissing;
Under a brazier, green with verdigris,
A wry-necked flagon lay dejectedly;
Then there were pilchards, salt-fish too, I think,
A jug betrayed them by the filthy stink,
A powerful smell that even reeked beyond
The brackish water in a fishy pond.
What else? Cheese from Toulouse its presence told,

XII.33

Ut pueros emeret Labienus vendidit hortos.
  Nil nisi ficetum nunc Labienus habet.

A blackened wreath of flea-bane, four years old,
And onion-ropes—but only ropes were left—
And garlic-strings—of garlic all bereft;
A pot of resin, from your mother's lair,
That Jezebels use to strip themselves of hair.
But say, why seek new lodgings for your crew
To taunt the rent-collectors yet anew,
When you could lodge yourself and baggage free
Upon the Bridge—with all your company?

                              Olive Pitt-Kethley

Labienus sold an orchard
to buy some slave boys:
he traded fruit trees
for real live fruits.

        Donald Goertz

XII.34

Triginta mihi quattuorque messes
Tecum, si memini, fuere, Iuli.
Quarum dulcia mixta sunt amaris,
Sed iucunda tamen fuere plura;
Et si calculus omnis huc et illuc
Diversus bicolorque digeratur,
Vincet candida turba nigriorem.
Si vitare velis acerba quaedam
Et tristis animi cavere morsus,
Nulli te facias nimis sodalem:
Gaudebis minus et minus dolebis.

XII.41

Non est, Tucca, satis, quod es gulosus:
Et dici cupis et cupis videri.

Just half our three-score years & ten
I mind me, *Julius*, spent with thee,
The bitter & the blessed blent—
The bless'd preponderant.
                              Count here,
There, the parti-colored pebbles:
White beats the black!
                              If sorrow's ruth
Thou 'ldst void, her heart-bite parry,
Caution in comradeship be thine:
Less sorrow, as less joy, thou 'llt know.

                                    Peter Whigham

To *be* a glutton's not enough, Tucca! Oh no,
You want to be said to be, seen to be so.

                                    J. P. Sullivan

XII.42

Barbatus rigido nupsit Callistratus Afro,
    Hac qua lege viro nubere virgo solet.
Praeluxere faces, velarunt flammea vultus,
    Nec tua defuerunt verba, Talasse, tibi.
Dos etiam dicta est. Nondum tibi, Roma, videtur
    Hoc satis? expectas numquid ut et pariat?

XII.43

Facundos mihi de libidinosis
Legisti nimium, Sabelle, versus,
Quales nec Didymi sciunt puellae
Nec molles Elephantidos libelli.
Sunt illic Veneris novae figurae,
Quales perditus audeat fututor,
Praestent et taceant quid exoleti,
Quo symplegmate quinque copulentur,
Qua plures teneantur a catena,
Extinctam liceat quid ad lucernam.
Tanti non erat, esse te disertum.

Callistratus wed Afer yesterday.
Man married man in just the selfsame way
A virgin takes a spouse. The bride's bent head
Was veiled and all the wedding service read;
Even the settlements were quite *de rigueur.*
What more d'you want? Do you expect his figure
To swell till, after nine or ten months' gap,
A pledge of his affection's in his lap?

Brian Hill

Fluent the salacious verses
Read by you to me, Sabellus.
Didymus' girls know less; less
Permissive Elephantis' verse.
Such forms of Venery are here
Only the dedicated lecher
Tries—performs and speaks not of:
The copulatory daisy-chain,
Five love-locked in links together.
Matter for the lamp turned down,
Matter that demeans your manner.

Peter Whigham

XII.47

Vendunt carmina Gallus et Lupercus.
Sanos, Classice, nunc nega poetas.

XII.56

Aegrotas uno decies aut saepius anno,
    Nec tibi, sed nobis hoc, Polycharme, nocet:
Nam quotiens surgis, soteria poscis amicos.
    Sit pudor: aegrota iam, Polycharme, semel.

Lupercus and Gallus sell verse of their own:
That poets are sane is conclusively shown.

Paul Nixon

Every month, my Polycharmus,
With some ailment you alarm us,
Whose event is sure to harm us
  Though yourself no ill befall.
For each monthly convalescing
In return for such a blessing
Brings you gifts, our joy expressing.
  Can't you sicken once for all?

A. L. Francis and H. F. Tatum

XII.57

Cur saepe sicci parva rura Nomenti
Laremque villae sordidum petam, quaeris?
Nec cogitandi, Sparse, nec quiescendi
In urbe locus est pauperi. Negant vitam
Ludi magistri mane, nocte pistores,
Aerariorum marculi die toto;
Hinc otiosus sordidam quatit mensam
Neroniana nummularius massa,
Illinc balucis malleator Hispanae
Tritum nitenti fuste verberat saxum;
Nec turba cessat entheata Bellonae,
Nec fasciato naufragus loquax trunco,
A matre doctus nec rogare Iudaeus,
Nec sulphuratae lippus institor mercis.
Numerare pigri damna quis potest somni?
Dicet quot aera verberent manus urbis,
Cum secta Colcho Luna vapulat rhombo.
Tu, Sparse, nescis ista, nec potes scire,
Petilianis delicatus in regnis,
Cui plana summos despicit domus montis,
Et rus in urbe est vinitorque Romanus
Nec in Falerno colle maior autumnus,
Intraque limen latus essedo cursus,
Et in profundo somnus, et quies nullis
Offensa linguis, nec dies nisi admissus.
Nos transeuntis risus excitat turbae,
Et ad cubilest Roma. Taedio fessis
Dormire quotiens libuit, imus ad villam.

Is there a question my small house
I seek—its comf'table disorder—
Your parched acres, *Nomentum*?
If poor in *Rome*, small likelihood
Of studious hours in quiet spent.
Ushers at dawn, bakers at night,
Noontide hamm'ring of copper-smiths.
The bankers at their greasy count-
ers negligently sift *Nero's* bits.
Spanish gold-diggers with polished
Pestle pound the smoothened mortar.
Ceaseless uproar of the soldiery . . .
Garrulous salts with false peg-legs . . .
Yiddish kids Mamma set begging . . .
Blank-eyed vendors of match-boxes. . . .
The hours reposeful rest shall lose
Mate the multitude of pots &
Pans clanged by the citizenry
When the *Colchian* rhombus clamors
To the moon's eclipse.
                              You, *Sparsus*,
Can never know what such things mean
From your so elegant estate,
Where the first floor tops the hill-tops,
Where (*rus in urbe*) you've a *Roman*
As curator of your vines (fine
As *Falernian* vineyards yield),
Where th' entrance widens for your coach,

XII.61

Versus et breve vividumque carmen
In te ne faciam, times, Ligurra,
Et dignus cupis hoc metu videri.
Sed frustra metuis cupisque frustra.
In tauros Libyci ruunt leones,
Non sunt papilionibus molesti.
Quaeras, censeo, si legi laboras,
Nigri fornicis ebrium poetam,
Qui carbone rudi putrique creta
Scribit carmina, quae legunt cacantes.
Frons haec stigmate non meo notanda est.

Where realms of sleep, tranquility,
Are not by tongues nor daylight torn
Unless admitted.
                        I, *Martial,*
Have street laughter as my alarum.
Rome is at my pillow. When worn
Down, feel like catching up on sleep,
I've one place left to go—
                        Nomentum.

                        Peter Whigham

Ligurra's fearful I'll contrive
Some pungent piece, some sprightly ditty
And longs to be considered worth it.
Longings baseless! Baseless fears!
The Libyan lion paws the Libyan bull
But does not bat the butterfly.
What people write of you'll find
In dismal dives where sodden poets
Scrawl their rhymes on toilet walls.
Your forehead shan't disgrace my brand.

                        Peter Whigham

XII.63

Uncto Corduba laetior Venafro,
Histra nec minus absoluta testa,
Albi quae superas oves Galaesi
Nullo murice nec cruore mendax,
Sed tinctis gregibus colore vivo:
Dic vestro, rogo, sit pudor poetae,
Nec gratis recitet meos libellos.
Ferrem, si faceret bonus poeta,
Cui possem dare mutuos dolores.
Corrumpit sine talione caelebs,
Caecus perdere non potest quod aufert:
Nil est deterius latrone nudo:
Nil securius est malo poeta.

XII.73

Heredem tibi me, Catulle, dicis.
Non credam, nisi legero, Catulle.

Cordoba! Luxuriating more in
Oils than Istria, Venafrum, in
Flocks fairer than Galaesian whites,
Not by counterfeit of conch or blood
But by their Guadalquivir dyed,
Pump, pray, with shame your poetaster,
Bid him not recite my verses
Free. I'ld bear it, had he merit—
Could soon inflict the like on him.
Th' unwed adult'rer goes unscored;
Unscored the eyeless one that blinds.
What further fear has a naked thief?
Who safer than a bogus poet?

Peter Whigham

You tell me that you're leaving—
Me everything in your will.
Since seeing is believing,
I can't be sure until . . .

James Michie

XII.77

Multis dum precibus Iovem salutat
Stans summos resupinus usque in ungues
Aethon in Capitolio pepedit.
Riserunt homines, sed ipse divom
Offensus genitor trinoctiali
Adfecit domicenio clientem.
Post hoc flagitium misellus Aethon,
Cum vult in Capitolium venire,
Sellas ante petit Paterclianas
Et pedit deciesque viciesque,
Sed quamvis sibi caverit crepando,
Compressis natibus Iovem salutat.

XII.80

Ne laudet dignos, laudat Callistratus omnes.
    Cui malus est nemo, quis bonus esse potest?

XII.81

Brumae diebus feriisque Saturni
Mittebat Umber aliculam mihi pauper;
Nunc mittit alicam: factus est enim dives.

Mr. Bishop was devoutly religious, but once
Standing up and almost on tiptoe
He farted loudly in St. Paul's Cathedral.
The congregation lost some of its gravity.
But receiving no invitations
To dinner for weeks,
Mr. Bishop took it that God was offended.
Now before attending Sunday services,
Mr. Bishop visits the nearby lavatory,
Farting away ten or twenty times.
But for all his loud precautions,
Mr. Bishop now prays with clenched cheeks.

J. P. Sullivan

The worthy not to overpraise
   And be misunderstood,
He praises all: if no one's bad,
   Who can he think is good?

Roy F. Butler

Hard up: Umber showered me with presents
   and regard.
Now he's rich: I'm lucky if I get a card.

Lee Hatfield

XII.82

Effugere in thermis et circa balnea non est
    Menogenen, omni tu licet arte velis.
Captabit tepidum dextra laevaque trigonem,
    Inputet acceptas ut tibi saepe pilas.
Colliget et referet laxum de pulvere follem,
    Et si iam lotus, iam soleatus erit.
Lintea si sumes, nive candidiora loquetur,
    Sint licet infantis sordidiora sinu.
Exiguos secto comentem dente capillos
    Dicet Achilleas disposuisse comas.
Fumosae feret ipse propin de faece lagonae,
    Frontis et umorem colliget usque tuae.
Omnia laudabit, mirabitur omnia, donec
    Perpessus dicas taedia mille "Veni!"

XII.84

Nolueram, Polytime, tuos violare capillos,
    Sed iuvat hoc precibus me tribuisse tuis.
Talis eras, modo tonse Pelops, positisque nitebas
    Crinibus ut totum sponsa videret ebur.

I defy you to escape him at the baths.
He'll help you arrange your towels;
While you're combing your hair, scanty as it may be,
He'll remark how much you resemble Achilles;
He'll pour your wine and accept the dregs;
He'll admire your build and spindly legs;
He'll wipe the perspiration from your face,
Until you finally say, "Okay, let's go to my place."

Philip Murray

You begged me, boy, to cut your flowing hair
And, after all, I'm glad I heard your prayer.
For you're like Pelops now and, older,
You show the beauty of an ivory shoulder.

Anthony Reid

XII.91

Communis tibi cum viro, Magulla,
Cum sit lectulus et sit exoletus,
Quare, dic mihi, non sit et minister.
Suspiras; ratio est, times lagonam.

XII.94

Scribebamus epos; coepisti scribere: cessi,
    Aemula ne starent carmina nostra tuis.
Transtulit ad tragicos se nostra Thalia coturnos:
    Aptasti longum tu quoque syrma tibi.
Fila lyrae movi Calabris exculta Camenis:
    Plectra rapis nobis, ambitiose, nova.
Audemus saturas: Lucilius esse laboras.
    Ludo levis elegos: tu quoque ludis idem.
Quid minus esse potest? epigrammata fingere coepi:
    Hinc etiam petitur iam mea palma tibi.
Elige, quid nolis—quis enim pudor, omnia velle?—
    Et si quid non vis, Tucca, relinque mihi.

Your husband's bed you share;
Your husband's boy you share;
   Tell me, Magulla, why
   His cup you'll never try.
Is there something of which you're aware?

J. P. Sullivan

It occurred to me to write an epic:
   you followed suit; I ceased, not to compete.
My Thalia assumes Melpomene's buskins:
   you try her tragic finery yourself.
I strike up Songs of the South, like Flaccus:
   pushy, you filch my scarce-tried plectrum.
I turn satiric: you're Lucilius now.
   Light elegies. . . . Must yours be lighter still?
What's left but *nugae?* Martial carves a few.
   Even in epigram you withhold the palm.
Show what you don't want, Tucca—manners leaving
   something over—and what that is, I'll take.

Peter Whigham

XII.96

Cum tibi nota tui sit vita fidesque mariti,
    Nec premat ulla tuos sollicitetve toros,
Quid quasi paelicibus torqueris inepta ministris,
    In quibus et brevis est et fugitiva Venus?
Plus tibi quam domino pueros praestare probabo:
    Hi faciunt ut sis femina sola viro;
Hi dant quod non vis uxor dare. "Do tamen," inquis,
    "Ne vagus a thalamis coniugis erret amor."
Non eadem res est: Chiam volo, nolo mariscam:
    Ne dubites quae sit Chia, marisca tua est.
Scire suos fines matrona et femina debet:
    Cede sua pueris, utere parte tua.

XII.98

Baetis olivifera crinem redimite corona,
    Aurea qui nitidis vellera tinguis aquis;
Quem Bromius, quem Pallas amat; cui rector aquarum
    Albula navigerum per freta pandit iter:
Ominibus laetis vestras Instantius oras
    Intret, et hic populis ut prior annus eat.
Non ignorat, onus quod sit succedere Macro:
    Qui sua metitur pondera, ferre potest.

Knowing as you do that your husband is faithful,
and that no female dints or rumples your bed,
why do you excruciate irrelevantly
as if your lads (whose passion is fugitive, brief)
were concubines? I'll prove that the slave-boys
avail you more than they do their master,
contrive that you are the only woman for him:
they give what his wife does not wish to give.

"I give it, though, lest roving Love should stray
from the conjugal bed." It's not the same thing!
I want a prime fig, not common or garden piles.
(What's prime? Well, yours is common or garden.)
A woman and matron should know her limitations:
concede their part to boys, make use of your own.

                                             W. G. Shepherd

Guadalquivir! Tresses twined with olive boughs,
    brilliancies that tint the sheep-fold gold,
Whom Bacchus, whom Athene bless, whose sounding
    channels Tiber has made navigable—
Bring with rejoicings Rufus to your banks,
    let this year be, for all, as good as last.
Tough to follow Macer; Rufus knows it:
    who tests the burden first, best bears it.

                                       Peter Whigham

BOOK XIII
XENIA
(A.D. 84 OR 85 DECEMBER)

Xenia were gifts given by a host to his friends, or gifts in general. Tags or messages, sometimes humorous, might be attached to them. Martial's ingenious collection of these was for general use and is interesting mainly as a document of foodstuffs favored by the Romans.

XIII.3

Omnis in hoc gracili XENIORUM turba libello
   Constabit nummis quattuor empta tibi.
Quattuor est nimium? poterit constare duobus,
   Et faciat lucrum bybliopola Tryphon.
Haec licet hospitibus pro munere disticha mittas,
   Si tibi tam rarus, quam mihi, nummus erit.
Addita per titulos sua nomina rebus habebis:
   Praetereas, si quid non facit ad stomachum.

XIII.53   TURTURES

Cum pinguis mihi turtur erit, lactuca valebis:
   Et cocleas tibi habe. Perdere nolo famem.

XIII.66   COLUMBINI

Ne violes teneras periuro dente columbas,
   Tradita si Gnidiae sunt tibi sacra deae.

This slim book, my *Xenia*,
  costs four sesterces.
Is that excessive? At two,
  Tryphon profits still.
If poor as I, these couplets
  you'll as guest-gifts use.
All have titles: each dish, glass
  not to your taste—skip.

Peter Whigham

TURTLE DOVES

Plump turtle dove? Farewell lettuce bowl,
The snails are yours! I'll keep my hunger whole.

Peter Whigham

DOVES

No devotee of *Venus'* rite
With tooth profane shall this bird bite.

Peter Whigham

XIII.77   CYCNI

Dulcia defecta modulatur carmina lingua
  Cantator cycnus funeris ipse sui.

XIII.81   RHOMBI

Quamvis lata gerat patella rhombum,
  Rhombus latior est tamen patella.

XIII.82   OSTREA

Ebria Baiano veni modo concha Lucrino:
  Nobile nunc sitio luxuriosa garum.

XIII.120   SPOLETINUM

De Spoletinis quae sunt cariosa lagonis
  Malueris, quam si musta Falerna bibas.

SWANS

The swan his own death's minstrel's sung
Sweet measured songs with failing tongue.

Fiona Pitt-Kethley

TURBOTS

However wide the plate that holds the fish,
The flat-fish is still wider than the dish.

Fiona Pitt-Kethley

OYSTERS

Tipsy from *Baiae's* streams but lately sent,
This wanton bi-valve thirsts for condiment.

Peter Whigham

SPOLENTINE WINE

Than *Falernian* e'er its time,
Better a well-aged *Spolentine*.

Peter Whigham

BOOK XIV
APOPHORETA
(A.D. 84 OR 85 DECEMBER)

Apophoreta were presents for guests to carry away from feasts and entertainments, which often involved lotteries and various playful games. Sometimes rebus-like descriptions or verse messages accompanied them. The season of the Saturnalia at the winter equinox was particularly the time for gifts in general.

XIV.2

Quo vis cumque loco potes hunc finire libellum:
Versibus explicitumst omne duobus opus.
Lemmata si quaeris cur sint adscripta, docebo:
Ut, si malueris, lemmata sola legas.

XIV.30 VENABULA

Excipient apros expectabuntque leones,
Intrabunt ursos, sit modo firma manus.

XIV.34 FALX

Pax me certa ducis placidos curvavit in usus.
Agricolae nunc sum, militis ante fui.

XIV.39 LUCERNA CUBICULARIS

Dulcis conscia lectuli lucerna,
Quidquid vis facias licet, tacebo.

You don't have to read the whole book through.
I present each item in a couplet.
As for the added titles—you may wonder;
They're for people who read only titles.

Peter Whigham

HUNTING SPEARS

They'll capture boars and be for lions ready,
They'll pierce bears if the hand be steady.

Fiona Pitt-Kethley

A SICKLE

Bent by *Caesar's* Peace to gentle purpose,
That now a farmer's, once a soldier's was.

Peter Whigham

A BEDSIDE LAMP

To me are bedroom joys revealed;
Enjoy at will, my lips are sealed.

Peter Whigham

xiv.40   CICINDELA

Ancillam tibi sors dedit lucernae,
Totas quae vigil exigit tenebras.

xiv.75   LUSCINIA

Flet Philomela nefas incesti Tereos, et quae
  Muta puella fuit, garrula fertur avis.

xiv.119   MATELLA FICTILIS

Dum poscor crepitu digitorum et verna moratur,
  O quotiens paelex culcita facta mea est!

xiv.134   FASCIA PECTORALIS

Fascia, crescentes dominae compesce papillas,
  Ut sit quod capiat nostra tegatque manus.

A CANDLE

A lantern's handmaid, I who stay
Awake to keep the dark at bay.

Peter Whigham

THE NIGHTINGALE

Her incest-rape must *Philomel* bewail,
The tongue-torn maiden, now a nightingale.

Peter Whigham

A CLAY CHAMBERPOT

I snap my fingers; the slave is slow:
So often a pillow absorbs the flow.

J. P. Sullivan

A BRASSIÈRE

Go, little bra, confine that swelling breast,
That on it my own hand may smoothly rest.

J. P. Sullivan

XIV.149   AMICTORIUM

Mammosas metuo; tenerae me trade puellae,
   Ut possint niveo pectore lina frui.

XIV.165   CITHARA

Reddidit Eurydicen vati: sed perdidit ipse,
   Dum sibi non credit nec patienter amat.

XIV.189   MONOBYBLOS PROPERTI

Cynthia—facundi carmen iuvenale Properti—
   Accepit famam, non minus ipsa dedit.

XIV.191   SALLUSTIUS

Hic erit, ut perhibent doctorum corda virorum,
   Primus Romana Crispus in historia.

A WRAP

Big breasts scare me: on adolescent
Bosoms I make a snowy present.

J. P. Sullivan

A ZITHER

It drew *Eurydice* to one who drove her thence,
Lacking love's patience & self-confidence.

Peter Whigham

PROPERTIUS, VOLUME ONE

In his young song she brought *Propertius* fame,
So doing, *Cynthia* brought herself the same.

Peter Whigham

SALLUST

Sallust all scholars now declare
Prince of historians, beyond compare.

J. P. Sullivan

XIV.193   TIBULLUS

Ussit amatorem Nemesis lasciva Tibullum,
   In tota iuvit quem nihil esse domo.

XIV.194   LUCANUS

Sunt quidam, qui me dicant non esse poetam:
   Sed qui me vendit bybliopola putat.

XIV.195   CATULLUS

Tantum magna suo debet Verona Catullo,
   Quantum parva suo Mantua Vergilio.

XIV.203   PUELLA GADITANA

Tam tremulum crisat, tam blandum prurit, ut ipsum
   Masturbatorem fecerit Hippolytum.

TIBULLUS

Sensuous Nemesis so fired Tibullus' flame
That even his household scarcely knew his name.

J. P. Sullivan

LUCAN

There are some who say I'm not a poet:
But the bookseller selling me wouldn't know it.

J. P. Sullivan

CATULLUS

What great *Verona* to *Catullus* owes
Virgil on little *Mantua* bestows.

Peter Whigham

THE GADES GIRL

Those swaying hips, so sweetly lewd, would straight
Hippolytus himself make masturbate.

Peter Whigham

XIV.205 PUER

Sit nobis aetate puer, non pumice levis,
 Propter quem placeat nulla puella mihi.

XIV.220 COCUS

Non satis est ars sola coco: servire palatum
 Nolo: cocus domini debet habere gulam.

XIV.222 PISTOR DULCIARIUS

Mille tibi dulces operum manus ista figuras
 Extruet: huic uni parca laborat apis.

XIV.223 ADIPATA

Surgite: iam vendit pueris ientacula pistor
 Cristataeque sonant undique lucis aves.

A YOUNG BOY

Give me a young boy with cheeks soft and gay,
And any girl alive I'd turn away.

Anthony Reid

A COOK

Skill in a cook's not all, for he must have
The palate of a master, not a slave.

Peter Whigham

THE PASTRY COOK

His hands a thousand sweet shapes form,
For whom the thrifty bee shall swarm.

Peter Whigham

CROISSANTS

Children sleepy-eyed eat the baker's rolls.
Sleepy-head rise, the birdsong calls.

W. S. Milne

APPENDIX OF
OLDER VERSIONS

I.10

Petit Gemellus nuptias Maronillae
Et cupit et instat et precatur et donat.
Adeone pulchra est? immo foedius nil est.
Quid ergo in illa petitur et placet? Tussit.

I.15

O mihi post nullos, Iuli, memorande sodales,
    Si quid longa fides canaque iura valent,
Bis iam paene tibi consul tricensimus instat,
    Et numerat paucos vix tua vita dies.
Non bene distuleris videas quae posse negari,
    Et solum hoc ducas, quod fuit, esse tuum.
Expectant curaeque catenatique labores,
    Gaudia non remanent, sed fugitiva volant.
Haec utraque manu conplexuque adsere toto:
    Saepe fluunt imo sic quoque lapsa sinu.
Non est, crede mihi, sapientis dicere "Vivam":
    Sera nimis vita est crastina: vive hodie.

Gemellus, Maronilla fain
  would have unto his wife:
He longs, he likes, he loves, he craves
  with her to lead his life.
What? Is she of such beauty brave?
  Nay, none more foul may be:
What then is in her to be liked
  or loved? Still cougheth she.

Timothe Kendall

Thou, whom (if faith or honour recommends
  A friend) I rank amongst my dearest friends,
Remember, you are now almost threescore;
  Few days of life remain, if any more.
Defer not, what no future time insures:
  And only what is past, esteem that yours.
Successive cares and trouble for you stay;
  Pleasure not so; it nimbly fleets away.
Then seize it fast; embrace it ere it flies:
  In the embrace it vanishes and dies.
"I'll live to-morrow," will a wise man say?
  To-morrow is too late, then live to-day.

William Hay

1.32

Non amo te, Sabidi, nec possum dicere quare:
Hoc tantum possum dicere, non amo te.

1.34

Incustoditis et apertis, Lesbia, semper
   Liminibus peccas nec tua furta tegis,
Et plus spectator quam te delectat adulter
   Nec sunt grata tibi gaudia si qua latent.
At meretrix abigit testem veloque seraque
   Raraque Submemmi fornice rima patet.
A Chione saltem vel ab Iade disce pudorem:
   Abscondunt spurcas et monumenta lupas.
Numquid dura tibi nimium censura videtur?
   Deprendi veto te, Lesbia, non futui.

1.46

Cum dicis "Propero, fac si facis," Hedyle, languet
   Protinus et cessat debilitata Venus.
Expectare iube: velocius ibo retentus.
   Hedyle, si properas, dic mihi, ne properem.

I do not love thee, Doctor Fell;
The reason why I cannot tell.
But this I'm sure I know full well,
I do not love thee, Doctor Fell.

Tom Brown

Lesbia, thou sinn'st still with an unpinn'd door,
And open, and ne'er cloak'st thy pleasure o'er,
Thy peepers more than active friends delight,
Nor are thy joys in kind if out of sight:
But yet the common wench with veil and key
Strives to expel the witness far away.
No chink doth in a brothel-house appear;
Of vulgar strumpets learn this modest care;
Stews hide this filthiness: but, *Lesbia*, see
If this my censure seem too hard to be?
  I don't forbid thee to employ thy prime,
  But to be taken, *Lesbia*, there's the crime.

Robert Fletcher

When you cry, "Now it comes—stand to me": then
My courage flags, my lust abates. But when
You cry "Forbear," I faster come, restrain'd.
If you would have me do it, ride me rein'd.

Egerton MS 2982

1.86

Vicinus meus est manuque tangi
De nostris Novius potest fenestris.
Quis non invideat mihi putetque
Horis omnibus esse me beatum,
Iuncto cui liceat frui sodale?
Tam longe est mihi quam Terentianus,
Qui nunc Niliacam regit Syenen.
Non convivere, nec videre saltem,
Non audire licet, nec urbe tota
Quisquam est tam prope tam proculque nobis.
Migrandum est mihi longius vel illi.
Vicinus Novio vel inquilinus
Sit, si quis Novium videre non volt.

1.90

Quod numquam maribus iunctam te, Bassa, videbam
    Quodque tibi moechum fabula nulla dabat,
Omne sed officium circa te semper obibat
    Turba tui sexus, non adeunte viro,
Esse videbaris, fateor, Lucretia nobis:
    At tu, pro facinus, Bassa, fututor eras.
Inter se geminos audes committere cunnos
    Mentiturque virum prodigiosa Venus.
Commenta es dignum Thebano aenigmate monstrum,
    Hic ubi vir non est, ut sit adulterium.

My neighbour Hunks's house and mine
Are built so near they almost join;
The windows too project so much,
That through the casements we may touch.
Nay, I'm so happy, most men think,
To live so near a man of chink,
That they are apt to envy me,
For keeping such good company:
But he's as far from me, I vow,
As London is from good Lord Howe;
For when old Hunks I chance to meet,
Or one or both must quit the street.
Thus he who would not see old Roger,
Must be his neighbour—or his lodger.

Jonathan Swift

That I ne'er saw thee in a coach with man,
    Nor thy chaste name in wanton satire met;
That from thy sex thy liking never ran,
    So as to suffer a male-servant yet;
I thought thee the Lucretia of our time:
    But, Bassa, thou the while a Tribas wert,
And clashing cunts, with a prodigious crime,
    Didst act of man th' inimitable part.
What Oedipus this riddle can untie?
Without a male, there was adultery.

Sir Charles Sedley

I.107

Saepe mihi dicis, Luci carissime Iuli,
    "Scribe aliquid magnum: desidiosus homo es."
Otia da nobis, sed qualia fecerat olim
    Maecenas Flacco Vergilioque suo:
Condere victuras temptem per saecula curas
    Et nomen flammis eripuisse meum.
In steriles nolunt campos iuga ferre iuvenci:
    Pingue solum lassat, sed iuvat ipse labor.

Oft, noble Lucius, thou dost this repeat
Th'art idle, Martial, *write something that's great.*
Then give me ease, such as Maecenas gave,
When the like work from Virgil he would have;
I'll frame a verse with such immortal flame,
As to all ages shall preserve my name.
The yoke does pinch that's born in barren soil,
The rich ground tires, but sweeter is the toil.

Henry Killigrew

II.53

Vis fieri liber? mentiris, Maxime, non vis:
  Sed fieri si vis, hac ratione potes.
Liber eris, cenare foris si, Maxime, nolis,
  Veientana tuam si domat uva sitim,
Si ridere potes miseri chrysendeta Cinnae,
  Contentus nostra si potes esse toga,
Si plebeia Venus gemino tibi vincitur asse,
  Si tua non rectus tecta subire potes.
Haec tibi si vis est, si mentis tanta potestas,
  Liberior Partho vivere rege potes.

Would'st thou be free? I fear thou art in jest
But if thou would'st, this is the only law;
Be no man's tavern nor domestic guest:
Drink wholesome wine which thy own servants draw.

Of knavish Carlo scorn the ill-got plate,
The num'rous servants and the cringing throng:
With a few friends on fewer dishes eat,
And let thy clothes, like mine, be plain and strong.

Such friendships make as thou may'st keep with ease;
Great men expect what good men hate to pay;
Be never thou thyself in pain to please,
But leave to fools and knaves th' uncertain prey.

Let thy expense with thy estate keep pace;
Meddle with no man's business, save thine own:
Contented pay for a plebeian face,
And leave vain fops the beauties of the town.

If to this pitch of virtue thou canst bring
Thy mind, thou 'rt freer than the Persian king.

Sir Charles Sedley

II.58

Pexatus pulchre rides me, Zoile, trita.
Sunt haec trita quidem, Zoile, sed mea sunt.

II.88

Nil recitas et vis, Mamerce, poeta videri.
Quidquid vis esto, dummodo nil recites.

III.90

Vult, non vult dare Galla mihi: nec dicere possum,
Quod vult, et non vult, quid sibi Galla velit.

In velvet clad, and lace so fine,
You scorn this thread-bare suit of mine.
—Thread-bare I grant ye, Mr. Beau,
—But then—'twas paid for long ago.

Nathaniel Brassey Halhed

Arthur, they say, has wit. "For what?
For writing?" No—for writing not.

Jonathan Swift

You will and you won't—half no and half yes,
I'm quite at a loss for your meaning, dear Miss.
Long enough in all conscience you've shuffled and
    shamm'd:
—Say yes and be kissed—or say no, and be ———.

Nathaniel Brassey Halhed

III.93

Cum tibi trecenti consules, Vetustilla,
Et tres capilli quattuorque sint dentes,
Pectus cicadae, crus colorque formicae;
Rugosiorem cum geras stola frontem
Et araneorum cassibus pares mammas;
Cum conparata rictibus tuis ora
Niliacus habeat corcodilus angusta,
Meliusque ranae garriant Ravennates,
Et Atrianus dulcius culex cantet,
Videasque quantum noctuae vident mane,
Et illud oleas quod viri capellarum,
Et anatis habeas orthopygium macrae,
Senemque Cynicum vincat osseus cunnus;
Cum te lucerna balneator extincta
Admittat inter bustuarias moechas;
Cum bruma mensem sit tibi per Augustum
Regelare nec te pestilentia possit:
Audes ducentas nuptuire post mortes
Virumque demens cineribus tuis quaeris
Prurire. Quid si Sattiae velit saxum?
Quis coniugem te, quis vocabit uxorem,
Philomelus aviam quam vocaverat nuper?
Quod si cadaver exigis tuum scalpi,
Sternatur Acori de triclinio lectus,
Talassionem qui tuum decet solus,
Ustorque taedas praeferat novae nuptae:
Intrare in istum sola fax potest cunnum.

When thou hast worn three hundred consuls out,
Hast but three hairs, four teeth as black as soot,
A grasshopper's skinny breast, a pismire's thigh,
A face—thy gown shows not so ruggedly—,
Dugs hanging like the cobwebs of a spider,
A filthy seam-rent mouth that yawns far wider
Than Nilus' crocodile, to it but narrow;
And chatters worse than any frog can harrow;
Sings harsher than a gnat; and sees as well
As owls do in the morning; breathes a smell
More deadly than a goat's in's lust can make,
And hast a rump as dry as a lean drake,
A bony thing withall more hard and thin
Than an old Cynic's; art glad to come in
Amongst the hedge whores, and bathe thee there with dark.
Deep'st winter at mid-August, art so stark
And stiff with cold the very plague itself
Is not enough to thaw thee. And yet, thou elf,
Thou wither'd ghost, when th 'ast already shed
Two hundred husbands, thou wouldst yet be wed,
And for thy itching ashes seekst out one,
When thou as well may'st bid him grind a stone.
Whoe'er will let his tongue run so random
To call thee wife, whom each old sire calls grandam?
But if thou would'st have thy carcass scratch'd indeed,
Send for the hangman Cloris for a weed,
And let him make thy nuptial bed and sing
Thy Hymenaeus. Let the burner bring
His torch and carry it before the bride.
'Tis only a firebrand that must pierce this hide.

MS Donington d.58

IV.21

Nullos esse deos, inane caelum
Adfirmat Selius: probatque, quod se
Factum, dum negat haec, videt beatum.

V.13

Sum, fateor, semperque fui, Callistrate, pauper,
    Sed non obscurus nec male notus eques,
Sed toto legor orbe frequens et dicitur "Hic est",
    Quodque cinis paucis, hoc mihi vita dedit.
At tua centenis incumbunt tecta columnis
    Et libertinas arca flagellat opes,
Magnaque Niliacae servit tibi glaeba Syenes,
    Tondet et innumeros Gallica Parma greges.
Hoc ego tuque sumus: sed quod sum, non potes esse:
    Tu quod es, e populo quilibet esse potest.

V.64

Sextantes, Calliste, duos infunde Falerni,
    Tu super aestivas, Alcime, solve nives,
Pinguescat nimio madidus mihi crinis amomo
    Lassenturque rosis tempora sutilibus.
Tam vicina iubent nos vivere Mausolea,
    Cum doceant, ipsos posse perire deos.

That in the Heavens no gods there be
Selius affirms, and proves, 'cause he
Still thinking so lives happily.

Thomas May

I am, and always was, I confess, poor,
But yet a well-known knight, and not obscure,
Whom the whole world reads, and sayeth, *This is he.*
Few dead so famous, as I living be.
But your vast piles on hundred columns rest,
Your massy wealth is in cramm'd coffers press'd,
Your granaries from Egypt stor'd each year,
And Parma's wool your numerous flocks do bear,
Thus we are each. Yet you can't be like me.
What you are every vulgar man may be.

Egerton MS 2982

Boy! Let my cup with rosy wine o'erflow,
Above the melting of the summer snow:
Let my wet hair with wasteful odour shine,
And loads of roses round my temples twine:
Tombs of the Caesars, your sad honours cry,
"Live, little men, for lo! the gods can die."

William Hay

VI.11

Quod non sit Pylades hoc tempore, non sit Orestes,
  Miraris? Pylades, Marce, bibebat idem,
Nec melior panis turdusve dabatur Orestae,
  Sed par atque eadem cena duobus erat.
Tu Lucrina voras, me pascit aquosa peloris:
  Non minus ingenua est et mihi, Marce, gula.
Te Cadmea Tyros, me pinguis Gallia vestit:
  Vis te purpureum, Marce, sagatus amem?
Ut praestem Pyladen, aliquis mihi praestet Oresten.
  Hoc non fit verbis, Marce: ut ameris, ama.

VI.12

Iurat capillos esse, quos emit, suos
Fabulla: numquid illa, Paule, peierat.

You wonder now that no man sees
Such friends as those of ancient Greece.
Here lies the point—Orestes' meat
Was just the same his friend did eat;
Not can it yet be found his wine
Was better, Pylades! than thine.
In home-spun russet I am drest,
Your cloth is always of the best.
But, honest Marcus, if you please
To choose me for your Pylades,
Remember, words alone are vain;
Love—if you would be lov'd again.

Samuel Johnson

The golden hair that Galla wears
Is hers: who would have thought it?
She swears 'tis hers, and true she swears,
For I know where she bought it.

Sir John Harrington

VI.39

Pater ex Marulla, Cinna, factus es septem
Non liberorum: namque nec tuus quisquam
Nec est amici filiusve vicini,
Sed in grabatis tegetibusque concepti
Materna produnt capitibus suis furta.
Hic, qui retorto crine Maurus incedit,
Subolem fatetur esse se coci Santrae.
At ille sima nare, turgidis labris
Ipsa est imago Pannychi palaestritae.
Pistoris esse tertium quis ignorat,
Quicumque lippum novit et videt Damam?
Quartus cinaeda fronte, candido voltu
Ex concubino natus est tibi Lygdo:
Percide, si vis, filium: nefas non est.
Hunc vero acuto capite et auribus longis,
Quae sic moventur, ut solent asellorum,
Quis morionis filium negat Cyrtae?
Duae sorores, illa nigra et haec rufa,
Croti choraulae vilicique sunt Carpi.
Iam Niobidarum grex tibi foret plenus,
Si spado Coresus Dindymusque non esset.

OF CINNA

Thou father'st for thy wife sev'n births, which I
Can't children call, no, nor yet free-born. Why?
For thou thyself not one of them, nay, not
Thy friend, or honest neighbor, ever got:
But all on mats conceiv'd or couches they,
E'en by their looks, their mother's stealths betray.
This that with curled hair Moor-like doth look
Proves himself issue of the swarthy cook.
He with flat nose and blubber lips, you'd swear
The wrestler Pannicus his picture were.
Damas, the third, who (that did him e'er see)
Knows not the blear-eyed baker's son to be?
The fourth, a sweet-fac'd boy with wanton mine*
Was got by Lygdus, thy he-concubine.
Use him so too: thou needst no incest fear.
But this, with 's taper-head and his long ear,
Which like an ass's moves, who can deny
To be the idiot Gyrrha's progeny?
Two daughters, this fox-red, that bacon-brown
One's Crote's, the piper; t' other Carp's, the clown.
Thy mongrels' number had been now complete
Could Dindymus and Cores children get.

                              Egerton MS 2982

---

* I.e., mien.

VI.93

Tam male Thais olet quam non fullonis avari
    Testa vetus media sed modo fracta via,
Non ab amore recens hircus, non ora leonis,
    Non detracta cani transtiberina cutis,
Pullus abortivo nec cum putrescit in ovo,
    Amphora corrupto nec vitiata garo.
Virus ut hoc alio fallax permutet odore,
    Deposita quotiens balnea veste petit,
Psilothro viret aut acida latet oblita creta
    Aut tegitur pingui terque quaterque faba.
Cum bene se tutam per fraudes mille putavit,
    Omnia cum fecit, Thaida Thais olet.

Worse than a fuller's tub* doth Thais stink,
Broke in the streets and leaking through each chink;
Or lion's belch; or lustful, reeking goats;
Or skin of dog that, dead, o' the bankside floats;
Or half-hatched chicken from broke rotten eggs;
Or tainted jars of stinking mackerel dregs.
This vile rank smell, with perfumes to disguise,
Whene'er she naked bathes, she doth devise.
She's with pomatum smudg'd or paint good store;
Or oil of bean flour varnished o'er and o'er.
A thousand ways she tries to make all well.
In vain. For still she doth of Thais smell.

                    Egerton MS 2982

* The Romans used urine for cleaning clothes and placed vats as urinals at
city corners. Accidents would happen.

VII.61

Abstulerat totam temerarius institor urbem,
  Inque suo nullum limine limen erat.
Iussisti tenuis, Germanice, crescere vicos,
  Et modo quae fuerat semita, facta via est.
Nulla catenatis pila est praecincta lagonis,
  Nec praetor medio cogitur ire luto,
Stringitur in densa nec caeca novacula turba,
  Occupat aut totas nigra popina vias.
Tonsor, copo, cocus, lanius sua limina servant.
  Nunc Roma est, nuper magna taberna fuit. *

* Domitian's urban regulations widened and regulated the main Roman
streets.

When the bold huckster bore the town away,
  And within bounds no boundary would stay;
Thou bad'st obstruction sound a quick retreat;
  And what was not a lane became a street.
Concatenated pots no post surround:
  No praetor waddling in mid-mud is found.
No razor, drawn in darkness, now we feel:
  Whole streets of tipplers dance no more their reel.
The tonsor, taverner, the butcher, look;
  Who, each forsaking, curst the bounds forsook;
All their respective mounds submiss explore:
  And she is ROME, that was a stall before.

                                James Elphinston

VIII.3

"Quinque satis fuerant: nam sex septemve libelli
    Est nimium: quid adhuc ludere, Musa, iuvat?
Sit pudor et finis: iam plus nihil addere nobis
    Fama potest: teritur noster ubique liber;
Et cum rupta situ Messalae saxa iacebunt
    Altaque cum Licini marmora pulvis erunt,
Me tamen ora legent et secum plurimus hospes
    Ad patrias sedes carmina nostra feret."
Finieram, cum sic respondit nona sororum,
    Cui coma et unguento sordida vestis erat:
"Tune potes dulcis, ingrate, relinquere nugas?
    Dic mihi, quid melius desidiosus ages?
An iuvat ad tragicos soccum transferre coturnos,
    Aspera vel paribus bella tonare modis,
Praelegat ut tumidus rauca te voce magister
    Oderit et grandis virgo bonusque puer?
Scribant ista graves nimium nimiumque severi,
    Quos media miseros nocte lucerna videt.
At tu Romano lepidos sale tinge libellos:
    Agnoscat mores vita legatque suos.
Angusta cantare licet videaris avena,
    Dum tua multorum vincat avena tubas."

Five had suffic'd; six books or seven do cloy,
Why dost as yet delight, my muse, to toy?
Give o'er, for shame: Fame has not more to grace
My verse, the business made in ev'ry place.
And when proud tombs, in which for fame men trust,
O'erthrown and broken lie reduc'd to dust,
I shall be read, strangers will make 't their care,
Unto their sev'ral soils my works to bear.
    She of the sacred nine (when I had spoke),
Whose locks with odours drop, thus silence broke:
"And wilt thou then thy pleasant verse forsake?
What better choice, ungrateful, canst thou make?
Exchange thy mirthful for a tragic vein;
Thunder harsh wars in an heroic strain;
Which strutting pedants, till they're hoarse, may rant,
While the ripe youth detest to hear the cant:
Let the o'er-sour and dull that way delight,
Whose lamps at midnight see the wretches write.
But season thou thy lines with sharpest wit,
That all may read their vices smartly hit.
Altho' thou seem'st to play but on a reed,
Thy slender pipe the trumpet does exceed."

                                        Henry Killigrew

VIII.6

Archetypis vetuli nihil est odiosius Eucti
   —Ficta Saguntino cymbia malo luto—,
Argenti furiosa sui cum stemmata narrat
   Garrulus et verbis mucida vina facit.
"Laomedonteae fuerant haec pocula mensae:
   Ferret ut haec, muros struxit Apollo lyra.
Hoc cratere ferox commisit proelia Rhoetus
   Cum Lapithis: pugna debile cernis opus.
Hi duo longaevo censentur Nestore fundi:
   Pollice de Pylio trita columba nitet.
Hic scyphus est, in quo misceri iussit amicis
   Largius Aeacides vividiusque merum.
Hac propinavit Bitiae pulcherrima Dido
   In patera, Phrygio cum data cena viro est."
Miratus fueris cum prisca toreumata multum,
   In Priami calathis Astyanacta bibes.

In leathern jack* to drink much less I hate,
Than in Sir William's antique set of plate.
He tells the gasconading pedigree,
Till the wine turns insipid too as he.
"This tumbler, in the world the oldest toy,"
Says he, "was brought by Brute himself from Troy.
That handled cup, and which is larger far,
A present to my father from the Czar:
See how 't is bruis'd, and the work broken off;
'T was when he flung it at Prince Menzikoff.
The other with the cover, which is less,
Was once the property of good Queen Bess:
In it she pledg'd Duke d'Alençon, then gave it
To Drake, my wife's great uncle: so we have it.
The bowl, the tankard, flagon, and the beaker,
Were my great-grandfather's, when he was Speaker."
What pity 't is, that plate so old and fine
Should correspond no better with the wine.

                                    William Hay

* Jug or tankard.

VIII.19

Pauper videri Cinna vult; et est pauper.

VIII.32

Aera per tacitum delapsa sedentis in ipsos
    Fluxit Aretullae blanda columba sinus.
Luserat hoc casus, nisi inobservata maneret
    Permissaque sibi nollet abire fuga.
Si meliora piae fas est sperare sorori
    Et dominum mundi flectere vota valent,
Haec a Sardois tibi forsitan exulis oris,
    Fratre reversuro, nuntia venit avis.

When humble Cinna cries, I'm poor and low,
You may believe him—he is really so.

Colley Cibber

Through silent air the gentle dove does glide,
And into Aretulla's bosom slide.
This seemed to be by chance, had it not stayed
And, as loath to be begone, a nest there made.
Why should she not from hence take augury;
It came to say: Caesar would not deny
Revocal of her banish'd brothers doom,
Did she now beg it, and would call him home.

Egerton MS 2982

IX.28

Dulce decus scaenae, ludorum fama, Latinus
   Ille ego sum, plausus deliciaeque tuae,
Qui spectatorem potui fecisse Catonem,
   Solvere qui Curios Fabriciosque graves.
Sed nihil a nostro sumpsit mea vita theatro,
   Et sola tantum scaenicus arte feror:
Nec poteram gratus domino sine moribus esse;
   Interius mentes inspicit ille deus.
Vos me laurigeri parasitum dicite Phoebi,
   Roma sui famulum dum sciat esse Iovis.

IX.56

Spendophoros Libycas domini petit armiger urbis:
   Quae puero dones tela, Cupido, para,
Illa quibus iuvenes figis mollesque puellas:
   Sit tamen in tenera levis et hasta manu.
Loricam clipeumque tibi galeamque remitto;
   Tutus ut invadat proelia, nudus eat:
Non iaculo, non ense fuit laesusve sagitta,
   Casside dum liber Parthenopaeus erat.
Quisquis ab hoc fuerit fixus, morietur amore.
   O felix, si quem tam bona fata manent!
Dum puer es, redeas, dum vultu lubricus, et te
   Non Libye faciat, sed tua Roma virum.

AN EPITAPH OF LATINUS

The stage's fame and pleasing glory, I
(Thy pleasure and applause once) here now lie:
That could have Cato made look on awhile,
Grave Curios and Fabricios forc'd to smile.
Yet was my life untainted by my trade:
My looser parts myself ne'er looser made.
I could not else with Caesar favour find.
He, god-like, searches to the inward mind.
Apollo's parasite you may me call:
Whil'st Rome knows me for her Jove's menial.

Egerton MS 2982

To Libya goes Spendophorus to war.
Cupid thy shafts for this fair boy prepare,
Those shafts which youths and tender virgins wound;
Let thy spear in his soft hand be found.
The breast-plate, helm and shield I leave to thee;
To fight in safety, let him naked be.
No arrow, sword, nor dart could hurt in war
Parthenopaeus, whilst his face was bare.
He whom this youth shall wound will die of love,
And happy too so sweet a fate to prove.
Whilst yet thy chin is smooth, fair boy, come home;
Grow not a man in Afric, but at Rome.

Thomas May

IX.80

Duxerat esuriens locupletem pauper anumque
Uxorem: pascit Gellius et futuit.

IX.97

Rumpitur invidia quidam, carissime Iuli,
   Quod me Roma legit, rumpitur invidia.
Rumpitur invidia quod turba semper in omni
   Monstramur digito, rumpitur invidia.
Rumpitur invidia tribuit quod Caesar uterque
   Ius mihi natorum, rumpitur invidia.
Rumpitur invidia quod rus mihi dulce sub urbe est
   Parvaque in urbe domus, rumpitur invidia.
Rumpitur invidia quod sum iucundus amicis,
   Quod conviva frequens, rumpitur invidia.
Rumpitur invidia quod amamur quodque probamur:
   Rumpatur quisquis rumpitur invidia.

Feignlove, half-starved, a rich old hag has wed:—
Poor Feignlove, doom'd to earn his board in bed.

Nathaniel Brassey Halhed

There is a certain man, my dearest jewel!
That bursts with envy, spite, and malice cruel,
He bursts with envy, 'cause with wit I'm read;
And let him burst; Gods, curse him till he's dead;
Because I'm pointed out, where-e'er I go,
He bursts with envy; let him burst in two.
Because restored unto my right I am,
He bursts with envy; let him burst and damn;
Because, in town, I've got a little box;
He bursts with envy; let him burst and pox;
And in the country too, a rural cot,
He bursts with envy; let him burst and rot;
Because I'm loved for mirth, and reckoned droll,
He bursts with envy; let him burst his soul;
Because in feasts, I'm asked to take a part
He bursts with envy; let him burst his heart;
Let all such wretches ever be accurst,
And burst with envy, who with envy burst.

The Gentleman's Magazine (1753)

x.5

Quisquis stolaeve purpuraeve contemptor,
Quos colere debet, laesit impio versu,
Erret per urbam pontis exul et clivi,
Interque raucos ultimus rogatores
Oret caninas panis inprobi buccas;
Illi December longus et madens bruma
Clususque fornix triste frigus extendat:
Vocet beatos clamitetque felices,
Orciniana qui feruntur in sponda.
At cum supremae fila venerint horae
Diesque tardus, sentiat canum litem
Abigatque moto noxias aves panno.
Nec finiantur morte supplicis poenae,
Sed modo severi sectus Aeaci loris,
Nunc inquieti monte Sisyphi pressus,
Nunc inter undas garruli senis siccus
Delasset omnis fabulas poetarum:
Et cum fateri Furia iusserit verum,
Prodente clamet conscientia "Scripsi."

Whoe'er, despising what should be rever'd,
The stole and purple in lewd rhythms hath jeered,
Wretched'st of beggars, may he have no shed,
But, wandring 'bout the town, for broken bread,
Fit for the dogs, beg till he's hoarse again.
On long wet winters may he still complain.
And, in 's bleak cell, feeling sharp frosts increas'd,
May he the dead, that feel no cold, think bless'd.
When Death begins, long-wish'd for, to arrive,
May snarling dogs his carcase tear alive.
A scarecrow then in 's rags may he be show'd
Nor let his pains in single death conclude:
But now with Aeacus' scourge cut to the bone,
Then tir'd with restless Sisyphus' rolling stone,
Then thirsting 'midst the waves of Tantalus,
Outvie all poets' lyred fables thus:
Then, ask'd who was that writ them, may he cry:
His conscience wracking truth from him, "'Twas I!"

Egerton MS 2982

X.20

Nec doctum satis et parum severum,
Sed non rusticulum tamen libellum
Facundo mea Plinio Thalia
I perfer: brevis est labor peractae
Altum vincere tramitem Suburae.
Illic Orphea protinus videbis
Udi vertice lubricum theatri
Mirantisque feras avemque regis,
Raptum quae Phryga pertulit Tonanti;
Illic parva tui domus Pedonis
Caelata est aquilae minore pinna.
Sed ne tempore non tuo disertam
Pulses ebria ianuam, videto:
Totos dat tetricae dies Minervae,
Dum centum studet auribus virorum
Hoc quod saecula posterique possint
Arpinis quoque conparare chartis.
Seras tutior ibis ad lucernas:
Haec hora est tua, cum furit Lyaeus,
Cum regnat rosa, cum madent capilli:
Tunc me vel rigidi legant Catones.

My book not learn'd enough, enough severe,
But yet not rude, to fluent Pliny bear,
Sportive Thalia. The Suburran way
Pass'd, with short labour the next hill you may
Ascend: from whence thou Orpheus (set on high,
Dash'd by the theatre) plainly shalt descry;
The wond'ring beasts, the king of birds and air,
Which the young Phrygian to the Thund'rer bear:
There thy friend Pedo's house stands also by,
Showing a lesser eagle carv'd on high.
But to learn'd Pliny make not thy address
Wanton, but when time suits for thy access;
He in severer studies spends the day,
How he the Hundred Judges best may sway.
Studies, which ours, nor no age, will forbear
With Tully's noblest labours to compare.
Thou'lt safeli'st go when it is candle-light;
This is the hour when Bacchus mads the night;
When odours reign, when roses crown the head,
By rigid Cato then thou may'st be read.

Henry Killigrew

X.23

Iam numerat placido felix Antonius aevo
    Quindecies actas Primus Olympiadas
Praeteritosque dies et tutos respicit annos
    Nec metuit Lethes iam propioris aquas.
Nulla recordanti lux est ingrata gravisque;
    Nulla fuit, cuius non meminisse velit.
Ampliat aetatis spatium sibi vir bonus: hoc est
    Vivere bis, vita posse priore frui.

At length, my friend (while time with still career
Wafts on his gentle wing this eightieth year),
Sees his past days safe out of Fortune's pow'r,
Nor dreads approaching fate's uncertain hour;
Reviews his life, and, in the strict survey,
Finds not one moment he could wish away,
Pleas'd with the series of each happy day.
Such, such a man extends his life's short space,
And from the goal again renews the race:
For he lives twice who can at once employ
The present well, and e'en the past enjoy.

Alexander Pope

X.47

Vitam quae faciant beatiorem,
Iucundissime Martialis, haec sunt:
Res non parta labore, sed relicta;
Non ingratus ager, focus perennis;
Lis numquam, toga rara, mens quieta;
Vires ingenuae, salubre corpus;
Prudens simplicitas, pares amici;
Convictus facilis, sine arte mensa;
Nox non ebria, sed soluta curis;
Non tristis torus, et tamen pudicus;
Somnus, qui faciat breves tenebras:
Quod sis, esse velis nihilque malis;
Summum nec metuas diem nec optes.

A new translation appears on page 375 above. This familiar poem has been translated so many times that it seems appropriate to reprint its first known rendering, written ca. 1540, and some of the less familiar. For seven other versions, see *The Classical Outlook* 63 (1986), 112–14.

Martial, the things that do attain
The happy life be these I find:
The riches left, not got with pain,
The fruitful ground, the quiet mind:
The equal friend, no grudge, no strife,
No charge of rule, no governance,
Without disease the healthful life,
The household of continuance,
The mean diet, no delicate fare,
True wisdom joined with simpleness,
The night discharged of all care,
Where wine the wit may not oppress,
The faithful wife without debate,
Such sleeps as may beguile the night,
Content thyself with thine estate,
Ne wish for death, ne fear his might.

                    Henry Howard, Earl of Surrey

Things that can bless a life and please,
   Sweetest Martial, they are these:
A store well left, not gain'd with toil,
   A house thine own and pleasant soil,
No strife, small state, a mind at peace,
   Free strength, and limbs free from disease,
Wise innocent friends, like and good,
   Unarted meat, kind neighborhood,
No Drunken rest, from cares yet free,
   No sadd'ning spouse, yet chaste to thee,
Sleeps, that long Nights abbreviate,
   Because 'tis likening thy wish'd state,
Nor fear'd, nor joy'd at Death or Fate.

Abraham Cowley

These are things that being possest
Will make a life that's truly blest:
Estate bequeath'd, not got with toil;
A good hot fire, a grateful soil.
No strife, warm clothes, a quiet soul,
A strength entire, a body whole.
Prudent simplicity, equal friends,
A diet that no Art commends.
A night not drunk, and yet secure;
A bed not sad, yet chaste and pure.
Long sleeps to make the nights but short,
A will to be but what thou art.
Naught rather choose; contented lie,
And neither fear nor wish to die.

Sir Thomas Randolph

XI.29

Languida cum vetula tractare virilia dextra
    Coepisti, iugulor pollice, Phylli, tuo:
Nam cum me murem, cum me tua lumina dicis,
    Horis me refici vix puto posse decem.
Blanditias nescis: "dabo" dic "tibi milia centum
    Et dabo Setini iugera culta soli;
Accipe vina, domum, pueros, chrysendeta, mensas."
    Nil opus est digitis: sic mihi, Phylli, frica.

XI.60

Sit Phlogis an Chione Veneri magis apta, requiris?
    Pulchrior est Chione; sed Phlogis ulcus habet,
Ulcus habet Priami quod tendere possit alutam
    Quodque senem Pelian non sinat esse senem,
Ulcus habet quod habere suam vult quisque puellam,
    Quod sanare Criton, non quod Hygia potest:
At Chione non sentit opus nec vocibus ullis
    Adiuvat, absentem marmoreamve putes.
Exorare, dei, si vos tam magna liceret
    Et bona velletis tam pretiosa dare,
Hoc quod habet Chione corpus faceretis haberet
    Ut Phlogis, et Chione quod Phlogis ulcus habet.

Think'st thou shrunk prick with thy shrivel'd hand
To raise? Such strokings make it fall, not stand.
When thou call'st me Thy Life, Light of thine eyes,
Ten hours to fetch it up will scarce suffice.
Thou knowst not what will do 't. Say, Thousands take,
Thee heir of all my seats and lands I make:
My wine, house, boys, plate, household stuff, coin, and
Thus tickle me. 'Twill do 't without thy hand.

Sir John Harrington

Sophy and Jane the Bond-Street beaus divide:
Their merits all can judge—for all have tried.
Sophy's the belle—but Jane's eternal spunk
Would tempt a Brahmin and exhaust a monk.
Jane into love-worn Wilkes new life would pour,
And bid old Queensbury be old no more.
Jane's am'rous flame all wish their nymphs to catch:
The *Brighton Taylor** is not half her match.
No fires in Sophy's marble bosom glow,
Tame as St. Austin'st bed-fellow of snow.
Ah, might we ask the gods one precious boon,
Too great, perhaps, for aught below the moon:
'Tis, that they'd Sophy's charms on Jane confer,
And breathe Jane's ardent feelings into her.

Nathaniel Brassey Halhed

* A well-known lady of pleasure.

† St. Augustine.

XI.104

Uxor, vade foras, aut moribus utere nostris:
    Non sum ego nec Curius nec Numa nec Tatius.
Me iucunda iuvant tractae per pocula noctes:
    Tu properas pota surgere tristis aqua.
Tu tenebris gaudes: me ludere teste lucerna
    Et iuvat admissa rumpere luce latus.
Fascia te tunicaeque obscuraque pallia celant:
    At mihi nulla satis nuda puella iacet.
Basia me capiunt blandas imitata columbas:
    Tu mihi das, aviae qualia mane soles.
Nec motu dignaris opus nec voce iuvare
    Nec digitis, tamquam tura merumque pares:
Masturbabantur Phrygii post ostia servi,
    Hectoreo quotiens sederat uxor equo,
Et quamvis Ithaco stertente pudica solebat
    Illic Penelope semper habere manum.
Pedicare negas: dabat hoc Cornelia Graccho,
    Iulia Pompeio, Porcia, Brute, tibi;
Dulcia Dardanio nondum miscente ministro
    Pocula Iuno fuit pro Ganymede Iovi.
Si te delectat gravitas, Lucretia toto
    Sis licet usque die: Laida nocte volo.

Prythee die and set me free
   Or else be
Kind and brisk and gay like me.
I pretend not to the wise ones,
   To the grave,
To the grave or the precise ones.

Prythee, why those bolts and locks,
   Coats and smocks?
And those drawers? With a pox!
I would wish, could nature make it,
   Nakedness,
Nakedness itself more naked.

Prythee, why the room so dark?
   Not a spark
Left to light me to the mark.
I love daylight or a candle,
   And to see,
And to see as well as handle.

There is neither art nor itch
   In thy breech;

Nor provoking hand or speech.
And when I expect thy motion,
    Fall'st asleep,
Fall'st asleep, or to devotion.

But if a mistress I must have
    Wise and grave,
Let her so herself behave:
By daylight a Susan Civil,
    Nell by night,
Nell by night, or such a devil.

                    Sir John Davies

Sweet spouse, you must presently troop and be gone,
    Or fairly submit to your betters;
Unless for the faults that are past you atone,
    I must knock off my conjugal fetters.

When at night I am paying the tribute of love—
    You know well enough what's my meaning—
You scorn to assist my devotions, or move,
    As if all the while you were dreaming.

At cribbage and put and all-fours I have seen
    A porter more passion expressing
Than thou, wicked Kate, in the rapturous scene,
    And the height of the amorous blessing.

Then say I to myself, "Is my wife made of stone,
    Or does the old serpent possess her?"

Better motion and vigour by far might be shown
   By dull spouse of a German professor.

So, Kate, take advice and reform in good time,
   And while I'm performing my duty,
Come in for your club, and repent of the crime
   Of paying all scores with your beauty.

All day thou may'st cant, and look grave as a nun,
   And run after Burgess the surly;
Or see that the family business be done,
   And chide all thy servants demurely.

But when you're in bed with your master and king,
   That tales out of school ne'er does trumpet,
Move, wriggle, heave, pant, clip round like a ring:
   In short, be as lewd as a strumpet.

                      Tom Brown

XII.46

Difficilis facilis, iucundus acerbus es idem:
Nec tecum possum vivere, nec sine te.

XII.50

Daphnonas, platanonas et aerios pityonas
Et non unius balnea solus habes,
Et tibi centenis stat porticus alta columnis,
Calcatusque tuo sub pede lucet onyx,
Pulvereumque fugax hippodromon ungula plaudit,
Et pereuntis aquae fluctus ubique sonat;
Atria longa patent. Sed nec cenantibus usquam
Nec somno locus est. Quam bene non habitas!

In all thy humours, whether grave or mellow,
Thou'rt such a touchy, testy, pleasant fellow;
Hast so much wit, and mirth, and spleen about thee,
There is no living with thee, or without thee.

Joseph Addison
(*The Spectator*, no. 68 [1711])

None equal you in trees for ever green:
Your bath's the most majestic can be seen:
Your colonnade is lofty, spacious, fine:
And under-foot your marble pavements shine:
Round your wide park the fleeting courser bounds:
Many cascades salute us with their sounds:
Apartments grand: no place to eat or sleep!
What a most noble house you do not keep.

William Hay

XII.61

Versus et breve vividumque carmen
In te ne faciam, times, Ligurra,
Et dignus cupis hoc metu videri.
Sed frustra metuis cupisque frustra.
In tauros Libyci ruunt leones
Non sunt papilionibus molesti.
Quaeras, censeo, si legi laboras,
Nigri fornicis ebrium poetam,
Qui carbone rudi putrique creta
Scribit carmina, quae legunt cacantes.
Frons haec stigmate non meo notanda est.

XII.90

Pro sene, sed clare, votum Maro fecit amico,
    Cui gravis et fervens hemitritaeos erat,
Si Stygias aeger non esset missus ad umbras,
    Ut caderet magno victima grata Iovi.
Coeperunt certam medici spondere salutem.
    Ne votum solvat, nunc Maro vota facit.

Sir Inigo* doth fear it, as I hear,
And labours to seem worthy of that fear,
That I should write upon him some sharp verse,
Able to eat into his bones, and pierce
Their marrow. Wretch! I quit thee of thy pain,
Thou'rt too ambitious, and dost fear in vain:
The Libyan lion hunts no butterflies,
He makes the camel and dull ass his prize.
Seek out some hungry painter, that for bread
With rotten coal or chalk upon the wall
Will well design thee to be view'd of all;
Thy forehead is too narrow for my brand.

Ben Jonson

When all men thought old Cosmus was a-dying,
And had by Will giv'n thee much goods & lands,
Oh, how the little Cosmus fell a-crying!
Oh, how he beat his breasts & wrung his hands!
How fervently for Cosmus' health he pray'd!
What worthy Alms he vow'd, on that condition:
But when his pangs a little were allayed,
And health seem'd hoped, by the learn'd Physician,
     Then, though his lips all love and kindness vanted,
     His heart did pray his prayer might not be granted.

Sir John Harrington

*Jonson's imitation of this poem is directed at Sir Inigo Jones (1573–1651), the famous Palladian architect, who ousted him from favor at the royal court.

XIII.2

Nasutus sis usque licet, sis denique nasus,
    Quantum noluerat ferre rogatus Atlans,
Et possis ipsum tu deridere Latinum:
    Non potes in nugas dicere plura meas,
Ipse ego quam dixi. Quid dentem dente iuvabit
    Rodere? carne opus est, si satur esse velis.
Ne perdas operam: qui se mirantur, in illos
    Virus habe, nos haec novimus esse nihil.
Non tamen hoc nimium nihil est, si candidus aure,
    Nec matutina si mihi fronte venis.

Be nosed, be all nose, till thy nose appear
So great that Atlas it refuse to bear;
Though even against Latinus thou inveigh,
Against my trifles thou no more canst say
Than I have said myself. Then to what end
Should we to render tooth for tooth contend?
You must have flesh if you'll be full, my friend!
Lose not thy labour, but on those who do
Admire themselves thy utmost venom throw;
That these things *nothing* are, full well we know.

Charles Cotton (after Montaigne)

SELECT BIBLIOGRAPHY OF
ENGLISH TRANSLATIONS
AND SOURCES

Amos, A. *Martial and the Moderns*. Cambridge, 1858.

Ashmore, John. *Certain Selected Odes of Horace . . . New Epigrams*. London, 1621.

BL Add. 27343, British Library, London.

Bohn, Henry George, ed. *The Epigrams of Martial*. London, 1860.

Bovie, Palmer. *Epigrams of Martial*. New York, 1970.

Brown, Thomas. *The Works . . . Serious and Comical in Prose and Verse*. Ed. James Drake. London, 1730.

Carrington, A. G. *Aspects of Martial's Epigrams*. Eton, Windsor, 1960.

Cotton, Charles. *Essays of Montaigne newly rendered into English*. London, 1685–1686.

Courthope, W. J. *Selections from the Epigrams of M. Valerius Martialis. Translated or Imitated in English Verse*. London, 1914.

Cowley, Abraham. *Poems*. London, 1656.

———. *Poems*. Ed. A. R. Waller. Cambridge, 1905.

Cunningham, J. V. *Collected Poems and Epigrams*. Chicago, 1971.

Egerton MS 2982, British Library, London.

Eliot, John. *Poems: Consisting of Epistles and Epigrams*. London, 1658.

Ellis, H. D. *English Verse Translations of Selections from Odes of Horace, Epigrams of Martial and Other Writers*. London, 1920.

Elphinston, James. *Martial*. London, 1782.

Fanshawe, Sir Richard. *The Faithfull Shepheard*. London, 1647.

———. *Shorter Poems and Translations*. Ed. N. W. Bawcutt. Liverpool, 1964.

Fitts, Dudley. *Sixty Poems of Martial in Translation*. New York, 1967.

Fletcher, Robert. *Ex Otio Negotium, or, Martiall his Epigrams Translated*. London, 1656.

Francis, A. L., and H. F. Tatum. *Martial's Epigrams: Translations and Imitations*. Cambridge, 1924.

Goertz, Donald C. *Select Epigrams of Martial*. New Hyde Park, N.Y., 1971.

Grant, Michael, ed. *Latin Literature: An Anthology.* Harmondsworth, 1979.

Halhed, Nathaniel Brassey. *Epigrams of Martial Imitated.* London, 1793.

Harrington, Sir John. *Alcilia.* London, 1613.

———. *Epigrams Both Pleasant and Serious.* London, 1615.

Harrison, Tony. *U.S. Martial.* Newcastle-upon-Tyne, 1981.

Hay, William. *Select Epigrams of Martial. Translated and Imitated by William Hay, Esq., and some by Cowley and Other Hands.* London, 1755.

Herrick, Robert. *Hesperides: or Works Both Humane and Divine.* London, 1648.

———. *Poetical Works.* Ed. L. C. Martin. Oxford, 1956.

Heyrick, Thomas. *Miscellaneous Poems.* London, 1691.

Hill, Brian. *Ganymede in Rome: Twenty Eight Epigrams of Martial.* London, 1971.

———. *An Eye for Ganymede: Forty Epigrams of Marcus Valerius Martial.* London, 1972.

Howard, Henry. See *Tottel's Miscellany.*

Humphries, Rolfe. *Selected Epigrams of Martial.* Bloomington, 1963.

Jonson, Ben. *Epigrams; the Forrest.* In *Workes,* London, 1616.

———. *Poems.* Ed. Ian Donaldson. London, 1975.

Kendall, Timothe. *Flowers of Epigram.* London, 1577.

Killigrew, Henry. *Select Epigrams of Martial Englished.* London, 1689.

———. *Epigrams of Martial Englished. With some Other Pieces, Ancient and Modern.* London, 1695.

Lind, L. R., ed. *Latin Poetry in Translation.* Boston, 1957.

Marcellino, Ralph. *The Pensive and the Antic Muse: Translations from Martial.* West Hempstead, N.Y., 1966.

———. *Martial: Selected Epigrams.* Indianapolis, 1968.

May, Thomas. *Selected Epigrams of Martial Englished.* London, 1629.

Michie, James. *Martial: The Epigrams Selected and Translated.* London, 1973.

Mills, Barriss. *Epigrams from Martial: A Verse Translation.* Lafayette, Indiana, 1969.

MS Donington d.58, Cambridge University Library.

Murray, Philip. *Poems after Martial.* Middletown, Conn., 1967.

Nixon, Paul. *A Roman Wit. Epigrams of Martial Rendered into English.* Boston & New York, 1911.

O'Connell, Richard. *Epigrams from Martial.* Philadelphia, 1976.

———. *More Epigrams from Martial.* Philadelphia, 1981.

Pecke, Thomas. *Parnassi Puerperium . . . Six Hundred of Owen's Epigrams, Martial de Spectaculis, Sir Thomas More; Libellus de specta-*

culis, or, An account of the most memorable monuments of the Romane glory . . . now periphrastically translated into English verse. London, 1659.

Pestell, Thomas. *The Poems of T. P.* Ed. Hannah Buchan. Oxford, 1940.

Porter, Peter. *After Martial.* London, 1972.

Pott, J. A. and F. A. Wright. *Martial, The Twelve Books of Epigrams.* London, 1924.

Randolph, Thomas. *Poems, With the Muses Looking-glasse and Amyntas.* Oxford, 1638.

———. *Poems.* Ed. G. Thorn-Drury. London, 1929.

Raymond, Oliver. *To Be Plain: Translations from Greek, Latin, French and German.* Florence, Kentucky, n.d.

Rieu, E. V. *A Book of Latin Poetry.* London, 1925.

Sala, George Augustus, E. Sellon, et al. *The Index Expurgatorius of Martial, Literally Translated.* London, 1868.

Scott, Rev. William. *Epigrams of Martial . . . Translated, Imitated, and Addressed to the Nobility, Clergy, and Gentry.* London, 1773.

Sedley, Sir Charles. "Epigrams or Court Characters." In *The Poetical and Dramatic Works,* ed. V. de Sola Pinto, pp. 51–62. London, 1928.

———. *The Miscellaneous Works.* Ed. Capt. Ayloffe. London, 1702.

Sellon, E. *See* Sala, George Augustus.

Shaw, William Francis. *Juvenal, Persius, Martial, and Catullus: An Experiment in Translation.* London, 1882.

Sherburne, Sir Edward. *Salmacis, Lyrian and Sylvia, the Rape of Helen, A comment thereon,* with Severall other poems and Translations. London, 1651.

———. *Works.* Ed. F. J. Beeck. Assen, 1961.

Smith, Goldwin. *Bay Leaves: Translations from the Latin Poets.* Toronto, 1890.

Stevenson, Robert Louis. *Poems (1880–1894).* In *Collected Poems,* ed. Janet Adam Smith. London, 1950.

Stoneman, Richard, ed. *Daphne into Laurel: Translations of Classical Poetry from Chaucer to the Present.* London, 1982.

Street, A. E. *Fifty Epigrams from the First Book of Martial, Translated into English Verse.* Eton College, London, 1900.

———. *Martial: 120 Selected Epigrams Metrically Rendered in English.* Eton College, London, 1907.

Sullivan, J. P. "Themes and Variations from Martial." *Helix* 18 (1983), 47–55.

———. "Some Versions of Martial 10.47: The Happy Life." *The Classical Outlook* 63 (1986), 112–14.

Tatum, H. F. *See* Francis, A. L.

Tomlinson, Charles, ed. *The Oxford Book of Verse in English Translation*. Oxford, 1980.

Tottel's Miscellany, i.e. Songes and Sonettes, written by the ryht honorable Lorde Henry Haward late Earle of Surrey, and other. London, 1557.

Webb, W. T., *Select Epigrams from Martial for English Readers*. London, 1879.

Wender, Dorothea, trans. *Roman Poetry: From the Republic to the Silver Age*. Carbondale, Ill., 1980.

West, Alfred Slater. *Wit and Wisdom from Martial Contained in 150 of his epigrams chosen and done into English with Introduction and Notes*. London, 1912.

Westcott, J. H., *One Hundred and Twenty Epigrams of Martial*. Boston, 1894.

Whigham, Peter. *Letter to Juvenal: 101 Epigrams from Martial*. London, 1985.

Wright, F. A. *See* Pott, J. A.

Wright, James. *Sales Epigrammaton, Being the choicest Disticks of Martial's Fourteen Books of Epigrams . . . Made English*. London, 1663.

INDEX OF EPIGRAMS TRANSLATED

INDEX OF TRANSLATORS

VIII.28, *293*; VIII.40, *297*; VIII.68,
301; VIII.73, *303*; IX.92, *341*; X.2,
347; X.4, *349*; X.8, *351*; X.35, *363*;
X.36, *365*; X.37, *367*; X.38, *369*;
X.42, 44, *371*; X.45, *373*; X.47, *375*;
X.48, *377*; X.51, *379*; X.58, *381*;
X.78, *393*; X.92, *399*; X.103, *405*;
X.104, *407*; XI.15, *417*; XI.18, *419*;
XI.26, *425*; XI.75, *447*; XI.91, *451*;
XII.2, *461*; XII.18, *465*; XII.21, *467*;
XII.31, *471*; XII.34, *477*; XII.43,

479; XII.57, *483f.*; XII.61, *485*;
XII.63, *487*; XII.94, *493*; XII.98,
495; XIII.3, *53, 66, 499*; XIII.82,
120, *501*; XIV.2, *34, 39, 505*;
XIV.40, *75, 507*; XIV.165, *189, 509*;
XIV.195, *203, 511*; XIV.220, *222,
513*
Wright, F. A.: II.49, *115*; V.24, *201*

Young, James M.: V.73, *213*

INDEX OF LATIN FIRST LINES

Designer: Mark Ong
Compositor: Graphic Composition, Inc., Athens, Georgia
Text: 10/13 Trump
Display: Trump
Printer: Braun-Brumfield, Inc.
Binder: Braun-Brumfield, Inc.

Epigrams of Martial
Englished by Divers Hands
Edited by J. P. Sullivan
and Peter Whigham

Martial (Marcus Valerius Martialis) was a
compatriot of the Senecas and of Lucan. He
came to Rome in his early twenties and lived
there for thirty-four years under several
emperors, including Nero, Vespasian, Titus,
and Domitian. Martial was the perfect urban
poet, and his epigrammatic form—wry and
disenchanted, always graphic, frequently gross
and obscene—reflects the mixed society of the
capital more tellingly than any other lyricist.
Because of his use of obscenities, he has never
been given his due as a poet in his own right,
being overshadowed by more prominent fig-
ures such as Catullus and Horace. However,
Martial's influence on English literature was
enormous.

This volume presents a generous selection
of his best poems in both Latin and English.
The broad range of his work is represented,
including most of his satiric portraits and
poems written to solicit patronage and to flat-
ter the emperors through whose reigns he
lived. The reader is also able to see the unex-
pectedly great influence Martial had on Eliza-
bethan, Jacobean, and Restoration poets and
how he continues to provide poetic inspiration
in the twentieth century.

In addition to displaying Martial's versatility,
this collection shows the different techniques
adopted by translators through five centuries.
It will be of interest to classicists, English
scholars, specialists in comparative literature,
and amateurs of the art of translation.